T3-BGL-938

J. EDGAR HOOVER SPEAKS CONCERNING COMMUNISM

Compiled by

JAMES D. BALES

The Capitol Hill Press
Washington, D. C.

J. EDGAR HOOVER SPEAKS
CONCERNING COMMUNISM

Published by The Capitol Hill Press in
cooperation with The Craig Press,
Nutley, New Jersey

© Copyright 1970 by The Craig Press

Capitol Hill Press Editions

December, 1971
July, 1972
March, 1973

HX
86
·H7

Printed in the United States of America

The Capitol Hill Press

Division of
Prospect House, Inc.
1825 Connecticut Avenue, N.W.
Washington, D.C. 20009

TABLE OF CONTENTS

iii

ALMA COLLEGE
MONTEITH LIBRARY
ALMA, MICHIGAN

DEDICATION

To

J. EDGAR HOOVER

Who, with a voice of authority based on information and insight, has warned America and Christendom of the menace of Communism for a longer period of time than has any other public or private figure.

Mr. Hoover had nothing to do with the compilation and publication of this collection of material from his pen.

INTRODUCTION

J. Edgar Hoover has served in the Justice Department for fifty-three years. For forty-six years he has been Chief of the Federal Bureau of Investigation. The most eloquent testimony to the capable service which he has rendered this country is found in the fact that he has served under ten Presidents and more than fourteen Attorney Generals. After all these years of service he was asked by President Johnson, who waived his compulsory retirement, to remain "for an indefinite period of time."[1] President Nixon has also asked him to continue to serve.

He has been praised by men from various walks of life and from various social and political positions. William S. White has called him "perhaps the most authentic anti-Communist in the United States."[2] In speaking of the Communists, Bishop G. Bromley Oxnam said, "Our FBI is qualified to ferret him (Communist, J. D. B.) out. Its thorough work, its loyalty to American traditions, and its splendid leader, J. Edgar Hoover . . . ."[3] Senator Kuchel said "Mr. Hoover's contribution to America, her freedom, and her security extends over a long lifetime under seven American Presidents. He occupies a unique and respected position among all his fellow citizens."[4] Thus it is not surprising that a Harris Poll indicated that the public's confidence in the FBI remained at a high level, and even higher was the confidence in which they held J. Edgar Hoover.[5] In 1962, fifty Governors commended him for his work.[6]

Daniel A. Poling spoke of him as the one who "above all other living Americans deserves the title 'Mr. America.' " "He stands shoulder-high above the tumult and the shouting, the charges and the countercharges, with the confidence of his fellow Americans—a man to be trusted in our fated

vii

hour."[7]   Harry and Bonaro Overstreet spoke of him as one "who deals with the actualities of the Communist threat."[8] George S. Benson wrote of him: "J. Edgar Hoover, FBI Director, has been one of America's greatest public servants. Through one of the most trying and dangerous eras in our history as a Republic, he has continued to demonstrate the highest quality of leadership in a position of decisive importance to the security of our Nation and the future freedom of every citizen.   Constantly he has been the smear target of the powerful Communist conspiracy and the unending variety of dupes whose influence the Reds so skillfully use."[9] Robert F. Kennedy has praised him,[10] as did President John F. Kennedy who spoke of having "the greatest respect for its Director, Mr. Hoover, who is one of the most distinguished public servants who have occupied positions of high responsibility in the long history of this Republic, and also because of the extraordinary men who have rallied to the standard of the FBI over the years and have served the public interest."[11]   The then Vice President Lyndon Johnson said: "And I take great pride in saying to you this morning that in the thirty-two years I have spent in Federal service, and the hundreds of thousands and millions of people who have come from all of the states in the Union, I can say without fear of contradiction and with the complete confirmation of my wife who has brought a great many groups to the FBI here, one thing that has most impressed, indelibly impressed, the citizenry who have come to this capital of the free has been the efficiency and the competence and the courtesy and the justice of this great organization headed by this great American, J. Edgar Hoover."[12]   Attorney General Katzenbach said of Hoover: "The FBI, under Mr. Hoover's leadership, has won worldwide renown for its speed, skill, and service.   Equally important is that throughout the years, the FBI has never exceeded its proper investigative responsibility.

"If this says much for Mr. Hoover's judgment and restraint and for the quality of men working with him, the FBI Academy says as much about Mr. Hoover's understanding.   His pioneering efforts in assisting local law enforcement within the strict confines of the Federal system may well prove to be among the most appreciated of his contributions to law and law enforcement in America."[13]

Another remarkable thing about J. Edgar Hoover is that in all the years of his public service he has never been wrong about the nature, the objectives, the strategy and tactics of communism. The Communist writer Art Shields unconsciously paid tribute to J. Edgar Hoover's knowledge of the conspiracy fifty years ago when he spoke of: "The disgraceful 'Red Raids,' when Hoover arrested thousands of innocent workers on January 2, 1920."[14] Herbert Aptheker, one of the leading, if not the leading, Communist theoretician in America paid a similar tribute when he said: "The ultra-reactionary views of J. Edgar Hoover are notorious; he has publicly expressed them ten thousand times since 1919, before American Legion Conventions, in 'guest columns' for the Hearst press, in hectoring and threatening letters to various editors and publicists, and in his occasional books. Above all, these views are shown in his witch-hunting specialization, again ever since he was in direct charge of the notorious Palmer Raids just after World War I."[15]

The testimony of J. Edgar Hoover in 1920, which we have reprinted in chapter three of this volume, indicates how long ago he understood the nature of communism. It also underscores the fact that there has been no excuse for anyone to be ignorant of the nature of communism since its words and deeds have been well documented throughout the years.

There is still a great need in America for more people to become informed upon the subject of communism. In an effort to help do this we have prepared this book of quotations and materials from J. Edgar Hoover's pen. We have not dealt with the material found in his two excellent books: *Masters of Deceit* and *A Study of Communism*. Instead we have drawn upon the material from Director Hoover which is found in the public record.

The first chapter of this book is made up of a series of articles which J. Edgar Hoover wrote for *Christianity Today*. It emphasizes the irreconcilable conflict between Christianity and communism.

This is followed with a long chapter, which makes up most of the book, of quotations alphabetically arranged on a wide variety of subjects related to communism. The third chapter of the book is a reprint of the brief on the Communist Party which J. Edgar Hoover wrote fifty years ago. The fourth chapter is a brief history of communism in the United States. The fifth chapter is on the New Left.

It should be observed that these statements of J. Edgar Hoover were made over a period of many years. Thus there may be some cases where a statement would be descriptive of one period of time but not as descriptive of another. The Communists, for example, can change their number one current objective from one year to the next, or even in one day. Therefore, a statement by Hoover concerning their emphasis and main thrust at one time might not be true at another period of time. For example, the Communist influence on some religious leaders could have been more pronounced and widespread in one period than in another.

Quotation marks have not been used because all of the statements in the book, with the exception of the introduction, are from the pen of Mr. Hoover. In most cases the material is taken from speeches or from testimony before governmental committees.

The compiler thinks that this material from J. Edgar Hoover underscores his determination, dedication and faith which he expressed a number of years ago when referring to his feelings at the time he became Director of the FBI. "I feel today, as on May 10, 1924, the challenge to be a servant of my fellow man and my God. For behind that challenge lies a basic truth of the universe: good *will* triumph over evil; fidelity, bravery, and integrity *will* make men great."[16]

CR has reference to the *Congressional Record*, HCUA has reference to the House Committee on Un-American Activities, and SISS to the Senate Internal Security Subcommittee. Their publications are issued by the Government Printing Office.

The page references in the *Congressional Record* in the daily issues and in the yearly bound volumes may differ. In some cases quotations have been taken from the daily issues, and in other cases from the bound volumes. All of them can easily be located in the bound volumes by using the indexes to locate the insertions of materials by J. Edgar Hoover. In most cases the articles which we have taken from other sources will also be found in the *Congressional Record*.

The compiler wishes to express his appreciation to the following for permission to quote from articles by J. Edgar Hoover which appeared in their publications. *The American Legion Magazine. Christian Herald. Christianity Today. The Elks Magazine. The Lion. Harvard Business Review. Nation's Business. Newsweek.*

Work on this compilation was started around twenty years ago.

FOOTNOTES

INTRODUCTION

[1] *U. S. News and World Report*, May 18, 1964, p. 20; also *Commercial Appeal*, Memphis, November 27, 1964, p. 16; and the *Congressional Record*, July 26, 1967, p. H9467.

[2] *Congressional Record*, September 25, 1961, p. A7707.

[3] G. Bromley Oxnam, "How to Un-Cover Communists," *Parade*, June 28, 1953, p. 9.

[4] *Congressional Record*, February 11, 1965, p. 2582.

[5] *Arkansas Gazette*, Little Rock, February 18, 1965, p. 7A.

[6] *Arkansas Gazette*, August 16, 1962, p. 1.

[7] *Christian Herald*, August 1965, p. 76.

[8] *Strange Tactics of Extremism*, p. 46.

[9] "Looking Ahead" July 23, 1958.

[10] Robert Kennedy praised Hoover as "a vigilant, experienced American who has real credentials as a Communist fighter. . . . " (Robert F. Kennedy, *The Pursuit of Justice*, New York: Harper and Row, Publishers, 1964, pp. 61-62). See also *Arkansas Gazette*, August 8, 1962, p. 2A.

[11] *FBI Law Enforcement Bulletin*, January 1963, p. 10.

[12] *FBI Law Enforcement Bulletin*, August 1963, p. 9. See also the tribute by Herbert A. Philbrick, "Tribute to J. Edgar Hoover," *Dollar Hollar*, Columbus, Ohio, 43125, Dollar Federal Savings and Loan Association, June 1964.

[13] *FBI Law Enforcement Bulletin*, August 1965, p. 8.

[14] *The Worker*, February 16, 1965, p. 7.

[15] *Political Affairs*, November 1962, pp. 10-11.

[16] Quoted in the *Congressional Record*, July 26, 1967, p. H9466. Richard Nixon wrote that: "J. Edgar Hoover, to his eternal credit, was conducting constant investigations of Communist infiltration in the United States generally and the government in particular, despite the fact that the official Administration policy was to 'get along with Stalin.' But Hoover had the power only to conduct investigations. He could not follow them up with prosecutions or other required action without the approval of his superiors in the Justice Department and in the White House." (*Six Crisis*, New York: Pyramid Books, 1968, p. 5).

Chapter One

THE COMMUNIST MENACE: RED GOALS AND CHRISTIAN IDEALS

I

The twentieth century has witnessed the intrusion into its body fabric of a highly malignant cancer—a cancer which threatens to destroy Judaic-Christian civilization. One-fourth of the world's land surface has been seared and blackened by this cancer, while one out of every three human beings is caught in its tentacles. At this very hour, some are wondering whether we as a free nation can survive the frontal and underground assaults of this tumorous growth of communism.

Just 100 years ago communism was a mere scratch on the face of international affairs. In a dingy London apartment, a garrulous, haughty, and intolerant atheist, Karl Marx, callous to the physical sufferings and poverty of his family, was busy mixing the ideological acids of this evil philosophy. Originally of interest only to skid row debaters and wandering minstrels of revolution, Marx's pernicious doctrines were given organizational power by a beady-eyed Russian, V. I. Lenin, who, with his Bolshevik henchmen, seized state power for communism in 1917. From that wintry day in St. Petersburg, communism began to flow in ever greater torrents. After Lenin came the crafty and cunning Joseph Stalin and now the ebullient master prevaricator, Nikita Khrushchev. Communism is today literally a violent hurricane, rocking not only the chanceries of the world but seeking to capture the bodies, minds, and souls of men and women everywhere.

1

Universal Domination the Goal

The full implications of the Communist challenge are shocking. The ultimate Communist goal—as defined by Marx, Lenin, and other Communist leaders—is the ruthless overthrow of our Judaic-Christian heritage and the establishment of a worldwide Communist society. By its very nature, communism is expansionist and universalist. In fact, the Communists feel that they can find their true fulfillment only by conquering non-Communist areas and bringing the whole planet under their dominion.

This overriding Communist goal of universal domination becomes the key to Party activities. Feeling that history has destined communism for ultimate victory, the Communists believe that permanent peace with non-Communists is impossible, that life must be an inevitable struggle between the two. "It is inconceivable," Lenin proclaimed, "that the Soviet Republic should continue to exist for a long period side by side with imperialist states. Ultimately, one or the other must conquer."

Rejection of Ojective Morality

Hence, there arises the ugly manifestation of Communist "ethics"—namely, the Communist belief that morality must be subordinated to the class struggle, the inevitable conflict between communism and its opponents. What is moral? Anything which serves to destroy the enemy and promote communism. Lenin was most explicit: "Morality is that which serves to destroy the old exploiting society and to unite all the toilers around the proletariat, which is creating a new Communist society."

Communist morality, of course, is rooted in total rejection of a belief in God and in the values of the Christian moral code. Supernatural concepts and divine revelation play no role in communism. "We repudiate all morality that is taken outside of human, class concepts," Lenin proclaimed. "We, of course, say that we do not believe in God, and that we know perfectly well that the clergy, the landlords, and the bourgeoisie spoke in the name of God in order to pursue their own exploiters' interests."

This rejection of God gives communism a demonic aspect—transforming it into a fanatical, Satanic, brutal

2

phenomenon. Morality is not determined by ethical standards grounded in an Absolute, but in the expedient interpretations of the Party—meaning, in actual practice, the whims and desires of the ruling clique or Party leader. This leads to the terrifying doctrine that "the end justifies the means." Proof of the cynical ruthlessness of such morality is the following description by long-time American revolutionaries:

> With him the end justifies the means. Whether his tactics be "legal" and "moral," or not, does not concern him, so long as they are effective. He knows that the laws as well as the current code of morals, are made by his mortal enemies . . . . Consequently, he ignores them in so far as he is able and it suits his purposes. He proposes to develop, regardless of capitalist conceptions of "legality," "fairness," "right," etc., a greater power than his capitalist enemies. . . .

A SOCIETY WITHOUT GOD

Hence, under communism we see a decisive break from and thrust against the Judaic-Christian heritage. Communism is not just another political party, social organization, or economic philosophy which can be understood within the framework of our traditional Western heritage. So to regard communism is radically to misunderstand its terrific driving power, insidious persuasion, and terrifying intent. The Communists are not interested in remodeling or reforming our society, but in organizing a completely different society—a society which by denying God hopes to create a new type of man: Communist Man. St. Paul, the great Apostle, could say, "If any man be in Christ, he is a new creature." The Communists would pervert this profound truth to say: "If any man be in the Communist Party, he is a new creature."

CONFRONTING THE RED CHALLENGE

The question arises: how can a philosophy so *anti-God, anti-religious, anti-human* be so provocative and appealing to some people in our country? Perhaps in this strategic question we can find some of the challenges of—and answers to—this demonic way of life.

Let's take a look at some of the Communist challenges today and see what we as Christians can do about them.

3

1. *The Communists appeal to man's idealism and ask the very best of his life.* Communist propaganda proclaims Marxism-Leninism "the greatest cause in the history of mankind," worthy of man's highest devotion. The Communist appeal is always to the noblest, the best, the most admirable in man. "The great vision and courage of us Communists has never been matched by that of any past heroes in the annals of mankind. In this respect we have every reason to be proud. . . ."

Answer: Have we in America and in the Church given sufficient emphasis to Christian ideals, and called for heroic effort in the attainment of great goals? In particular, have we imbued our young people with the moral idealism which helps to mold their lives for Christ? Perhaps we have contented ourselves with catering to man's mediocrity, rather than attempting to bring out the noblest and deepest strands of character. Like Isaiah of Jerusalem, we must ever keep the awe, the majesty, and the holiness of God before us— and call men to ever greater efforts in His service. Are we pressing on toward the high calling in Christ, toward the goals of a Christian society? The Christian Church—as history has proved—has the power to capture men and lead them to divine levels. By exalting God and His purposes in the lives of men, the Church can unmask the utter falsity of communism's siren calls.

2. *The Communists do not doubt the validity of their cause; they press ever onward for their secularized Utopia, confident of ultimate victory.* "We Communists must possess the greatest courage and revolutionary determination of mankind. . . . While we clearly see the difficulties confronting the cause of communism, we are not in the least daunted by them. . . ."

Answer: Are there too many pessimists, waverers, and people of little faith in the ranks of the Church today? Is there the enthusiasm among our people to match this Communist aggressiveness and certainty? The Church of Christ has a great message to sing, a great responsibility to fulfill. Never must she feel pessimistic, daunted, or uncertain.

3. *The Communists expect from their members a deep sense of personal sacrifice and dedication.* "To sacrifice one's personal interests and even one's life without the

4

slightest hesitation and even with a feeling of happiness, for the cause of the Party . . . is the highest manifestation of Communist ethics." This is a sacrifice of the members' time, talents, and personal resources, financial and otherwise. Casual effort is not a Communist trait.

Answer: Do we in the church and society really expect a deep sense of personal sacrifice and dedication? Do too many individuals come to church exerting only a "casual effort" and not giving sacrificially of their time, talents, and personal resources? The Communists have discovered that a demand for the very best actually brings forth the very best from the individual. If the Communists can create such responses on the basis of a cold, cynical materialism, just think of the accomplishments which can be wrought by the power of the Holy Spirit!

4. *The Party stresses the need for fidelity and loyalty to the mission of communism and the necessity of members to shun all temptations which would distract them from their assigned tasks.* "But if for the sake of . . . the Party . . . he is required to endure insults, shoulder heavy burdens, and do work which he is reluctant to do, he will take up the most difficult and important work without the slightest hesitation and will not pass the buck."

Answer: In our society today is there too much tendency to "pass the buck," to let George do it. Do we not often start out enthusiastically in civic or church work, and then let temptations sidetrack us from our task? Are we embarrassed when we are criticized for doing Christ's work? Are we ready to shoulder heavy burdens? Are too many following the easy road of conformity with secularism and not holding sufficiently high the banner of Christ?

5. *The Communists proclaim that working for the Party brings internal peace, joy, and happiness to the member.* He finds here creative achievement and self-fulfillment. "He will also be capable of being the most sincere, most candid, and happiest of men."

Answer: The Christian Gospel tells of the deep joy, peace, and blessings which come from belief in Christ as Saviour and Lord. Is the Church doing enough to overcome the loneliness of contemporary man, his feelings of insecurity and frustration in a world growing more secular every day?

Fear, personal unhappiness, and uncertainty stalk the streets today. Crime, juvenile delinquency, and disrespect for law and order are rife. Are we meeting these challenges in the Christian spirit, offering with maximum effort the true answer of the Gospel, telling people that belief in God is the true way to a peace of mind which passes all understanding?

PERVERSION OF THE TRUTH

These are some of the challenges of communism today, and the problems they pose for Christians. Communists, in fact, attempt to capture the historic values of Christian civilization, such as love, mercy, and justice, and after grossly perverting their true meaning, they actually turn these values against their parent!

With shameless perfidy the Communists hail themselves as the great exponents of love—most truly, one of mankind's most sublime virtues. Under communism, it is proclaimed, "there will be no oppressed and exploited people, . . . no darkness, ignorance, backwardness. In such a society all human beings will become unselfish. . . . The spirit of mutual assistance and mutual love will prevail among mankind." We know, in fact, however, that communism means terror, fear, and slavery. Communism represents a new age of barbarism, which is repealing the centuries of progress of Western man toward tolerance, understanding, and human brotherhood. Communist Man—the product of this system— is a brute, ideologically trained, who unhesitantly conducts purges, runs concentration camps, butchers the Hungarian Freedom Fighters. He is immune to the emotions of pity, sorrow, or remorse. He is truly an alarming monster, human in physical form, but in practice a cynically godless and immoral machine.

ROLE OF THE MINISTRY

If communism is to be defeated, the task must rest largely upon the theologians and the ministers of the Gospel. Communism is a false secular religion with pseudo-theological explanations of the great verities of life, such as the creation, life on earth, and the world to come. Communism is an all-encompassing system with explanations—though wrong ones

—for this great universe of God. The Party offers answers —though perverted ones—for the hopes, joys, and fears of mankind.

In the final analysis, the Communist world view must be met and defeated by the Christian world view. The Christian view of God as the Creator, Sustainer, and Lord of the universe is majestically superior to the *ersatz* approach of dialectical materialism concocted by Marx and Lenin. The task of our clergy today is to translate this Holy Truth into the daily lives of our men and women. This truly is their responsibility as Christian clergymen.

Strong, responsible, and faithful Christians, wearing the full armor of God, are the best weapons of attack against communism and the other problems of our day. "Seek ye first the kingdom of God, and his righteousness." In this way you will be playing a vital role also in helping defend our cherished way of life.

II

COMMUNIST PROPAGANDA AND THE CHRISTIAN PULPIT

The Communists are today spraying the world with ideological and propaganda missiles designed to create a deadly radioactive cloud of Marxism-Leninism. From bases behind the Iron Curtain and in the non-Communist world, this cloud of Communist propaganda is drenching many lands, with a particularly heavy fall-out in this nation.

The deadliest of these Communist missiles—whose warheads are exceptionally heavy—are being directed against the Christian pulpit. Communist gunners, with special ideological training and schooled in atheistic perversity, are "sighting in" the clergy—hoping to shatter, immobilize, and confuse this powerful forum of idealism, morality, and civic virtue. No assignment is more strategic in the Communist world today than the disruption of the Church of God—both *within* and *outside* the Iron Curtain.

Why does the Church which has no military forces— merit the most explosive of Communist rockets, the most venomous of Communist hate, the most vituperative of Communist scorn? Because religion, of all facets of Western civilization, represents the eternal "thorn in the flesh" of communism, that jagged rock which is constantly puncturing, exposing, and unmasking Communist claims, performances, and hopes. The Communists realize that unless the Christian pulpit—that mighty fortress of God—is liquidated, pitilessly, mercilessly, finally, the very existence of communism itself stands in jeopardy. The spiritual firepower of the Christian Church—based on the love of God—is sufficient to destroy all the Soviet man-made missiles and rockets and extirpate this twentieth century aberration.

And the Communists know it—and fear it.

THE RELIANCE ON ATHEISM

To understand the Communist attack against the Christian pulpit, we must, so to speak, transplant ourselves into the control room of Party strategy. Let's see the Communist high command at work as it executes its attack against the Church. Let's note its mode of approach, its variable tactics, and ultimate goal.

The basic Communist weapon is the materialism of the Communist dialectic. Communism is atheistic, utterly denying God. This has been a fundamental premise of communism since the days of Marx and remains so today under the mendacious huckstering of Nikita Krushchev. "It is not religion that creates man, but man who creates religion . . . . It is the opium of the people" (Karl Marx). "Religion is a kind of spiritual gin . . ." (V. I. Lenin). "In my outlook on life there is no place for religion" (William Z. Foster, Chairman Emeritus of the Communist Party, USA). "We remain the atheists that we have always been" (Khrushchev).

Just why, we may ask, does the Party rely so greatly on these missiles of atheism? Just why do other phases of Communist strategy alter, but never the dependence on this weapon?

The answer is simple and fundamental to any progress which communism hopes to achieve. Atheism is an all-out weapon of highly destructive and devastating power. If properly launched, atheistic missiles can mangle, cut, and obliterate the spiritual tendons of life—belief in God, faith in Judaic-Christian values, love of the Church. The very

8

existence of Communist Man—that fanatical atheist imbued with the ethics of expediency—is proof of the paralyzing power of atheism in destroying the taproots of spiritual strength which flow into the individual personality in a Christian civilization. Hence, in Communist strategy, these missiles of atheism are the ultimate weapons, the essential ideological artillery designed not to damage partially but to destroy ruthlessly.

However, as we watch from the Communist control room, we note that, in launching these missiles of atheism toward America, the Communist rocketeers are experiencing considerable trouble. These mighty missiles are propelled, but then, like meteors, they seem to burn up as they approach the atmosphere of America, a proud Christian land. In simple language, here is the problem of Party strategists: how can an atheistic Communist Party operate in the United States where the vast majority of people believe in God?

To attack directly, with an open appeal for atheism, is to risk defeat, frustration, and loss of faith. To stand on the street corner and proclaim, "We the Communists believe in atheism," will not gain recruits. To denounce God in open Party appeals will cause open resentment and hostility. What is to be done?

A STRATEGY OF DECEIT

The Communist answer: *employ a strategy of deceit*— a technique designed to hoodwink non-Communists. This is today one of the Party's most potent attacks against the Christian pulpit.

The strategy means primarily three things:

1. *A false claim that the Communists stand for tolerance of religion.* The Party's tactic in the Christian world is to de-emphasize the importance of religion, to talk and write little about it, and emphasize other topics, such as social, economic, and political issues. A leader of the Communist Party, USA, recently commented: "We know there is no God or Supreme Being, but we can't go out and tell this to church people." "We do not declare and must not declare in our programme that we are 'atheists'. . . " (Lenin). If questions are asked, Communists pose as being "tolerant,"

9

and say that religion is a "private matter" for the individual. "The people's state holds that the question of religious belief is a private matter; belief or nonbelief in religion relates to the personal freedom of an individual."

Actually, however, religion is not a private affair for the Communist. "Religion is an ideological foe of communism, and the reconciliation of the two is impossible." As a Marxist, he must be an atheist. He has absolutely no personal choice. "Personal freedom of an individual" is a deceptive Party shibboleth. Any non-Communist believing this double talk is being trapped—and "softened up" for the next tactic in this strategy of deceit.

2. *To achieve a mutuality of agreement with the Christian pulpit on "common issues" (as defined by the Communists).* This tactic is being actively pursued by the Communist Party, USA, today. "Look," the Communists are saying "we are tolerant of religion, we do not want to attack your faith. Rather, let's work together on issues in which we are both interested—peace, civil liberties, economic justice. We Communists are believers in love, justice, and the brotherhood of man. We too want a world of peace and good will. Let's not fight but work together."

Here is the deadly "come along" of communism, directed today at the Christian pulpit. This enables the Party to move close to unsuspecting ministers and laymen who see only the exterior verbiage and not the concealed danger. How does the Party work here? In many ways: encouraging churchmen to endorse, support, and even participate in Communist front groups; to sign Communist-sponsored petitions; to neutralize clerical opposition to communism (if a minister can be influenced to even keep silent about the dangers of communism, the Party has gained).

At the same time the Party, through infiltration tactics, is attempting to reach inside the churches. In one instance, a Communist official instructed Party members to join churches and become active in their organizations. Another member was working in the church office, while still another Party official helped conduct the financial affairs of his parish. Most important, of course, is the youth field. A national Party leader recently commented that Communist youth must find "common ground" with church youth groups, "not only for ideological reasons but also for the use of their facilities!"

3. *Exploit the church for their own Communist ends.* This "brotherliness" of Communists is most purposive: the Communists want to hitch as much of the influence of the Christian church as they can capture to the Party's cause. This means that if clergymen or laymen participate (knowingly or unknowingly) in fronts, sign Communist-sponsored petitions, speak favorably of Communist objectives—these points must be exploited to strengthen the Party's position. To a prospective "customer," a Communist canvasser will say, "The Rev. X has signed this petition, why don't you sign too?" "The Rev. Y has endorsed this organization. You know him. Why don't you help us and contribute some money?" "The Rev. Z has spoken favorably of this proposal. This shows that it's in the spirit of the Church."

To the Communists, any support gained from church circles enables them to break down the moral antipathy of the community and gives them a desperately desired "respectability."

Hence, this strategy of Communist deceit is aimed to *undermine, hoodwink,* and *exploit* the Christian pulpit.

A WAR FOR THE MINDS OF MEN

Now, we may ask, what is the answer to this ideological attack? What can the clergy of America do to defeat this Communist strategy?

First, we must make this assertion. The Christian pulpit is today one of America's most formidable barriers against communism. The spiritual dedication of thousands of clergymen, in large and small churches across the nation, is a powerful antidote to the danger. America owes a great debt of gratitude to the stalwart example of our religious leadership.

Yet the Communist attack toward the Church continues. What can you, as clergymen, do to help blunt this tactic?

In our nation one of communism's most potent allies is *apathy toward* and *lack of knowledge of* communism. Very strangely, many citizens will be highly conversant about the diseases of azaleas, the weathering qualities of automobile paints, the latest ways to play a new card game—yet

11

know nothing about communism, that deadly plague which threatens to extinguish our way of life. That is one of the anomalies—and tragedies—of modern-day America.

Perhaps we can pose several questions.

Have you, as a minister, preached any sermons describing the frightful challenge which communism poses for the spiritual heritage of America?

Have you encouraged members of your church to read about communism and to learn about its evil nature?

Have you urged the formation of discussion groups to acquaint men and women with this challenge?

The approach must not be one of *fear* but *knowledge*. Communism is not a monstrosity to be hidden from sight, never spoken about publicly, or shunted into a side closet. Communism is not a controversial subject, best to be left untouched. Communism is not so overpowering as to throw us into a state of hysterical fear, anger, or violence. Like an epidemic of polio, the solution lies not in minimizing the danger or overlooking the problem—but rapidly, positively, and courageously finding an anti-polio serum.

THE GREAT CHRISTIAN ANSWER

We in America have this anti-communism serum, the answer to the Communist challenge. It lies in *the strength of our Judaic-Christian tradition, the power of the Holy Spirit working in men.* Too frequently, both clergy and laymen, do not realize the full resources at their command in the Christian tradition—*the tremendous power of God* to turn men toward good, to make personalities bloom with the living courage of sainted men. The job of you as clergymen is to help channel this divine power into the hearts, minds, and souls of men. Literally, *the Gospel has the power* to turn the world upside down. *That should be your mission.*

No greater challenge has ever faced the Christian Church. Communism has caused the deaths of millions of people. No enemy in all these 2,000 years has held such a deadly challenge to the Christian pulpit. As spokesmen of God, your task is to enable men to know the truth, so the truth will set them free.

SOVIET RULE OR CHRISTIAN RENEWAL?

"What is past is prologue" was William Shakespeare's magnificent summation of man's position in the vast stream of history. The time has arrived for us, as *Christians* and as *Americans,* to peer ahead and see what we as individuals and church members can do to help make this a better world in which to live. Atheistic communism has now been with us as a state power for almost a half century. Talk as we will concerning the past, we cannot undo, revise, or alter the events of the years. "What is past is prologue"—and we must build for the future.

Today two vast ideological worlds confront each other, worlds which embody different deities and conceptions of man. Casting our eyes down the avenue of the next generation, we may pose the issue between the worlds as *Communist domination or Christian rededication.* Shall the world fall under the cold hand of dialectical materialism where every man must conform to the atheistic, irrational, and immoral laws of a way of life which is contrary to the Divine Intelligence? Or shall the answer be a rededication to Christian moral values, a digging deep of the wells of personal faith in the bottomless ocean of God's love and the creation of a society which is in harmony with the laws of God?

Will it be the cold world of Communist conformity, or the eager, active, and genuine world of religious dedication?

Unfortunately today many people, watching the Communist world in action, have become defeatist. They see bustling energy, teeming exhilaration, and powerful personal energies keyed to promoting self-sacrifice, fanatical zeal, and Party accomplishments. In deep anguish, they say, "How can we compete against such a powerful and dynamic ideology?"

The answer to this skepticism (highly unwarranted, as we shall see) lies in understanding the dynamics of motivation in a Communist society.

Communism has the power to stimulate intense, fanatical, and sustained effort. If we would peer into the day-to-day activities of the Communist Party (USA), for example, we would see a vast panorama of demonic rushing and counter-rushing. Members are eternally busy making speeches, collecting money, and passing out handbills. The moment one emergency is surmounted, another arises, more breath-taking and earth-shaking than the former. Like ants scurrying on a hot summer day, Party members are whirling fanatical action at all levels of the Party.

This incessant Party activity arises, to a large extent, because of what the Communists call *ideological cultivation*—which means an educational program designed to immerse the individual in Communist thought for the purpose of making him a more effective Party member. Communists speak of ideological cultivation as a weapon of attack. Actually it is the foundation stone of Marxism-Leninism.

Training New Recruits

A recruit joins the Party. Immediately he is sent to a Party school to learn, among other things, the ideas, opinions, and prejudices of the Communist "masters" (Marx, Engels, and Lenin; Stalin is now "out of date"). Regardless of how busy a member may be in everyday Party work or how long he's been in the Party, he must continue to attend indoctrination schools and do homework. Among Party slogans is "One night a week for Marxist study."

The idea is to make the member think like the Party "masters," to imbue him with the Communist personality of these men. To the Communists, the reading, studying, and discussion of Communist "classics," such as Marx's *Capital* and Lenin's *State and Revolution*, as well as the latest works of the current Party leaders, help raise the Communist qualities of the members. "Strive to become the best pupils of Marx, Engels and Lenin. . . ." These source books of Communist doctrine, in the Party's eyes, give the members a sense of Communist purpose and direction and a zeal to push forward to achieve the Party's goals.

Hence, to the Communists, the member must, in the Party's language, constantly raise his own *ideological level*, that is, increase his knowledge of the Party's doctrines. Gradually, under such an educational program, the member becomes an "advanced" or "mature" Communist able to handle the most difficult of Party assignments. Such an individual, because of his indoctrination, automatically thinks

14

as the Party wants him to think, subordinates his personal desires to the interests of the Party, and works only for Communist goals.

Here arises the dynamics of motion in communism. In the Party there is a close relationship between theory and practice. Ideological training is designed to make the member a man of action—*revolutionary action*. The member is steeled in revolutionary discipline, armed for battles in the fields of infiltration, agitation, and propaganda.

At first blush communism may seem almost like an invincible monster. Admittedly, it can engender tremendous personal effort and zeal, but it has a *tragic flaw*, a flaw which heralds its eventual destruction.

Communism is anti-God: this is its fatal weakness. Hence, it is contrary to divine laws which give meaning, validity, and depth to the dignity of human personality. The world of communism, despite its overt bustling, energy, and action, is a cold world of sterility, conformity, and monotony. One is no longer regarded as a child of God, to bloom from spiritual roots. Rather, a deadly sameness is enforced, and the individual becomes a robot of the state, servile in thought, and groveling in attitude. The great seedbeds of dissent are deracinated. Critical thought and independent judgment are hunted down and destroyed. Freedom of expression is prohibited. Purges, concentration camps, and faked trials betray the poisonous hand of communism which corrupts everything it touches, creates error, evil, and sin, and transforms love into hate, justice into slavery, and truth into falsehood.

Contrasted to the world of Communist conformity, we as Christians have the unmatched power of Christ. The task for us is *spiritual rededication*—the creation of a world of love, justice, and truth. This is the Christian ethic which is part of our heritage. Ministers have a vital role in helping to roll back the iron curtain of communism and making real the world of divine love.

How Communism Works

In discussing such a mission, let us see what we can learn from the Communists by noting the way in which they inspire their members.

15

1. *Note the Communists' emphasis on returning to the original source of their beliefs to secure inspiration for their members.* Communists encourage members, young and old, to study the Party's "classics." To read such books, they say, is to gain personal guidance and raise the members' Communist qualities "in every respect to the same level as those of Marx, Engels, Lenin. . . ."

Answer: Think how much more enriching, rewarding, and satisfying are the original sources of Christian belief than the writings of the bigoted minds of the Communist "masters." The Bible is the Word of God. But besides the Bible, the writings of men of God, both clerical and lay, over 20 centuries are also guidelines to personal action. Do we as Christians take enough time to read the Bible—and these other affirmations of our faith? Do we quench our spiritual thirst (symbolized by the troubles, tensions, and anxieties of the day) with the truth ground in such sources? Are we digging deep enough in the wells of our faith? Most truly, the Bible gives inspiration, zeal, and guidance for life. To neglect it, is to reduce our national vitality and strength.

2. *Communists stress not only the reading of Marx, Engels, and Lenin, but reading them constantly—on a daily or weekly schedule—and never neglecting this habit even though the member becomes older.* "Comrades! Of course it is no easy matter to take Marx, Engels, and Lenin . . . as our models in self-cultivation and to become their most faithful and best pupils. It calls for an iron will and firm determination. . . . It calls for a life-long devotion to studying Marxism-Leninism. . . ."

Answer: How many Christians read the Bible only on special occasions? How many Christians set aside a certain amount of time each day or week for reading religious literature? Do some Christians regard the Bible as a book only for children; do they think that as adults they have outgrown it? Do we view the Bible as an "antique book" which has no message to our modern age? Do we display the same "iron will and firm determination" to learn the Christian faith as the Communists do for their ideology?

These are key questions, striking at the very heart of our religious faith and practices.

16

3. *The Communists have no use for a mere ceremonial avowal of Marxism or members interested only in acquiring a minimum knowledge of ideology.* "Every one of our Party members should not merely be a member of minimum qualifications . . . but should rather seek to make progress and ceaselessly raise his or her own consciousness and understanding of Marxism-Leninism."

Answer: Here again serious challenges are posed. How many church members today are merely members in name, not knowing or even caring what membership in the church of God really means and entails? Do some members object to learning about the tenets of their faith, and say that a few minimum requirements are enough? Has our Christian heritage been diluted by the inroads of secularism and materialism? Is our faith in God a growing, creative experience? Or are we satisfied with lesser visions of inspiration? The answers to these questions will help chart our way.

4. *At all times the Communists stress the relationship between theory and action.* To study the Communist "masters" is to ready oneself for revolutionary action. Communists are not interested in preparing members to parade their Marxist IQ's or pass academic examinations. Their knowledge must become a weapon to turn the world upside down for communism. "We study for the sole purpose of putting into practice what we have learnt. It is for the Party and for the victory of the revolution that we study."

Answer: In Christianity the study of the Bible is a guide to action—action in building a deeper Christian experience for the individual, and a better, more wholesome community. Are we as Christians adapting to actual practice the teachings of Christ? Are our day-to-day actions in the secular world determined by our Christian beliefs? Is the church—the Christian pulpit—effective today in determining men's actions? Are there individuals who think the church is a "good" organization to have in the community but should not be taken too seriously in everyday community action? These are challenges to us today.

5. *The Party stresses the development of the "politically mature" comrade, the individual on whom it can depend to carry out its mission.* The whole purpose of ideological

cultivation is to produce the member who will become a better Communist and work for the revolution.

Answer: Christians are also working for a revolution —a revolution of the spirit, not the sword. Deeply-committed Christians are needed to carry on the work of the Church, to uphold the Judaic-Christian faith. We may raise the question, are we working tirelessly enough to create these deeply-committed Christians? Are we training our members to buckle on the full armor of God, to commit their full lives to Christ? Working for Christian goals is a full-time job, not just a task for Sundays or evening meetings.

THE STRUGGLE IS REAL

How can we compete against such a powerful and dynamic ideology as communism? By way of answer we must say that as Christians and as Americans we *can* compete. We can defeat this atheistic enemy by drawing upon our spiritual resources.

Make no mistake about it, the struggle ahead is real. The Communists are determined, rugged, and treacherous enemies. The ideology of communism, as we have seen, generates great power. But the faith of communism is a perverted faith, giving predominance to evil, sin, and wrong. It draws its strength from deceit, chicanery, and hypocrisy. That is its fatal flaw, the rotten core which spoils the fruit of its branches.

The future, to a large extent, will be determined by what we as Christians have to say and do. Those who are ministers of the Gospel can help determine this fateful decision: shall it be a world of Communist domination or Christian rededication? Shall it be the cold world of Communist inhumanity, sterility, and conformity, where the bodies, minds, and souls of men become as stone, lifeless in the darkness of atheistic perversity, or shall it be Christian regeneration, where the power of the Holy Spirit floods in with joy, love, and harmony?

No group in America has a more key responsibility than the clergy. The answer to communism must be on a spiritual level. As representatives of a great tradition, the clergymen of America must light men's souls with deep enthusiasm for the teachings of Christ. A God-centered nation, ever humble before the majesty of the Divine Creator, can keep alive freedom, justice, and mercy. This is the heritage of America.

(Reprinted by permission from *Christianity Today*, Washington Building, Washington, D. C. 20005. October 10, 24, and November 7, 1960).

Chapter Two

QUOTATIONS ON COMMUNISM

ACADEMIC FREEDOM. I do fear so long as school boards and parents tolerate conditions whereby Communists and fellow travelers under the guise of academic freedom can teach our youth a way of life that eventually will destroy the sanctity of the home that undermines faith in God, that causes them to scorn respect for constituted authority, and sabotage our revered Constitution." (House Committee on Un-American Activities, "Menace of Communism," Washington: Government Printing Office, March 26, 1947, p. 43 in bound volume of Hearings. Pamphlet edition, p. 11.)

Schools and colleges should be on the alert against Communist infiltration. To spread Communist propaganda and hate under the guise of academic freedom is not freedom but vicious license. Parents should take a greater interest in school affairs and know what organizations attract their children. Communists recruit future members through the high-sounding youth auxiliary, the American Youth for Democracy, formerly known as the Young Communist League. ("How To Fight Communism," *Newsweek*, June 9, 1947, reprint, p. 4.)

The minds of young people on college campuses form the soil in which the conspirator is determined to implant seeds from which to reap a communist harvest. The truth about communism will never be learned from a communist. Such a one is an experienced propagandist whose sole objective is concealment of the truth. One does not get the truth about the conspiracy from an alert and sober communist propagandist. Rather, the true intent is detailed in secret or is blurted out in unguarded moments. A Khrushchev threatening, "We will bury you!" is a far more accurate measure of communist intent than a Khrushchev cooing coexistence!

A communist conspirator plotting the destruction of our freedom in the underground would seem to be a long cry from the campus philosopher who propagates collectivism among naive, impressionable minds. Yet how far are they apart? The mind which is truly liberal should be the first to condemn that which is false and hypocritical. Surely nothing can equal the obscene spectacle of the communist corruptionist hiding behind the shield of academic freedom in order to utilize his concealed weapons more effectively in behalf of tyranny! ("How To Beat Communism," *The Lion,* October 1957, reprint, p. 3.)

Alarming, too, is the ease with which some major educational institutions have been duped, under the much-abused term of "academic freedom," into permitting underhanded attacks to be made on democratic institutions and officials of government by instructors responsible for the higher education of our young people.

When academic freedom fails to recognize the importance of truth as the basic requirement for college classroom lectures and discussions, then the usefulness of our colleges and universities is a thing of the past. ("America—Freedom's Champion," October 18, 1960, p. 7.)

It is indeed ironic that Communist Party speakers— whose minds and thoughts and actions are *in no manner free* —should demand the opportunity to parrot the Moscow line to young Americans under the guise of *academic freedom!*

Academic freedom is not an instrument for the perpetuation of conspiratorial ideologies. Nor is it an agent of self-destruction — a freedom to destroy freedom. As a free-flowing channel of truth and knowledge, academic freedom is not obligated to carry along the silted tributaries of lies and distortions of known communists. ("Keys to Freedom," November 16, 1963, p. 6.)

In full swing, also, is the Party's speaking campaign which brings leading Communists to college campuses. Through this program, the Party is provided with a platform from which to try to convince our young people that it is a legitimate American political group interested in improving our society. Here the Communists seek to gain the sympathy of idealistic youth, pleading that the Party is serving as a "martyr" in fighting for the "Bill of Rights." Under the guise of academic freedom, they promote a way of life which itself tolerates no academic freedom. ("America's Ideals— Its Mark of Greatness," *The Union Central Advocate*, 1965, reprint.)

ACCUSED WRONGLY——DO IF? Not only can he present his version, but the FBI welcomes any such person's coming in and relating his story. We are a fact-finding organization and we are just as zealous to protect the innocent as we are to detect those who pose a threat to the internal security of our country. ("Where Do We Stand Today With Communism in the United States?" *Congressional Record*, March 1, 1954, p. 2297.)

AGREEMENTS BROKEN. During the last 30 years, the United States has participated in hundreds of meetings with the Communists—Teheran, Yalta, Potsdam, Panmunjom and Geneva. These meetings led to many agreements, almost all of which have been broken by Soviet Russia.

We are at war with this sinister conspiracy. Every Communist today must be considered as enemy, wherever he may be, at home or abroad.

A "soft" approach toward the menace of communism can lead only to national disaster. ("An American's Challenge," *Congressional Record*, Oct. 12, 1962, p. 22069.)

AMERICA—WEAKNESS. The God-given ideals which are responsible for this country's greatness are being attacked on many fronts today. Moral lethargy, self-indulgence, neglect of duty—these lethal forces are undermining many facets of business, labor, industry and Government.

We find their influence in the repulsive attitude of "half-way Americans" to whom life in this country is the enjoyment of rights and privileges devoid of responsibilities.

We find their influence in those courts of law where the true purpose and intent of our Constitution as a document designed for the protection of society have too often been warped and distorted for the benefit of offenders.

We find their influence in the continuing increase of crime—a tragic national problem which is growing four times as fast as our expanding population.

Crime has no respect for age, nationality, sex, color or religious creed. It has turned our streets into virtual jungles of terror and fear.

Today, a brutal crime of violence—a murder, forcible rape or assault to kill—is committed every three minutes. The number of these senseless atrocities will continue to grow until men of strong moral conviction assert greater influence toward the prevention of crime and administration of justice.

Disrespect for law and order is a tragic moral sickness which attacks and destroys the American traditions of honesty, integrity and fair play. The moral strength of our Nation has slipped alarmingly. National corruption is the sum total of individual corruption. We must follow the teachings of God if we hope to cure this moral illness.

Law and order are bulwarks on which successful government must stand. Without law and order, society will destroy itself.

Fantasy and weakness have too often prevailed in the administration of justice where strength and realism are essential needs.

There are some misguided social workers and judges who have perverted the meaning of mercy. When so-called mercy aids society's enemies, it is no longer mercy. It is sheer stupidity, if not worse. Justice is needed—stern justice. Without such justice our streets—and our families—will continue to be endangered.

Justice is not served when the innocent victim and society suffer while the vicious criminal goes free.

Oliver Wendell Holmes, Jr., observed: "At the present time in this country there is more danger that criminals will escape justice than that they will be subjected to tyranny."

Judge Learned Hand said: "Our dangers do not lie in too little tenderness to the accused. Our procedure has been always haunted by the ghost of the innocent man convicted. It is an unreal dream. What we need to fear is the archaic formalism and the watery sentiment that obstructs, delays, and defeats the prosecution of crime."

Justice Benjamin N. Cardozo observed: "Justice, though due to the accused, is due to the accuser also. The concept of fairness must not be strained till it is narrowed to a filament. We are to keep the balance true."

Let us proceed to try armed robbers as armed robbers. Let the punishment fit the crime and let us "keep the balance true."

Wherever politics and opportunism remain primary considerations in the appointment of jurists, parole officials, and others charged with the administration of justice, the public should have more adequate guarantees for the immediate removal of those who prove by their unjustifiable actions that they cannot be entrusted with the important responsibilities of their offices.

The fact is millions of free Americans are taking our good way of life for granted. They have ceased to care about our foundation stones, the "rock from which we were hewn."

Let us never forget that religion has made us what we are, given us what we have. Every good thing we enjoy as free Americans came directly or indirectly out of our belief in God.

Our best offensive against crime, subversion, intolerance, and all enemies of America's heritage of freedom is brotherhood—a brotherhood such as yours, built upon a solid foundation of mutual trust, understanding, and faith in God.

There must be a moral reawakening in every home in our land.

History shows us the great accomplishments that can be attained by the combined efforts of selfless men and women who are sincerely dedicated to a noble cause. We have such a cause in America—to dispel intolerance, to preserve the rule of law, to protect and strengthen our God-given ideals and faith in freedom. ("Faith in Freedom" *Congressional Record*, December 5, 1963, p. A7435.)

AMERICAN—HALFWAY. Spineless indifference, apathy and neglect of civic duty such as this are a national disgrace. What has happened to the civic pride and the sense of decency of these citizens? Has the last ounce been drained from the chalice of courage and moral indignation within their communities?

Today, there are too many signs that Americans, as individuals, are pursuing the deadly course of irresponsibility which has led to the downfall of other nations and other cultures throughout the history of mankind.

I refer particularly to those halfway Americans who eagerly avail themselves of every right and privilege which our country guarantees its inhabitants while blatantly refusing to accept the duties that life in a free society necessarily entails. I refer also to those modern-day Rip Van Winkles who tolerate abuses of our democratic institutions and corrosive downgrading of America's high ideals by dangerous enemies of freedom. ("Our Heritage of Greatness," December 12, 1964, p. 3.)

AMERICAN LEGION. This Nation would not now have the noblest government of individual human dignity yet known were it not for the gallantry of veterans like you of the Legion who put country above convenience, patriotism above profit and service above self-interest. ("America—Freedom's Champion." October 18, 1960, p. 2.)

AMERICAN NAZI PARTY. This Bureau has under active investigation 9 hate-type groups having a total estimated membership of 500 individuals. The largest of these is the American Nazi Party led by George Lincoln Rockwell, with headquarters in Arlington, Va. This group has an approximate membership of 100 individuals. (*FBI Appropriation 1966,* p. 81.)

AMERICAN YOUTH FOR DEMOCRACY. Illustrative of how the Communists bury one organization and conceive another is the Young Communist League. In convention assembled in New York City, the Young Communist League was dissolved on October 16, 1943, and the next day The American Youth for Democracy was born.

At first the Communists denied paternity for the AYD, but in April of 1946 the Party's National Board indicated that the AYD was the successor to the YCL. William Z. Foster, the Communist Party head, at the AYD National Intercollegiate Conference in New York City in 1945, told the delegates in the concluding session that, "The atomic age is the age of socialism, of Communism. This is the greatest lesson that the youth of America can learn." This new front set up youth centers ostensibly to combat juvenile delinquency. More properly, these centers could be termed Communist youth recruiting centers. (House Committee on Un-American Activities, "Menace of Communism," Washington: Government Printing Office, March 26, 1947, p. 10. Page 42 in bound volume of Hearings.)

AMERICANISM. Today, our country faces the most severe test ever to confront a free people. Here and abroad, mortal enemies of freedom and deniers of God Himself conspire to undermine the fundamental forces which are the lifeline of our country's vitality and greatness—our most formidable weapons, in peace and in war.

What are these forces? They are:

FAITH—faith in a Supreme Being: God, the Author of Liberty.

INDIVIDUALISM—inherent dignity and worth of every sovereign individual with his personal rights and responsibilities.

COURAGE—the courage of a free people firmly dedicated to the noblest cause.

INTEGRITY—that quality of trustworthiness which is essential in dealings between men, *and* between countries.

DISCIPLINE—and self-discipline, which are vital in a nation governed by laws rather than by men.

VISION—such as led our founding fathers into the perilous dangers of a hostile wilderness that was to become the proud American Republic in which we live today.

These are America's great bulwarks. They are under savage attack today, just as they were so severely tested nearly 200 years ago at Bunker Hill and at Valley Forge.

Daniel Webster, that brilliant early American statesman, eloquently declared, "God grants liberty only to those who love it, and are always ready to guard and defend it." ("Keys to Freedom," November 16, 1963, pp. 2-4.)

We Americans must never lose sight of the fact that our power, wealth, and happiness come directly or indirectly from our belief in God. Let us commemorate Thanksgiving by refurbishing our religious ideals. And as we meet the forces throughout the world which seek to destroy our way

26

of life, let us find strength in the Biblical quotation, "If God be for us, who can be against us?" (*FBI Law Enforcement Bulletin,* November 1, 1964, p. 2.)

I subscribe to the words of our 26th President, Theodore Roosevelt, when he defined Americanism as "the virtues of courage, honor, justice, truth, sincerity and hardihood." There is an urgent need for those strong virtues in our Nation today as we face the threats and provocations of a godless conspiracy which is bent upon enslaving the entire world. ("Our Heritage of Greatness," December 12, 1964, p. 5.)

AMERICANISM—NEED TO UNDERSTAND. The Communists, above all else, fear the truth. They fear the traditions of liberty and justice bequeathed us by our freedom-seeking forefathers. That is why they seek to rewrite the past. The fine and loyal members of your great organization are to be congratulated for urging the study of American history. There can be no surer way to appreciate American democracy than to understand its origins and growth. We should understand also the things our forefathers were willing to fight for and the ideals in which they believed. (Remarks before the Continental Congress of the National Society Daughters of the American Revolution, April 22, 1954, p. 4.)

AMERICANISM: POSITIVE, NOT JUST NEGATIVE. Above all, American young people should know more about the principles of freedom which have made this country great. We are against communism—yes, but more than that we are for something—the basic values of human dignity and freedom.

REAL MEANING

As Americans, we should count our blessings one by one. America was created by men and women accepting duties and responsibilities as well as exercising their rights and privileges. Ours is a country built by hard work, dedication, and extreme personal sacrifice.

Parents and educators should emphasize the real meaning of our flag, our Constitution, our heritage of law. For too many young Americans, Valley Forge, Bunker Hill, Old Ironsides are nothing but names, vaguely comprehended and unappreciated.

We need to make this American heritage live with enthusiasm and interest, to encourage our young people to feel the impact of the living personality of Washington and Jefferson.

This heritage should inspire young people to be better citizens themselves, realizing that they are the heirs of this legacy upon whose shoulders our future exists.

An America humble before God; an America serving the needs of all its citizens—this must be our goal. (*Congressional Record,* June 10, 1964, p. A3132.)

ANTI-ANTI-COMMUNISM. My feelings concerning the Communist Party of the United States are well known. I have not hesitated over the years to express my concern and apprehension. As a consequence, its professional smear brigades have conducted a relentless assault against the FBI. You who have been members of this Committee also know the fury with which the Party, its sympathizers and fellow travelers can launch an assault. I do not mind such attacks. What has been disillusioning is the manner in which they have been able to enlist support often from apparently well-meaning but thoroughly duped persons.

Anyone who opposes the American Communist is at once branded as a "disrupter," a "Fascist," a "Red baiter," or a "Hitlerite," and becomes the object of a systematic campaign of character assassination. This is easily understood because the basic tactics of the Communist Party are deceit and trickery. (House Committee on Un-American Activities, "Menace of Communism," March 26, 1947, p. 2.)

ANTI-SEMITISM. Today the fires of anti-Semitism continue to burn with fierce intensity in many areas of the world. This is particularly true behind the Iron Curtain where communism, the bitter enemy of Judaism and of all other religions of the world, seeks to destroy your priceless heritage and the right of your people to live according to the tenets of God.

During the past generation, the conscience of decent men everywhere has been shocked by the continuing vicious atrocities that have been committed against Jews in the Soviet Union. Rabbis have been arrested and imprisoned or executed; synagogues have been desecrated; the traditional Jewish school system has been liquidated; and Hebrew literature, language and customs have been suppressed by the Russian Communists.

Despite Communist claims of improved conditions for Jews under the Khrushchev regime, the opposite actually is true. Additional forms of suppression have been introduced.

The observance of Passover no longer can be held according to tradition; sacred Hebrew burial customs have been obstructed; and a statewide program has been instituted to make Jews the scapegoats for criminal acts affecting the Russian economy. Jews are clearly identified by religion on the internal passport which all Soviet citizens must carry.

Last October, the outrageous extent of this program was disclosed by the Moscow newspaper *Izvestia* when it announced the arrests of several persons involved in an alleged criminal conspiracy. The leaders of this gang have "Jewish names," *Izvestia* told its readers in demanding a "show trial" and "death sentence."

Vicious outbursts of religious hatred such as this caused one American newspaper recently to warn its readers, "For reasons best known to themselves the Soviet leaders discriminate heavily against Jews. The evidence is overwhelming and incontrovertible and renewed almost daily by the Russians themselves."

In a joint statement released last summer, three American Jewish organizations denounced the Soviet press for conveying "a viciously negative image of the Jews," and indignantly proclaimed, "Soviet Jews are deprived by official policy of religious and cultural rights . . . and are the victims of discrimination." (*Congressional Record,* December 5, 1963, p. A7434.)

APATHY. "An attitude of complacency seems to have permeated the national mind to an almost unbelievable extent. There is a trend of softness toward wrong-doing that can cause irreparable harm. We are being stifled by technicalities and by the throwing of road blocks in the pathway of our traditional methods of justice." ("Legion Alert as Guest Speakers Decry Public Apathy to Dangers," *The American Legion Magazine,* November, 1957, p. 32.)

Mr. Hoover warned that apathy toward the threat of subversion continued to grow in 1958. "Sensing a more favorable atmosphere, the Communist Party, USA, and its dupes and sympathizers gained further courage and became more vocal in their attacks upon law enforcement and other professions which are dedicated to preserving our freedoms," he said. (FBI Release, December 22, 1958, p. 3.)

Communists know that apathy among American citizens is the chink in democracy's armor. One of the speakers at the 17th national convention revealed the basic Communist tactic of taking advantage of every weakness when he urged members of the Communist Party, U.S.A., to move in the primaries since 90 percent of the Congressmen are elected at the primaries.

The convention heard a report of a five-man committee which had made a study of what the party could do in the 1960 elections. It advocated, among other things, influencing both major political parties. Also, it recommended that the party attempt to exploit labor and Negro groups to wield independent political influence. This report was adopted by the convention. (Senate Internal Security Subcommittee, "Concerning the 17th National Convention, Communist Party, U.S.A., December 10-13, 1959," Washington: Government Printing Office, 1960, p. 9.)

Heartened by an atmosphere of continuing public complacency, and encouraged by its successes in invoking every legal technicality to thwart the interests of justice, the Communist Party is today a unified, ambitious, and destructive instrument of subversion operating within our midst. It has shown a brazen defiance and disrespect for America's laws, governmental institutions, and traditions. (*FBI Appropriation, 1962,* March 6, 1961, p. 48.)

Some persons may not believe that a Communist could reach a position of responsibility in Government through the election process. They have only to consider the thousands of votes cast for William Cottle Taylor, vice chairman of the party's southern California district, who publicly identified himself as a Communist while running in the California primary as an independent candidate for the Board of Supervisors of Los Angeles County. Although Taylor was defeated, he rolled up an impressive 33,576 votes, or some 13 percent of the total vote cast for this office on June 2, 1964. (*FBI Appropriation 1966,* p. 58.)

APATHY—IMMORAL. Where moral issues are concerned, there can be no compromise. Too many apathetic persons are unwilling to take an active part in the clearance of moral slums. Righteous anger is an inevitable ingredient of a truly noble life. Supine indifference always is a sign of moral deterioration.

Either we display the courage and determination to actively uphold our God-given heritage of freedom and decency, or we surrender ourselves to an evil cause. If the values we profess to hold dear are to be protected and nurtured, we must have a rebirth of faith and belief in their worth. ("Faith or Fear," *Congressional Record*, June 28, 1960, p. 13653.)

APATHY—RESULTS. If we fail—if we allow ourselves to be duped by communist cunning and the "new look" — we shall, with a casualness that is indecent, toss into discard our immortal heritage of freedom. ("Communist 'New Look' A Study in Duplicity," *The Elks Magazine*, August 1956, reprint, p. 4.)

Many times I have thought that if this young Republic is to fall before the grinding onslaught of a slave-driven regime, it will not be solely because an enemy-directed fifth column has worked its way into the body politic. Rather, it will be because we who are citizens are indifferent.

It is to me appalling that so few among all the citizens who daily enjoy the God-given blessings of being Free Americans are sufficiently interested in their future, and that of their children, to acquaint themselves fully with the facts of communism. Too many people condemn the word yet have not the vaguest notion of the evil which the word encompasses.

A handful of inspired men gave us our freedom. They cannot preserve it for us. That responsibility rests with the individual American. (*Ibid.,* p. 4.)

And what is that future to be? Will we sit at the feet of false prophets and supinely allow this devastating blight to spread and liquidate the free spirit of man? Will we stand by meekly as individual man is annihilated and transformed into a mechanized mass creature? Or will we rise against the destroyer by fearlessly bringing to young Americans the challenge, the vision, and the substance of a theistic philosophy which holds sacred the dignity of each human being? ("God and Country or Communism?" *The American Legion Magazine,* November, 1957, reprint, p. 9.)

"I wonder," Hoover declared, "how many stalwart, God-loving people there are in Poland, Hungary, Czechoslovakia, China and other red-controlled countries who today . . . condemn themselves for their failure to recognize the first signs of infiltration of subversive forces." ("Legion Alert as Guest Speakers Decry Public Apathy to Dangers," *The American Legion Magazine,* November, 1957, p. 33.)

Lethargy leads only to disaster. The communists have a savage plan of liquidation for a vanquished America. The blueprint can be found in the words of Mao Tse-tung, Chairman of the Chinese Communist Party, who reportedly said that it was necessary to liquidate 800,000 "enemies" to solidify communism in China. Another pattern is the plight of countless families in satellite countries who were torn apart and transported to the oblivion of Soviet labor camps. (*FBI Law Enforcement Bulletin,* March, 1960, p. 1.)

All our hopes for the future of our country, as well as for a world at peace, are bound up with our hopes for the future of our Nation's youth. They will not fail us if we do not fail them. Only our apathy and laxity in the face of the threat which Communist infiltration efforts represent can cause such a failure. It is the duty of all Americans to fully understand the true import of this threat to our heritage, to expose it, and to combat it with every weapon at our command. (House Committee on Un-American Activities, "Communist Target—Youth, Communist Infiltration and Agitation Tactics," Washington: Government Printing Office, 1960, p. 11.)

APATHY—SUICIDE. Public apathy is the sure way to national suicide—to death of individual freedom. It allowed the Communists to penetrate and make satellites of once-free countries, and it is presently enabling them to honeycomb and weaken the structures of the remaining countries, and there is today a terrifying apathy on the part of Americans toward the deadliest danger which this country has ever faced. Some of that apathy is deliberately induced.

The Communist Party in the United States is not out of business; it is not dead; it is not even dormant. It is, however, well on its way to achieving its current objective, which is to make you believe that it is shattered, ineffective, and dying. When it has fully achieved this first objective— . . . it will then proceed inflexibly toward its final goal.

Those who try to minimize its danger are either uninformed or they have a deadly axe to grind. (Quoted in HCUA, "Communist Infiltration and Activities in the South." Washington: Government Printing Office, 1958, p. 2754.)

APATHY—WHY. As a decent American citizen you mind your own business, work hard at your job, discharge your civic duties, and when you come home after a busy day you desire nothing so much as to stretch out in your favorite chair with the evening paper. The sense of well-being you experience is enhanced if the news happens to reflect even the most nebulous indication that the nightmare world of communism may be willing—sometime—somewhere—to make some slight concession toward civilized standards of behavior. So, you relax, and communism seems a threat that is sinister but distant, and one which, given time, might eventually recede and leave you and your loved ones untouched.

Would it surprise you to know that you are experiencing the very feeling of relaxation which the proponents of the most monstrous tyranny ever conceived desire to evoke in you? Would you be startled to learn that you are included in the Communist blueprint for the future and that as of now the Communist manipulators are striving to develop in you a frame of mind which will enable them to carry that blueprint through to a successful conclusion? ("Communist 'New Look' A Study in Duplicity," *The Elks Magazine,* reprint, August, 1956, p. 1.)

Mr. Director, I just wonder if you can give any explanation as to why so many organizations that are basically sound and dedicated to doing what is right—and I do not hesitate to name one of them, the National Council of Churches —why are some of the hierarchy of these organizations so naive to the threat posed by communism in this country?

Mr. Hoover. Mr. Congressman, I think it is due to the fact they have not fully informed themselves as to what the facts are. Many people have the idea that communism is not a serious threat because the movement is numerically small in this country. Its numerical strength is one thing but we must judge it by its fanatical, dedicated, and disciplined membership. Most non-Communists are not disciplined, fanatical believers in the theory and practice of American democracy as are the Communists in communism. That is a reason why some of these people err in their thinking.

Such erroneous thinking often results in a great deal of harm, particularly in many organizations where the practice is followed of having the rank-and-file elect delegates to represent them at conventions without exhibiting a sufficient degree of alertness and interest to determine the beliefs of their chosen representatives. As a result, these representatives commit large groups of the rank-and-file to a course of action which in reality is contrary to their true feeling and beliefs. As I pointed out previously in my testimony, apathy also plays a strong part in creating a prevailing atmosphere of indifference to this threat. (*FBI Appropriation 1962,* March 6, 1961, pp. 68-69.)

APPEASEMENT. In dealing with the treacherous Red Kremlin and its satellites, the road of appeasement is not the road to peace. It is surrender on the installment plan! ("America —Freedom's Champion," October 18, 1960, p. 3.)

We also have in our midst some timid souls who have so little faith in the strength of democrary that they would have our country yield to international threats and intimidation. I include those persons who urge "appeasement at any price" and those who chant the "better Red than dead" slogan.

America's emblem is the soaring eagle—not the blind and timid mole. Fear, apologies, defeatism, and cowardice are alien to the thinking of true Americans! As for me, I would rather be Dead than Red! ("The Faith to be Free," December 7, 1961, p. 6.)

Those who follow the road of appeasement do not know the true meaning of freedom. They do not comprehend the misery of Communist enslavement. You will not find their cheap slogans on the lips of the Hungarian refugees, the East German patriots, nor other freedom-loving peoples who have escaped from behind the Iron Curtain. (*Ibid.,* p. 6.)

Nor do you find their apologies in the writings of great American patriots such as: Patrick Henry, who asked the searching question, "Is life so dear, or peace so sweet, as to be purchased at the price of chains and slavery?"; or Benjamin Franklin, who declared, "They that can give up essential liberty to obtain a little temporary safety deserve neither liberty nor safety"; or Samuel Adams, who reminded us that "The liberties of our country . . . . are worth defending at all hazards; and it is our duty to defend them against all attacks. We have received them as a fair inheritance from our worthy ancestors . . . . [who] purchased them for us with toil and danger. . ." (*Ibid.*, p. 7.)

APOLOGISTS. Unfortunately, we are plagued with some Soviet apologists who, time after time, would have us betray the cause of international freedom and justice by yielding to the Red fascists in the Kremlin on vital moral issues. (*Ibid.*, p. 6.)

We must continue to stiffen our national backbone in dealing with the communists and their dupes, sympathizers, and apologists. If we relax our guard for one moment, we court national disaster. (*Ibid.*, p. 5.)

APTHEKER, HERBERT EUGENE. Also under provisions of the Internal Security Act of 1950, the Department of State revoked the passports held by Elizabeth Gurley Flynn and Herbert Eugene Aptheker, both national communist leaders. The revocation was based on testimony of witnesses supplied by the FBI concerning the Communist Party membership of Flynn and Aptheker. Both have filed suit in U. S. District Court, Washington, D. C., seeking to enjoin the Secretary of State from revoking their passports, and attacking the constitutionality of the passport section of the law. (*FBI Annual Report, Fiscal Year 1963*, p. 21.)

ATHEISM. And last year, Nikita Khrushchev, the present head of the Russian Communist Party, publicly proclaimed that Communists have not changed their opinion on religion and said: "We remain the atheists that we have always been; we are doing all we can to liberate those people who are still under the spell of this religious opiate."

When Communists temporarily and passively tolerate religion, it is for the purpose of furthering communism. But

35

time and again they have struck ruthlessly against Christians, Jews and other faiths, torturing, imprisoning, and murdering those who hold God above the State. Those who hate God always bring misery in their wake. They are brutal, cruel, and deceitful. Communism denies and destroys every spiritual value. No church and no church member can temporize with it. ("The Twin Enemies of Freedom," *FBI Law Enforcement Bulletin,* January 1957, reprint, p. 3.)

ATHEISM—COMMUNISM. International communism is the vilest form of atheism ever devised by the mind of man. It is completely unrestrained by moral considerations. Its methods are lies, immorality, treachery and deceit. Its agents are the almost 35 million fanatics who comprise the 83 Communist Parties throughout the world today. Here are the legions from which world atheism draws its strongest support. (*Congressional Record,* June 28, 1960, p. 13653.)

ATHEISM PAVES THE WAY FOR COMMUNISM. And what is that philosophy? To scholars, it is known as "dialectical materialism." While all Communists are materialists, not all materialists are Communists. Scores of individuals who have never been members of the Communist organization contribute to the spread of the philosophy of materialism. In so doing they are adding generously to the strength of the Communist movement. Among these philosophic materialists are numerous educators, authors, and lecturers. These materialists deny the existence of God. They deny the existence of the soul, of immortality, and of values derived from unchanging moral principles. Reality, the materialists maintain, consists only of matter. These people, as I stated, are not Communists; yet they are preparing mental soil for the seeds of communism. Their pernicious doctrine of materialism, fed to young Americans as something new and modern, readies the minds of our youth to accept the immoral, atheistic system of thought we know as communism.

It is a fact that the doctrines which the materialists hold to today are neither new nor modern. The basic philosophy of materialism predates modern communism by many centuries. It is broader and more diversified than communism, yet it places today's non-Communist materialists on common ground with the "idea men" who brought forth the curse of communism that now plagues the world.

The theoretical father of modern communism is the philosophic materialism of the ancients. And the children of this father—both inside and outside the Communist Party —are partisans and allies of each other in the campaign to debase man to the level of an animal.

Atheism—militant on the part of the Communist—is the common denominator of all materialists. Lenin spoke for all materialists, Communists and non-Communists alike, when he said:

"Our propaganda necessarily includes the propaganda of atheism. . . ."

The philosophy of materialism—in all its forms—is the intellectual problem of the future. ("God and Country or Communism?," *The American Legion Magazine,* November, 1957, reprint, pp. 8-9.)

ATTORNEY GENERAL'S LIST. At the close of the fiscal year, 274 organizations, both communist and non-Communist, appeared on the Attorney General's list of groups designated under Executive Order 10450. Under the Internal Security Act of 1950, the Subversive Activities Control Board has ordered 13 Communist fronts to register. Appeals have been filed in 11 of these cases, and the Court of Appeals for the District of Columbia has ordered further proceedings held in abeyance. (*Annual Report, Fiscal Year 1961,* p. 28.)

BLACK MUSLIM AND BLACK NATIONALIST EXTREMIST GROUPS. Through our responsibility to be aware of the formation of organizations which might require investigative attention to determine whether these organizations are engaged in activities in violation of any Federal statutes, various Negro organizations have come to our attention over the years. These include such organizations as the Nation of Islam, frequently called the Black Muslims, some members of which have refused to register under the provisions of the Selective Service Act, and the Revolutionary Action Movement, a highly militant, secretive organization which believes in replacing the capitalistic system with socialism.

Such activities require coverage and add to our work.

The Nation of Islam (NOI), an all-Negro, violently anti-white organization, which is frequently referred to as the

Black Muslims, teaches complete separation of the races; economic independence for the so-called Negro; and the black man in the United States will in the future own and occupy a separate black nation.

The national headquarters of this organization is located in Chicago, Ill., and its leader is a Georgia-born Negro who calls himself Elijah Muhammad who claims to have been selected by Allah, the Supreme Being, to lead the so-called Negro out of slavery. Muhammad and some other members of the NOI have refused to register under the provisions of the Selective Service Acts declaring that members of the organization owe no allegiance to the United States.

Members of the NOI have continuously been involved in violent conflict with local police. These altercations have resulted in injury to both NOI members and the local police officers.

The membership of the NOI has been estimated at 6,100 persons. However, the membership is decreasing as a result of the recent publication of charges filed against Elijah Muhammad asking support for illegitimate children. These charges indicate that Muhammad is the father of the children and the women have been employed as his secretaries. The disputes within the NOI have resulted in the formal organizing of splinter groups. One such group was formed by Wallace Muhammad, son of Elijah Muhammad, and was known as the Afro-Descendant Upliftment Society. This group has ceased to exist and Wallace Muhammad has been reaccepted by the NOI.

The Muslim Mosque, Inc. (MMI), was formed in March 1964, and headed by Malcolm X Little, former national functionary and leading spokesman of the NOI, until Little's murder on February 21, 1965. The MMI is also an all-Negro, violently antiwhite organization. The MMI, according to the statements of its former leader, advocates entrance into the civil rights movement in the United States and the formation of rifle clubs by Negro groups for the purpose of self-defence where the Federal Government will not afford adequate protection to civil rights demonstrators. The MMI also advocates the formation of Mau-Mau-type guerilla bands to obtain Negro rights. This organization teaches a Muslim religion.

38

The national headquarters of this organization is located in New York City. Efforts are being made to organize branches in various cities, including Boston and Philadelphia.

Members of the NOI and the MMI have engaged in altercations mainly arising out of the belief that the NOI has "declared war" upon the MMI and Little. This is a result of public utterances by Little indicating that Elijah Muhammad is the father of illegitimate children.

Little was shot and killed on the afternoon of February 21, 1965, while speaking at a meeting of the Organization of Afro-American Unity. The New York City Police Department has arrested Talmadge Hayer, Thomas Johnson, and Norman Butler in connection with this murder and is seeking others believed to have been involved. Hayer was previously arrested on November 8, 1963, and charged with receiving stolen goods in connection with the theft of firearms from the Liberty Firearms Co., Passaic, N. J. He was released on $3,500 bail. This matter is still pending in the courts. Sources of this Bureau have identified Hayer as a member of the Nation of Islam who attended meetings as recently as two months ago. Butler and Johnson were also previously arrested on November 8, 1963, and charged with shooting on January 6, 1965, of Benjamin Brown. Brown had defected from the Nation of Islam and had set up a Muslim worship hall. Butler and Johnson have been described as "enforcers" of Nation of Islam Temple No. 7 in New York City. At the time of their arrest in connection with the shooting of Little both were out on $10,000 bail in connection with the shooting of Brown.

Organization of Afro-American Unity (OAAU): The formation of this organization was announced in June 1964, by its then leader Malcolm X Little. The purpose of the OAAU is to bring before the United Nations the existing problems of the Negro in the United States. Membership of the OAAU is made up of members of the MMI, plus other individuals who do not desire to become involved in the religious teachings of the MMI.

Headquarters of the OAAU is located with the MMI headquarters and the same individuals direct both organizations.

Revolutionary Action Movement (RAM) is described as a highly militant, secretive organization following the Chinese-oriented Marxist-Leninist line and believes in replacing the capitalistic system with socialism. This group reportedly has a collective leadership representing Boston, Mass.; Chicago, Ill.; Cleveland, Ohio; and Detroit, Mich.

According to information we have received, RAM either follows or believes in the writings of Robert Franklin Williams, a Bureau fugitive currently residing in Cuba. Williams has visited Red China. In August 1961, Williams and others were charged with kidnaping a white couple at Monroe, N. C., during a racial incident. He fled to Cuba, where he has established a publication identified as "The Crusader" which advocates that Negroes arm themselves and fight violence with violence.

Although no timetable is known, RAM allegedly has its program organized into three stages, the first one being education and recruitment. The second stage is one of expropriation whereby efforts will be made to secure sufficient funds for the organization. This will include robbery and other means, legal or illegal. The third stage will be one of direct action whereby the present system of government will be replaced by RAM's Chinese-oriented society, to be accomplished by any means available.

Another militant Negro Organization is known as the Black Liberation Front. Members of this organization were involved in the conspiracy to destroy through the use of explosives several of our national monuments. Robert Steele Collier, a Negro, is the self-styled leader of this organization which has only a handful of members.

The joint investigation by the FBI and the New York City Police Department into the conspiracy to dynamite three symbols of liberty and freedom in the United States—the Statue of Liberty in New York City, the Liberty Bell in Philadelphia, and the Washington Monument in Washington, D. C.—led to the arrest on February 16, 1965, by the police and the FBI of three Negro men, Robert Steele Collier, Walter Augustus Bowe, and Khaleel Sultarn Sayyed; and Michelle Duclos, a white woman from Canada. A quantity of dynamite and blasting caps was also recovered. All were charged with conspiring to destroy Government property. The New York City Police Department also charged Robert Collier with the unauthorized possession of explosives. All are awaiting further prosecutive action.

Collier, in 1964, traveled to Cuba in a group under the auspices of the Student Committee for Travel to Cuba in violation of a U. S. Department of State ban on such travel. Another of the Negro men, Walter Augustus Bowe, has been a supporter of the Fair Play for Cuba Committee and Fidel Castro. (*FBI Appropriation, 1966*, March 4, 1965. pp. 59-60.)

The Organization for Black Power formally came into existence at a conference held in Chicago, Ill., over the July 4, 1965, weekend. According to its literature—"Membership in the Organization for Black Power shall be of organizations and individuals who accept the perspective of Black Power and the discipline of the organization in the struggle for this power." The organization states it—"is part of the revolutionary struggle of people all over the world to liberate themselves from the determination of the United States to impose its way of life on the whole world and to build a new world free from exploitation." (*FBI Appropriation, 1967*, February 10, 1966, p. 55.)

BLACK NATIONALIST MOVEMENT: FOREIGN INFLUENCES. The question of foreign influences in the black nationalist movement is a matter of grave concern to the FBI and during the course of our investigative activity in this field we are ever alert to this possibility. For one thing there has been travel abroad by such militant black nationalists as Stokely Carmichael of the Black Panther Party, James Forman of the Student Nonviolent Coordinating Committee, Milton and Richard Bullock Henry of the Republic of New Africa, and others.

In April 1968, black power posters were sent to the United States from Cuba. These posters urged "Retaliation to Crime: Revolutionary Violence" and were distributed by the Afro-Asian-Latin American Peoples Solidarity Organization. Havana, Cuba. (FBI, *1970 Appropriation*, April 17, 1969, p. 72.)

BLACK PANTHER PARTY. One of the most active black extremist groups is the Black Panther Party. It originated in Oakland, Calif., in 1966 and now has extended its activities to numerous cities throughout the United States.

41

Its members gained notoriety initially because of their practice of carrying rifles and pistols in plain view on the streets of Oakland while on "defense patrols" to prevent alleged police brutality.

On May 2, 1967, a group of Black Panther Party members armed with rifles, shotguns, and handguns, invaded the chamber of the California State Assembly, while that body was in session, to protest pending gun legislation.

More recently its "minister of defense," Huey Newton, is appealing his conviction on Sept. 8, 1968, for having shot and killed an Oakland police officer who had stopped him in connection with a motor vehicle violation in October 1967.

On still another occasion, eight other members of this black extremist organization were arrested for complicity in a gun battle with Oakland police on April 6, 1968, during which one Black Panther Party member was killed. Thirteen rifles, four handguns, and four shotguns were confiscated from the participants.

Leroy Eldridge Cleaver, minister of information of the Black Panther Party, achieved notoriety rivaling that of Stokely Carmichael during 1968. A parolee who was freed in December 1966 after serving 9 years in California prisons, Cleaver was returned to prison in April 1968 due to his involvement in a gun battle with Oakland, Calif., police. He was again released after 2 months following a court ruling that his parole had been improperly revoked for political activity. This decision was overruled by higher California courts and Cleaver was scheduled to return to prison on November 27, 1968. He failed to appear and on December 10, 1968, a Federal fugitive warrant was issued charging him with unlawful flight to avoid confinement.

Cleaver ran as presidential candidate of the Peace and Freedom Party and in this capacity made a series of speeches on college campuses. These received widespread publicity because of their extreme obscenity and calls for revolutionary action by black people.

Another active Black Panther leader is George Mason Murray, minister of education. He is also a member of the Central Committee of the San Francisco State College Black Student Union. The latter organization has been deeply involved in the campus agitation which has plagued that college during the current school year.

The political philosophy of the Black Panther Party is based in part on the writings of Mao Tse-tung of Communist China. It advocates that its members study the teachings of Mao Tse-tung. Instructions have been given to members on the making and the use of Molotov cocktails. Members have also been instructed in guerrilla warfare tactics in preparation for a showdown with established authority. It is reported that in the near future scheduled training sessions in California will teach guerrilla warfare tactics to selected members from all parts of the United States. (FBI, *1970 Appropriation*, April 17, 1969, pp. 69-70)

BLACK POWER—THIRD NATIONAL CONFERENCE ON BLACK POWER. Some 3,000 persons registered for the Third National Conference on Black Power held in Philadelphia, Pa., from August 29 through September 1, 1968. There were moderates and extremists and the extremism of some of the delegates to the conference was evident by some of the matters discussed in a workshop concerning the control of "white violence." These ranged from discussions of guerrilla warfare and terrorism, to the use of chemicals to make explosive and incendiary devices. (FBI, *1970 Appropriation*, April 17, 1969, p. 71.)

BLACKMAIL. Their use of blackmail and compromise is revolting. On two separate instances an American college professor and a woman tourist went to Moscow where they were drugged while separately visiting the Soviet Union, photographed while unconscious, participating in acts of sexual perversion, arrested and their cooperation in obtaining intelligence information solicited under threat of prosecution and exposure. (*FBI Appropriation, 1965,* January 29, 1964, p. 47.)

BOMBINGS. "During the national convention of the Students for a Democratic Society held in June, 1968, at Michigan State University, a workshop was held dealing with sabotage and explosives. It was only a short time after this convention that the wave of bombing and arson occurred throughout the country." (FBI Report by J. Edgar Hoover to the Attorney General, Dec. 31, 1968, p. 16.)

BUSINESS—TARGET. Exploiting their privileged status to the fullest, these diplomats have endeavored, by various means, to make friendly and personal contacts with American businessmen, scientists, engineers and others who they hoped might be developed as sources of information. This Soviet tactic was reported by the FBI in great detail in an article entitled "The U. S. Businessman Faces the Soviet Spy," which was published in the January-February, 1964, issue of the *Harvard Business Review.* This report not only identified Soviet spy techniques but suggested how American businessmen could recognize and thwart them. (*FBI Annual Report, Fiscal Year 1964,* p. 24.)

BUSINESSMAN DO? 1. Know more about communism, its strategy and tactics and how the communists are working to destroy our democratic principles. If you are an employer, encourage your employees to take the time to learn about the evil of this way of life. The distribution of reading material within your company is most desirable.

2. Be familiar with basic communist newspapers, magazines and periodicals. If they arrive in your plant, you and your staff will be able to recognize them. Perhaps you can help your employees identify them.

3. Know how communist fronts operate. Take the time to be informed about how fronts are formed, how they propagandize, issue literature and collect money.

4. Realize that business enterprises and labor unions are prime targets. The communists detest both business and labor unions. They regard both as part of the hated bourgeois society. Many people feel that because they are anti-communists the communists are not interested in them. This is wrong. The communists are constantly trying to influence the thinking of noncommunists.

5. Businessmen who are employers should be extremely conscious of plant security, realizing that the communists (especially Russian espionage agents) try to find weak points —both in personnel and physical facilities. Effective plant security is a vital and continuing responsibility.

6. Report to the FBI any information pertaining to espionage, sabotage and subversive activities. The FBI is the government agency charged with protecting the internal security of the nation.

You, as a businessman, stand today in a key position to help the FBI and protect our nation from the Russian espionage agent and the communist. Perhaps you may feel the information you possess is inconsequential. Resolve your doubts by reporting it immediately to the FBI. Many times a small piece of information, when placed with data already in our possession, may solve an important case.

We can defeat the communists by working together as a team. That is our challenge. ("Why Reds Make Friends With Businessmen," *Nation's Business,* May, 1962, reprint.)

CALIFORNIA—UNIVERSITY DEMONSTRATIONS. Demonstrations at the University of California were initiated October 1, 1964, by a small group of students who formed an organization called the Free Speech Movement (FSM) which demanded the right to engage in political activities on the campus in local, State, and National elections in violation of university regulations.

Demonstrations continued through October and November in spite of overtures and concessions by the university administration to the demands of the demonstrators. In this regard, on November 20, 1964, the board of regents endorsed a recommendation of the faculty committee that eight suspended students be reinstated and that soliciting of off-campus activities and funds be allowed on a modified scale. However, when the regents stated students would be held responsible for their activities on campus which would lead to "unlawful" off-campus deeds, the FSM immediately denounced the regents' ruling and continued sit-ins.

On December 2, 1964, approximately 1,000 demonstrators gathered in Sproul Hall, University of California, and refused to leave, resulting in Governor Brown of California issuing orders to arrest those who refused. Accordingly, at 3:45 a.m., December 3, 1964, over 600 police officers arrested 780 demonstrators who refused to leave Sproul Hall. The arrests were without violence or injuries.

Mario Savio, student leader and spokesman for FSM and the demonstrators, has a previous arrest record for sit-in demonstrations. During the period November 10-14, 1964, Savio was on a speaking tour of colleges in the Midwest and East seeking financial support for the arrested students. A close adviser who accompanied him on this tour was Bettina

Aptheker, member of the W.E.B. DuBois Club of Berkeley (a Marxist-oriented youth organization) and daughter of Herbert Aptheker, publicly identified in the Communist newspaper, *The Worker*, in its issue of July 30, 1961, as a member of the National Committee of the Communist Party, USA.

Individuals with subversive backgrounds who participated in the demonstrations included five faculty members and 38 individuals who were students or connected with the University of California in some capacity.

This is another example of a demonstration which, while not Communist originated or controlled, has been exploited by a few Communists for their own end. In this instance, a few hundred students contain within their ranks a handful of Communists that mislead, confuse, and bewilder a great many students to their own detriment.

Communist Party leaders feel that based on what happened on the campus of the University of California at Berkeley, they can exploit similar student demonstrations to their own benefit in the future. (*FBI Appropriation 1966*, pp. 61-62.)

CANNIBALISTIC. Free men and free governments would do well to reflect on the cannibalistic nature of communism. Whenever a united front includes Communists, the front often disappears and the Communists emerge, sleek and fat, seeking new fronts with which to "unite." In this game, the role of the smiling tiger seems always to be played by the Communists. ("Communist 'New Look' A Study in Duplicity," *The Elks Magazine*, August 1956, reprint, p. 3.)

CHANGE? The objective is fixed; the tactics remain fluid. We are presently witnessing a change in tactics and you, the American citizens, are the reason for that change. The Communist "new look" presently being put into effect was created for your benefit. Its purpose is to hoodwink you. (*Ibid.*, p. 1.)

Communism — the scourge of our generation — has not weakened. Its philosophy has not changed. The danger from it has not lessened. At this very moment, the same old communist crowd is doing business at the same old communist stand in the same old subversive way! And we are letting them do it! ("God and Country or Communism?," *The American Legion Magazine*, November 1957, reprint, p. 14.)

The current Communist tactics do not change the basic goals of Communist conquest; they do not change the basic Communist techniques; they do not mean independence from Soviet Communist leaders; and they do not represent any change of heart or a lessened antagonism toward religion. ("The Twin Enemies of Freedom," *FBI Law Enforcement Bulletin*, January, 1957, reprint, p. 4.)

Is the Communist Party succeeding in its purpose? *It is if you can be persuaded that the communist menace is lessening.*

The truth is that the global tyranny of the Twentieth Century has never been more deadly because it has never before been camouflaged with such shrewd effectiveness. ("Communist 'New Look' A Study in Duplicity," *The Elks Magazine*, August, 1956, reprint, p. 2.)

CHANGE—PARTY IN U.S. NOT. On May 28, 1942, Honorable Francis Biddle, then Attorney General, in reviewing the deportation proceedings of Harry Bridges, found that the Communist Party from the time of its inception in 1919 believes in, advises, advocates, and teaches the overthrow by force and violence of the Government of the United States.

Since then, much has happened. In 1944, the Party dissolved and became the Communist Political Association. The Constitution of the new CPA in 1944 omitted references to "Leninism" and the "Historic Mission." That was the era when Browder was preaching a second front and all-out production. But, even then, they secretly held to their historic mission, for in an injunction to Party members, Eugene Dennis, now General Secretary of the Party, said:

"Irrespective of name, we are and shall continue to be an American working class political organization, guided by the science of Marxism-Leninism."

But that era was short-lived. Immediately after Jacques Duclos, the French Communist leader, blasted the American Communists as deserting the Marxian cause, Browder was repudiated, the CPA was relegated to oblivion and the present Communist Party of the United States was reborn. A new Constitution adopted in July, 1945, as I have already indicated, referred to the Party as basing itself "upon the principles of scientific socialism, Marxism-Leninism" and reincorporated the reference to the Party's "historic mission."

47

In establishing the Party's illegal character in 1942, the then Attorney General Biddle based his findings on the contents of the same Communist publications which today are being sold and circulated in Party circles. The American Communist, like the leopard, cannot change his spots. (House Committee on Un-American Activities, *Menace of Communism*, March 26, 1947, pp. 3-4.)

In fact, there is nothing really new in the current Communist tactics. The American Communist Party from the time of its inception here in Chicago in 1919 until the present has changed its name 9 times. The constitution of the Communist Party in this country has been changed 17 times, zigging and zagging for the attainment of its diabolical ends through deception and double talk. ("The Twin Enemies of Freedom," *FBI Law Enforcement Bulletin*, January 1957, reprint, p. 4.)

That the Communist Party has not changed its objectives one iota is attested to by the following highlights of its 1957 convention:

1. Despite a year of debate, the party retained its old name and traditional organization.

2. The party continued the majority of its old leadership.

3. The party reaffirmed its adherence to the basic concepts of Marxism-Leninism.

4. The party reaffirmed its acceptance of "proletarian internationalism."

5. The party refused to take a stand against the Soviet rape of Hungary.

6. The party refused to take a stand against the tyranny and anti-Semitism in the Soviet Union.

7. The party at no time passed any resolution during the convention declaring its independence of the Soviet Union, nor did it urge freedom in the satellites, nor did it support American foreign policy to the detriment of Soviet foreign policy; and at no time did it disavow its dependence upon the Soviet Union or its loyalty to the Soviet Union. In fact, upon its conclusion, the Soviet-controlled press hailed the Communist Party, USA, for remaining loyal "to the principles of Marxism-Leninism."

8. The party reaffirmed its adherence to the basic Leninist concept of democratic centralism, even more than in prior conventions, through the selection of convention delegates who were primarily functionaries, and who ended the convention agreeing that "the party won" and that there was "unity." (Senate Internal Security Subcommittee, "An Analysis of the Sixteenth Annual Convention of the Communist Party of the United States," Washington: Government Printing Office, March 12, 1957, p. 3.)

CHANGES—TACTICAL. The record of the American Communists conclusively proves their true feelings. In the prewar days, when they were allied with Hitler, they marched on Washington, protesting Selective Service, Lend-Lease, shouting "The Yanks are not coming." The American Peace Mobilization picketed the White House until the day before the Nazis marched into Russia and then within less than a month reconverted it into the American People's Mobilization, demanded all-out production, and started the chant for the Second Front. (House Committee on Un-American Activities, "Menace of Communism," Washington: Government Printing Office, March 26, 1947, p. 4.)

In November of 1940, the Communist Party, in order to circumvent and evade the Voorhis Act, enacted on October 19, 1940, which would subject the party to registration as an organization subject to foreign control, called an emergency convention. At this convention the party proclaimed that it—"does hereby cancel and dissolve its organizational affiliation to the Communist International . . . for the specific purpose of removing itself from the terms of the so-called Voorhis Act. . ."

The Party then proclaimed that it— ". . . reaffirms the unshakable adherence of our party to the principles of proletarian internationalism, in the spirit of its greatest leaders and teachers, Marx, Engels, Lenin, and Stalin. . ." (Senate Internal Security Subcommittee, "An Analysis of the Sixteenth Annual Convention of the Communist Party of the United States," Washington: Government Printing Office, March 12, 1957, p. 4.)

CHILDREN'S FREEDOM AT STAKE. George Washington and his valiant troops fought not for themselves alone, but

49

for generations yet unborn. This too is our task. From our shoulders, the mantle of freedom—worn proudly for all the world to behold—must pass unstained to our children, and to our children's children. *No generation ever faced a more vital responsibility.*

A half century ago, one of our great Presidents, Theodore Roosevelt, warned, "If we stand idly by, if we seek merely swollen, slothful ease, and ignoble peace, if we shrink from the hard contests which men must win at hazard of their lives and at the risk of all that they hold dear, then the bolder and stronger peoples will pass us by and will win for themselves the domination of the world." ("The Courage of Free Men," *FBI Law Enforcement Bulletin,* April 1962, p. 19, Reprint, p. 5.)

CHINA RED—RECOGNIZE?. Mr. Hoover. Along the same line, the FBI continues to have heavy investigative responsibilities in the Cuban field. While there has been a lessening in open activities on the part of pro-Castro organizations such as the Fair Play for Cuba Committee, the Cuban Government has continued its efforts to infiltrate intelligence agents into this country.

Also, Communist China represents one of the gravest long-range security threats and the FBI is continuing to devote close attention to coverage of possible Chinese Communist agents and sympathizers in the United States. There is every likelihood that Chinese Communist intelligence activities in this country will increase in the next few years, particularly if Communist China is recognized by the United Nations and is thereby able to establish a diplomatic mission in this country. (*FBI Appropriation 1966,* p. 70.)

The potent threat to our national security posed by Red China still exists. In fact, the blatant, belligerent and illogical statements made by Red China's spokesmen during the past year leave no doubt that the United States is Communist China's No. 1 enemy. This bitterness towards the United States and other Western countries—even the Soviet Union—is a factor in Red China's ambition to equal other major powers economically, militarily and, especially, in scientific endeavors.

This Red Chinese goal has resulted in Chinese Communist intelligence activities in this country, overt as well as covert, to obtain needed material, particularly in the scientific field.

In one clandestine effort in 1967, which we thwarted, a Chinese American attempted to send electronic equipment to Hong Kong by way of Canada. This Chinese American headed an electronic company in the United States and the components involved, which could have been used in aerospace research, missile tracking, and radar, were sent to a Hong Kong businessman, temporarily in Toronto, Canada. Based on information furnished by the FBI, he was arrested by Canadian authorities in Toronto for making a false customs declaration, the electronics components being declared as replacement parts for printing machines. He was convicted and served a 60-day sentence.

We are being confronted with a growing amount of work in being alert for Chinese Americans and others in this country who would assist Red China in supplying needed material or promoting Red Chinese propaganda. For one thing, Red China has been flooding the country with its propaganda and there are over 300,000 Chinese in the United States, some of whom could be susceptible to recruitment either through ethnic ties or hostage situations because of relatives in Communist China.

In addition, up to 20,000 Chinese immigrants can come into the United States each year and this provides a means to send illegal agents into our Nation. There are active Chinese Communist sympathizers in the Western Hemisphere in a position to aid in operations against the United States.

The Chinese Communists do not have a legal base in the United States from which to conduct intelligence operations. In Canada, however, there is an office of the New China News Agency which poses as a legitimate news-gathering organization. Actually, its real function is to serve as a base for Red Chinese propaganda activity.

A growing problem which threatens to place a heavy burden on our investigative resources concerns the approximately 40,000 Hong Kong based Chinese seamen, many actually residing on the China mainland. We are aware of situations where they have served as couriers in intelligence operations. There have also been instances of mutinies on foreign ships by Chinese crews waving the book "Quotations From Chairman Mao Tse-tung."

Of the 40,000-odd crewmen, on any given day three-fourths of them are on vessels throughout the world. Some 27,000 of the total crew complement are members of the Chinese Communist-dominated Hong Kong Seamen's Union. In respect to the United States, there are thousands of entries made by these crewmen into the United States cities each year when their ships dock here. Although it is not necessary for a seaman to desert ship to perform an intelligence assignment, it is noted that there were over 700 desertions by Chinese crewmen in the United States in fiscal year 1967, and this accounted for more than 80 percent of the total desertions by Chinese crewmen throughout the world during that year. It is significant to note that desertions by Chinese crewmen jumped to some 930 during the fiscal year 1968. (FBI, *1970 Appropriation*, April 17, 1969, pp. 74-75.)

CHURCHES — OBJECT OF COMMUNIST PROPAGANDA.
The Communists are today spraying the world with ideological and propaganda missiles designed to create a deadly radioactive cloud of Marxism-Leninism. From bases behind the Iron Curtain and in the non-Communist world, this cloud of Communist propaganda is drenching many lands, with a particularly heavy fall-out in this nation.

The deadliest of these Communist missiles—whose warheads are exceptionally heavy—are being directed against the Christian pulpit. Communist gunners, with special ideological training and schooled in atheistic perversity, are "sighting in" the clergy—hoping to shatter, immobilize, and confuse this powerful forum of idealism, morality, and civic virtue. No assignment is more strategic in the Communist world today than the disruption of the Church of God—both *within* and *outside* the Iron Curtain.

Why does the Church—which has no military forces—merit the most explosive of Communist rockets, the most venomous of Communist hate, the most vituperative of Communist scorn? Because religion, of all facets of Western civilization, represents the eternal "thorn in the flesh" of communism, that jagged rock which is constantly puncturing, exposing, and unmasking Communist claims, performances, and hopes. The Communists realize that unless the Christian

52

pulpit—that mighty fortress of God—is liquidated, pitilessly, mercilessly, finally, the very existence of communism itself stands in jeopardy. The spiritual firepower of the Christian Church—based on the love of God—is sufficient to destroy all the Soviet man-made missiles and rockets and extirpate this twentieth century aberration.

And the Communists know it—and fear it. ("The Communist Menace: Red Goals and Christian Ideals," *Christianity Today*, October 10, 24, November 7, 1960 issues, reprint, pp. 3-4.)

CIVIL RIGHTS AND FBI. For more than a quarter century, we have maintained in the FBI training program a comprehensive indoctrination course on all phases of our work and more particularly on the handling of civil rights matters in an objective and penetrating manner. In addition, we have had conferences of our personnel dealing with civil rights matters at Washington, D. C. In many local areas of the country we have met with chiefs of police, sheriffs, and other law-enforcement officers to cover the jurisdiction of the FBI in civil rights matters. (*FBI Appropriation 1962*, p. 34.)

A record high 3,340 civil rights cases were handled during the fiscal year 1964. This is an increase of 648, or 24 per cent, over the heavy volume of such cases handled during the prior year and marks a continuation of the sharp upward climb in this work, which trend has now extended over a number of years. The heavy impact of this work is evidenced when it is considered that there has been a 139 per cent increase in the number of civil rights cases handled in just the past 5 years. In 1960 there were 1,398 cases. This climbed to 1,813 in 1961 and to 2,085 in 1962. In 1963 the volume mounted to 2,692 and climbed to a new record high of 3,340 cases in 1964.

These are matters which require immediate handling and in many instances involve the extraordinary assignment of manpower and other resources. (*FBI Appropriation 1966*, p. 16.)

CIVIL RIGHTS—EXPLOIT. The Party waged a constant effort in the fiscal year 1964 to exploit the civil rights issue. During the August 28, 1963, March on Washington, Communists and Party sympathizers sought to involve themselves in every aspect of this demonstration. Although attempting to conceal their Communist connections, approximately 200 Party members actually participated in the March.

Other recent racial demonstrations have attracted Communists, usually in a hidden role, and the legitimate leaders of these activities have been hard pressed to keep them out and minimize their influence.

The FBI does not investigate the legitimate activities of civil rights groups, but from an intelligence standpoint it is concerned with determining the extent of possible Communist infiltration of these organizations. (*FBI Annual Report Fiscal Year 1964*, p. 22.)

CLERGY—FRONTS. The strategy of the Communists to get others to front for them and do their dirty work cannot be underestimated. To illustrate, last Christmas 42 persons signed a petition to request Presidential amnesty for the Communist Party leaders convicted under the Smith Act for conspiring to teach and advocate the overthrow of the Government of the United States by force and violence. Not only did these persons ask the Government to release a group of Communist conspirators from prison to observe a Christian holiday which they would destroy, but they asked that the sentences of these criminal atheists be commuted to the time already served. Even more shocking is the fact that half of the signers of the petition were clergymen, professors of theology, or persons who were engaged in other religious positions. Another such petition is now in preparation to again ask for the release of those who would destroy the American way of life.

This is not an isolated example. Last year a legal brief was filed with the United States Supreme Court urging that the Internal Security Act of 1950 be declared unconstitutional. This legal brief had been initiated by 18 persons. Nine of these persons, exactly one half, were members of the clergy. Of the 360 persons who signed the brief, some 100 were clergymen.

Because they despise the church, the Communists continually attempt to infiltrate unsuspecting religious organizations. What better cloak of legitimacy can be found for their programs than to present them as the offerings of clergy-

54

men and churches? ("The Twin Enemies of Freedom," *FBI Law Enforcement Bulletin*, January 1957, reprint, p. 4.)

CLERGY—DO. The ultimate aim of Communism is to refashion the image of man—to make him a servile creature of the state, obedient to the whims of the ruling Party clique. Our clergymen are vitally needed today to help counteract the Communist challenge. Clergymen—and men who believe in God everywhere—literally stand on the front lines of this giant ideological battle. They have a vital task of helping strengthen the spiritual faith of our Nation. No group in America has a more significant role to play in protecting the historic values of our Judaic-Christian culture. ("Let's Fight Communism Sanely!" *Christian Herald*, January 1962, p. 63.)

CLERGY—LOYALTY. Over all, the Party has not had marked success in its attacks against the church. The Communists have found in religion a foe of the greatest tenacity, able to withstand the withering firepower of Marxist-Leninist chicanery. The overwhelming majority of America's clergy are loyal citizens, devoted to working for the best interests of the Nation. Being men of God, they realize that communism and religion are irreconcilable, that never can there be a truce between them.

Americans can be truly thankful for the magnificent contribution which these men have made to our national life. This Nation was founded by men and women who believed in the Eternal, and religion remains today the mainstream of our culture.

It is unfortunately true that, over the years, some clergymen—knowingly or otherwise—have lent their names and prestige to various Communist causes. In many instances, these individuals were supporting what they sincerely thought or had been led to believe were laudable social objectives and causes. They were sorely unfamiliar with the manner in which Communists continuously exploit legitimate issues for their own ulterior objectives.

Despite the fact that the Communists have had only limited success in exploiting the prestige of the clergy, we must face the tragic reality that any individual who aids the Communist conspiracy is one too many. Look at the example of Dr. Klaus Fuchs. He was just one of many thousands of workers on a highly confidential project in World War II —development of the atomic bomb. In fact, he was a rather undistinguished-looking fellow, not likely to impress anyone as a conspicuous leader. Yet that one man—Klaus Fuchs— was responsible for tremendous and irreparable damage to our national security.

Dr. Fuchs could steal only physical things, though they were vitally important. But our clergymen are dealing with properties of an incalculably higher value—the living souls of men and women, boys and girls. Their ideas, their actions, their example, are day after day helping to mold the spiritual values of our society. If they serve as sponsors of Party fronts, if they allow their names to be exploited in Party agitation programs, if they describe communism as offering legitimate solutions to the problems of life, they stray from their sacred duty—guiding hearts and souls into a deeper faith in God.

Clergymen, by the very nature of their calling, are dedicated, self-sacrificing individuals interested in social justice. The Communists, on the other hand, are cynically exploiting for their own ends all the deficiencies, real or imagined in our society. For this reason the Party's position, on occasion, may, for tactical reasons, coincide with the views of many clergymen on specific economic, political or social issues. We must be careful not to identify indiscriminately as Communists those clergymen whose views on a particular question may, at times, parallel the official Party position. Innuendoes, false accusations and unfounded charges can only weaken the fight against communism by diffusing the strength of the anti-communist forces. ("Let's Fight Communism Sanely!" *Christian Herald,* January 1962, pp. 62-63.)

CLERGY—INFILTRATION. I confess to a real apprehension so long as Communists are able to secure ministers of the gospel to promote their evil work and espouse a cause that is alien to the religion of Christ and Judaism. (House Committee on Un-American Activities, *Menace of Communism,* March 26, 1947, p. 11.)

Even the clergy, as I have said, are not without their undercover Reds. The Communists realize that religion is our strongest bulwark against the encroachment of Marxist

56

doctrines, and in some instances are trying to attack Christian faith at its wellsprings by influencing or winning over ordained ministers as recruits to aid the Party.

One concealed Communist minister, who we know is in constant contact with high-ranking Party leaders, preaches Red-slanted sermons to large congregations in an Eastern city, consistently praises Communist programs in speeches and articles which he writes, and serves as a mouthpiece for Red fronts.

Another Red-fronting minister, on the West Coast, is making a play for the minds of young people by holding "Youth Festivals" at his church and leading discussions which shed a favorable light on communism. Still another pulpit Red apologist recently told an audience: "We must not make a holy war against Russia . . . the Soviets are not opposed to freedom in Europe or anywhere else . . . it is only Fascism to which they are opposed." ("The Communists Are After Our Minds," *American Magazine*, October, 1954, reprint, p. 3.)

COEXISTENCE. A Communist will enter an alliance or "coexist" only to advance communism. ("America—Freedom's Champion," October 18, 1960, p. 7.)

COEXISTENCE AND WAR AT SAME TIME. Communism —mortal enemy of liberty and justice and of God—continues its relentless war against humanity. While the Kremlin and its corps of false propagandists incessantly speak of "peaceful co-existence," the roar of Communist cannon and the rattle of Red sabers continue around the world.

Week after week, gunfire of East German border guards heralds the continuing effort of persons behind the Iron Curtain to scale the Wall of Berlin.

In Laos, Vietnam and other countries bordering Slave China, guerrilla fires set to homes and villages—and guerilla bayonets cutting down defenseless men, women and children— have colored the earth and skies a sickening red.

And in Communist Cuba, less than 100 miles from our shores, a bearded disciple of the Kremlin shakes a bloodstained fist at the United States while belligerently conspiring to spread violence and subversion throughout the Americas. ("Our Heritage of Greatness," December 12, 1964, p. 5.)

COEXISTENCE—IMPOSSIBLE. Communism, like crime, advances and takes hold because men ignore God. The real danger in communism lies in the fact that it is atheistic and seeks to replace the Supreme Being. Communism is secularism on the march. It is the mortal foe of all the world's religions which acknowledge the existence of God. Either the Faith of our fathers will triumph or communism will engulf us. In this land of ours the two cannot live side by side. ("The Twin Enemies of Freedom," *FBI Law Enforcement Bulletin,* January, 1957, reprint, p. 3.)

Study the basic beliefs of communist woman and compare them with the beliefs generally accepted by the woman of the free world. You then can understand why the acts which flow from communist beliefs are so different from your own. You will see why individual rights cannot coexist with communism. You will understand also why the coexistence of which communist-controlled governments speak so eloquently is simply a lure to beguile the gullible. ("A View of Reality," *General Federation Clubwoman Magazine,* May-June, 1961, reprint, p. 2.)

COEXISTENCE—WHY?. Spurred by the realization of these capabilities, world communism has launched a broad political-economic offensive. The old fear of "capitalist encirclement," which motivated the defensive Soviet approach to international affairs during the 1920's and the 1930's, is gone. In its place, there has developed a dynamic, aggressive, competitive spirit. The time-tested Communist tactics—propaganda, front group activity, diplomatic maneuvers, and the united front—have not been abandoned. Now, however, they are being implemented by such programs as extensive economic aid, technical assistance, and the interchange of delegations. All of these are carefully planned and coordinated on a worldwide scale to promote communism. This multi-pronged offensive has been adroitly cloaked under the saccharine slogans of peaceful coexistence and peaceful competition, in an effort to lull the Free World into a false sense of security. ("Communist Illusion and Democratic Reality," December, 1959, p. 1.)

COLLEGE DEMONSTRATION CAUSES. "At the core of these campus disorders, and often below the surface, we find agitator personnel from organizations such as the communist W. E. B. DuBois Clubs of America and their comrades in the Students for a Democratic Society, a so-called 'New Left' group; members of the Progressive Labor Party, a pro-Red Chinese group; and individuals associated with organizations under the control of the subversive Socialist Workers Party and similar groups." (*FBI Law Enforcement Bulletin*, February 1, 1967, p. 1.)

COLLEGES—SPEAK AT. The increased number of public appearances by leaders of the Communist Party, USA in the last few years, whether it be in the form of press conferences, on radio programs, or on college campuses, is utilized in an effort to project the image that the Party is a legitimate political party; to gain increased acceptance and respectability for the Party; to generate an atmosphere of good will and understanding; and to spread Communist propaganda.

Since students constitute a primary Communist target group, Party leaders in their public appearances continue to concentrate on college and university campuses throughout the country. Over the past 3 school years, Party spokesmen have averaged 50 campus appearances each year. Their audiences ranged in size from an intimate 13 to a huge 4,000. The latter number heard Dorothy Healey, a member of the Party's national committee, when she spoke in the stadium of the California State College at Los Angeles, California, on May 20, 1964. Audiences from 500 to 800 were common.

While almost all of the public appearances of Party functionaries before students took place at colleges and universities, several speeches were made at secondary educational institutions.

That some success is achieved by the Party in the many appearances of its leaders on college campuses is indicated by the fact that Party youth clubs have been established recently at the University of Chicago and the University of California.

Skillfully imparting the Communist line with espousals paralleling Soviet views, party spokesmen made 44 appearances before college groups during the calendar year 1964. (*FBI Appropriation 1966*, p. 56.)

Skillfully imparting the Communist line with espousals paralleling Soviet views, party spokesmen appeared before 45 student groups, mostly at on-campus sites during the calendar year 1963.

That the Party is enjoying some success as a result of expanded contacts with college students is indicated in the comment of Daniel Rubin, national youth director of the Party, in June 1963 that of the number of young people attracted in its last recruiting drive, 65 percent were students. (*FBI Appropriation 1965*, January 29, 1964, p. 39.)

The Communists have attempted to infiltrate every segment of American society and have grown increasingly ambitious in their designs upon youth. Among the specific programs they have implemented is an intensive speech campaign which has seen Party functionaries appear at colleges and universities from Maine to California. This program has been spearheaded by the Party's lecture and information bureau, which operates out of Communist Party headquarters in New York City.

During 1963 top party leaders made 45 appearances before college groups. Set forth below is information concerning these appearances with the identity of the school, the party speaker, and the date of his or her appearance. (*FBI 1965 Appropriation*, January 29, 1964, pp. 63-64).

We have but to look at the Party's campus speech program which has seen Communist functionaries appear before student groups at colleges and universities from New York to California. On one campus alone, a crowd of nearly 12,000 turned out to hear the Party's general secretary, ex-convict Gus Hall, declare that the Communist Party, USA, is a legitimate political organization on the American scene and deny its subservience to Moscow, from which it has been established that it actually receives orders and financial support.

The success of these and other programs which the Communists have directed against American young people can be measured by the enthusiasm of top Party officials who predicted several weeks ago that 1,000 youths could be recruited as Party members before the end of the year.

Colleges should bear in mind that Communist speakers are not bound by any obligation to tell the truth. ("An

American's Challenge," *Congressional Record*, October 10, 1962, p. A7517.)

During the past two years, Communist spokesmen have appeared on nearly 100 campuses from coast to coast. Their purpose: To create confusion, raise questions and spread doubt among our young people concerning the American way of life.

If their constitutional right to free speech allows them to use the public school forum to promote the secular creed of Marxism-Leninism which *openly and avowedly denies God,* does their constitutional freedom of religion also *prohibit* the rest of us from using the same public school forum to express our faith that God does exist? ("Keys to Freedom," November 16, 1963, pp. 5-6.)

Probably more Americans saw and heard self-avowed members of the Communist Party, USA, in the fiscal year 1962 than in the preceding 10 years. Unquestionably, the Party unleashed one of the most intensive propaganda campaigns in its history.

Most successful of all its efforts was its speaking campaign, especially before college groups. From late October 1961, through May 1962, leaders of the Communist Party, USA, made 48 speeches before groups of college students all across the Nation. Approximately 43,000 persons heard these talks.

Encouraged by the early success of college appearances, the Party established a lecture and information bureau and early in 1962 sent a letter to college newspaper editors offering speakers on communism. Near the end of the 1962 fiscal year, the party already was lining up speeches for the coming academic year. (Senate Internal Security Subcommittee, "The Current Communist Threat," Washington: Government Printing Office, October 1962, p. 2.)

In October, 1963, a youth conference at Chicago, Illinois, sponsored by the Communist Party was guided by the Party's General Secretary, Gus Hall, toward the formation of a new, broad national youth organization. With the goal of the proposed new group established as the promotion of socialism, regional committees were named and plans made for a founding convention which was called in June, 1964. Approximately 450 young Marxist partisans attended this June meeting and set in motion one of the most ambitious communist youth movements in years, the W.E.B. DuBois Clubs of America. With this name, the group memorialized the late Dr. William E. B. DuBois, a prominent crusader for civil rights and supporter of communist fronts who at the age of 93 joined the Communist Party. (*FBI Annual Report Fiscal Year 1964*, pp. 21-22.)

The party has high hopes of utilizing the interests created by these campus appearances to get a nucleus of students interested in Marxism-Leninism and, subsequently, in a position to be recruited into the Communist Party. While party leaders understand that they may not have overwhelming success in recruiting the students, they are encouraged over their opportunities to appear on campuses and gain an aura of legitimacy. (*FBI Appropriation 1967*, p. 44.)

COLLEGE TOTALITARIANISM. "There is no place in the academic world, where unencumbered inquiry is essential, for a riot leader's recently voiced blackjack threat of 'if they do not accede to our demands, we'll close down their great and profitable university.' This is no calm, deliberate search for truth. This is the way of the totalitarian, seeking to enslave through force." (*FBI Law Enforcement Bulletin*, February 1, 1967.)

COMMUNISM DESCRIBED. The true menace of communism lies in the fact that it is a godless tyranny which holds that man has no dignity and is in fact a puppet of the State. It distorts human personality, imprisons the mind, and deadens the soul. The great values of our Western civilization —love, justice, mercy, a firm belief in God which has given life and meaning to all of us—are scorned and denounced by Communists.

Their motivation is based on the premise that the end justifies the means. They represent a satanic way of life that is a contradiction of every code of decency. Hate and terror and fear take over and man becomes a slave, physically and spiritually. (*Pathfinder*, November 5, 1952, quoted in *Congressional Record*, January 26, 1953, reprint.)

COMMUNISM—DON'T MISLABEL. I have also been encouraged to note that spokesmen generally are being circumspect in using the label of "Communist." The technique of the label is a Communist trick which anti-Communists are sometimes prone to use. It is deceptive and detrimental, however, to pin the label of "Communist" on honest American liberals and progressives merely because of a difference of opinion. Honesty and common decency demand that the clear-cut line of demarcation that exists between liberals and Communists be recognized. Despite the Communist technique of labeling themselves as progressives there is no more effective or determined foe of Communism than the millions of honest liberals and progressives. ("How To Fight Communism," *Newsweek*, June 9, 1947, reprint, p. 3.)

COMMUNISM IS DESTRUCTIVE. These doctrines threaten the happiness of the community, the safety of every individual, and the continuance of every home and fireside. They would destroy the peace of the country and thrust it into a condition of anarchy and lawlessness and immorality that passes imagination. (1919 statement. Quoted in the CR, May 8, 1964, p. 10071).

COMMUNISM—MAJOR IDEAS. I. *Nature Is All—There is no God.*

II. *Body Is All—There Is No Soul.*

III. *All Religions Are False and Harmful—All Religions Must Be Destroyed.*

IV. *Proletarian Utility Constitutes The Moral Code—All Existing Moral Codes Derived From Supernatural Concepts Are False.*

V. *History Is A Materialistic Process—It Is A History of Class Struggle—It Does Not Reflect The Spirit of Man.*

VI. *The Capitalistic State Is An Instrument Of Oppression—It Must Be Destroyed.*

VII. *Revolution And A Revolutionary Method Are Necessary—The Rulers Of Nations Will Not Surrender Peacefully.*

VIII. *Only A World-Wide Communist Social Order Conforms To The Nature of Men; Meets The Needs of Life; Is Adequate—All Other Social Orders Do Not Conform To The Nature Of Man; Do Not Meet The Needs Of Life; Are Inadequate. Therefore All Other Social Orders Must Be Destroyed.* ("A View of Reality," *General Federation Clubwoman Magazine*, May-June, 1961. Reprint, p. 2.)

COMMUNIST PARTY OBJECTIVE IN U.S. As such, it stands for the destruction of our American form of Government; it stands for the destruction of American Democracy; it stands for the destruction of free enterprise; and it stands for the creation of a "Soviet of the United States" and ultimate world revolution. (House Committee on Un-American Activities, "Menace of Communism," Washington: Government Printing Office, March 26, 1947, p. 3.)

CONGRESSIONAL COMMITTEES INVESTIGATING COMMUNISM. Some measure of the effectiveness of these investigative committees in exposing the aims, principles, and methods of communism is indicated by the bitterness and the intensity of communist attacks upon them, as well as by the continuous communist campaigns to abolish them. ("Communist Illusion and Democratic Reality," December, 1959, pp. 4-5.)

CONGRESSIONAL COMMITTEES—VALUE. While the FBI for years has exposed the Communist conspiracy, it cannot divulge the confidential details of its files as to specific individuals. A congressional committee having the power of subpoena and contempt citation is able to focus public attention on specific situations. ("Where Do We Stand Today With Communism in the United States?" *Congressional Record,* March 1, 1954, p. 2297.)

CONSPIRACY: Since 1949, 104 Party leaders have been convicted on charges of conspiring to teach and advocate the overthrow of the Government and 5 others have been convicted under the membership provision of the Act. (*Annual Report, Fiscal Year 1961,* p. 27.)

CONSTITUTION. Time and experience have proved our Constitution to be the greatest document for freedom ever drawn by man. This instrument of self-government is a reality envisioned by our Founding Fathers who were dedicated to the ideal that man is superior to the State. It embodies the fundamental principle of liberty which is dearer than life, the precept that men shall live as equals under government by law, not by men. (*FBI Law Enforcement Bulletin,* November 1964, pp. 1-2.)

CONSTITUTION—KNOWLEDGE OF NECESSARY. Knowledge of communism is only the first phase of the battle. This knowledge must be augmented by a continuous revitalization of our own inherently superior strength through the practical, daily exercise and development of our democratic principles. Too frequently, emphasis is placed on acquiring an understanding only of the mechanical functions of our Government, such as elections, the enactment of legislation, or judicial review. This knowledge, important as it is, becomes a mere collection of sterile facts without a deep appreciation and a continuing awareness of the reason for the very existence of our form of Government—the freedom of the individual under law. Without the realization of this fundamental philosophy of freedom, such basic individual rights as freedom of speech, the press, and religion are taken for granted. Forgotten is man's bitter fight through the centuries to wrest these freedoms from tyranny. ("Communist Illusion and Democratic Reality," December, 1959, pp. 5-6.)

CONTRADICTIONS. In the name of ending the exploitation of the common man, the Communist heirarchy has developed into a parasitic ruling class which has imposed a ruthless tyranny over millions. In the name of humanity, communism suppresses the most elementary human values and robs the individual of his inherent dignity and worth. In what is pictured as a workers' paradise, slave labor is commonplace and the working man is denied the right to strike. In the regime which claims to have eliminated all discrimination, anti-Semitism is virtually official policy. The pretension that communism stands for national independence is flagrantly contradicted by the brutal suppressions of the uprisings in East Germany, Hungary, and Tibet. ("Communist Illusion and Democratic Reality," December, 1959, p. 3.)

COURT DECISIONS. In recent years, the Communists have demonstrated an attitude of open defiance and contempt for our laws—an attitude which is fortified by their repeated ability to invoke loopholes, technicalities and delays in the law to thwart justice. One former judge found cause to warn last summer not only of "inexcusable" delays in the courts,

65

but also of what he considered to be a "trend of decisions in the last 10 years . . . . favorable to extreme left-wingers, communists and subversives in general."

Another student of court rulings in the internal security field was prompted to observe, "Unfortunately, subversive activities are well on the way to becoming a no-man's land in the law."

In 1957, a Federal judge in the Nation's capital assailed what he considered to be "an unfortunate trend of judicial decisions . . . . which strain and stretch to give the guilty, not the same, but vastly more protection than the law-abiding citizen." There has been no reversal of this alarming trend— a trend which is felt in our steadily rising national crime problem.

Justice in a free nation means protection for society as a whole, rather than leniency for the individual to the detriment of society.

Since 1957, when the Federal judge issued his warning, crime has increased nearly 40 per cent! Its victims continue to mount at a relentless rate. Four serious crimes are committed every minute; there is a crime of violence every 3 minutes; and property crimes—robberies, burglaries, larcenies and automobile thefts—occur within seconds.

Americans, in growing numbers, are developing a dangerously indulgent attitude toward crime, filth, and corruption. No one can deny that motion pictures are deliberately and defiantly pursuing an increasingly bold courtship with obscenity. No one can deny the role of the television industry in bringing lurid portrayals of violence and sadism into the living-rooms—and even the nurseries—of our homes. No one can deny that sensual trash is moving closer and closer to the children's books on the shelves of our newsstands and magazine stores. ("Keys to Freedom," November 16, 1963, pp. 9-11.)

Many developments on the national and international scene afforded American Communists encouragement during the fiscal year. Perhaps the most important, from the Party's point of view were the decision of the United States Court of Appeals for the District of Columbia which reversed the conviction of the Party for failing to register under the provisions of the Internal Security Act of 1950 and the subsequent refusal of the United States Supreme Court to review this decision. Party National Chairman Elizabeth Gurley Flynn hailed this action as a victorious turning point for the Communists in their 13-year struggle against the Internal Security Act. (*FBI Annual Report, Fiscal Year 1964*, p. 21.)

On December 1, 1961, a 12-count indictment was returned by a Federal Court Jury Washington, D. C., charging the Communist Party, USA, with failure to register as a Communist-action organization. The Party was convicted on all counts in U. S. District Court, Washington, on December 17, 1962, and a maximum fine of $120,000 was imposed. On December 17, 1963, the District of Columbia Court of Appeals reversed the conviction, holding that the Fifth Amendment privilege against self-incrimination was available to the officials of the Party as a legal justification for refusing to register. A request by the Government to the Supreme Court to review this decision was denied on June 8, 1964, and at the year's end the case was under review by the Department of Justice to determine whether a reindictment and retrial should be sought. (*FBI Annual Report Fiscal Year 1964*, pp. 22-23.)

CUBA: The proximity of danger is especially apparent to us here today, as less than 100 miles from our shores a gang of bearded bandits exhibit daily the chaos and corruption which closely follow the dictatorial usurpation of power. The Communist-inspired developments in Cuba graphically demonstrate the cold-blooded ruthlessness of tyrannical rule. They display how craftily an entire and basically peace-loving nation can be manipulated as a pawn to support the policies and programs of international communism, with its hypocrisy, guile, deceit, subversion, violence and thievery.

There, the Trojan snake of communism has discarded its disguise for brute force and slaughter. Communism, shed of all its false smiles, is on its bloody march again, not only in Cuba but in every country of the world. The resultant misery and mistreatment of the citizens of countries into which the tentacles of communism have reached should serve as a clear warning to all freedom-loving peoples of the world. ("America—Freedom's Champion," October 18, 1960, p. 6.)

CUBAN DANGER. Domestic intelligence problems springing from the Caribbean area have greatly increased in the past few years with the establishment of a Communist regime in Cuba. (*FBI Annual Report, Fiscal Year 1961*, p. 29.)

The threat posed to the Nation's security by the Communist regime of Fidel Castro in Cuba was made eminently clear in October, 1962, when the world faced possible war over the presence of Soviet missiles on the island less than 100 miles from the Florida shores.

Shortly after this major crisis came the discovery by FBI Agents of a large cache of weapons, explosives and incendiary devices in the hands of a group of pro-Castro Cubans who intended to create panic and destroy industrial sites in and around New York City. Three persons were arrested and two others, members of the Cuban Mission to the United Nations, were named as conspirators. Following a protest by the Department of State, the latter two, Jose Gomez Abad and his wife Elsa, left the country. Arrested were Roberto Santiesteban Casanova, a newly arrived member of the Cuban Mission to the United Nations who had not yet been granted diplomatic immunity, Antonio Sueiro and Jose Garcia Orellana. The three were charged with conspiracy to commit sabotage and other violations but were never brought to trial. All charges against them were dismissed in April, 1963, and they were returned to Cuba in connection with the release of Americans who were being held there. (*FBI Annual Report, Fiscal Year 1963*, p. 28.)

Developments such as the uncovering by the FBI of a sabotage plot engineered by a Cuban official in New York City with the assistance of pro-Castro followers and the continued efforts of the Castro regime to infiltrate intelligence agents into the United States show that we must maintain broad coverage in this area of our operations.

These factors, coupled with the continuing need to develop as much information as possible from sources available in this country concerning economic, political, and military development in Cuba and the necessity of covering the activities of pro-Castro groups and individuals in the United States (including their infiltration of the ranks of thousands of refugees entering this country from Cuba), will continue to demand the heavy assignment of manpower to this phase of our work. (*FBI 1965 Appropriation*, January 29, 1964, p. 47.)

CUBAN INFLUENCE. Ramifications of the Cuban situation have been responsible also for greatly accelerated activity among other Latin American exile groups in the United States, particularly those of Dominican, Venezuelan, and Nicaraguan nationals, all of whom have considerable strength in this country, (*FBI Appropriation 1926*, March 6, 1961, p. 51.)

Since Fidel Castro established a Communist beachhead in Cuba in 1959 he has from that point forward spared no effort to expand the Communist takeover to the remainder of Latin America. As a result, Cuba represents the greatest potential threat to peace in the Western Hemisphere. In this regard, Castro has not only publicly supported open rebellion by Communist-led groups in most of Latin America, but he has supplied men, material and logistical support in a further effort to overthrow existing democratic regimes in Latin-American countries.

Significantly, in addition to the training of guerillas for the exportation of Castro's revolution to other Latin-American countries, information has come to our attention that Negroes are being trained in Cuba for infiltration into the United States. This is particularly important when viewed in the light of open support given during several recent international Communist conferences held in Havana to the concept of armed insurrection by black power advocates and other black extremist groups in the United States.

Since Castro took over Cuba in 1958, over 400,000 Cubans have left their homeland for refuge in the United States, the flow since December 1965 having been at the rate of over 3,700 a month. This adds to our work in two areas. On one hand, many of the refugees carry on activities to overthrow Castro. These activities have ranged from the bombing of Cuban establishments as well as establishments of countries carrying on trade with Cuba, to sea and air attacks against the Cuban mainland. This continued militancy necessitates our keeping track of Cuban refugee activities and conducting appropriate investigations where there are indications that Federal statutes have been violated.

On the other hand, the possibility of Cuban intelligence agents being infiltrated into this country through the refugee stream is always present and requires continuing investigative attention.

Cuba, of course, as in the case of other Communist bloc countries, relies heavily on its only diplomatic establishment in the United States, the Cuban Mission to the United Nations in New York City, to serve as a legal base of operations for clandestine intelligence gathering activity. (FBI, *1970 Appropriation*, April 17, 1969, p. 74.)

CUBA—ORGANIZATIONS IN U.S. There are over 100,000 Cuban aliens in the United States and a number of pro-Castro organizations active in this country. Among these are The July 26 Movement and The Fair Play for Cuba Committee. The former group is composed chiefly of Cuban aliens and naturalized American citizens of Cuban extraction. As a result of FBI investigations, this organization was required to register with the Attorney General in July 1960, under provisions of the Foreign Agents Registration Act.

The Fair Play for Cuba Committee is one of the main outlets in this country for pro-Castro propaganda. Many of its members are United States nationals. This Bureau during the 1961 fiscal year determined that certain funds used by the Committee to pay for a newspaper advertisement had come from a Cuban official assigned to the United Nations, a fact later admitted by a Committee member in testimony before a Congressional Committee. FBI investigations also have shown that The Fair Play for Cuba Committee has been heavily infiltrated by the Communist Party and the Socialist Workers Party, and that these Parties have actually organized some chapters of the Committee. (*Annual Report, Fiscal Year 1961*, pp. 29-30.)

CULTURAL EXCHANGES. Mr. Hoover. East-West Exchange Program—The numerous Soviet scientific delegations which arrive in the United States to tour U. S. universities and scientific establishments invariably have among their members Soviet scientists who have been given special assignments by the KGB. It is established Soviet policy that among such groups are one or more full-time KGB officers who are in charge of the delegations.

Upon returning, Soviet scientists who have visited the United States under the exchange program are required by the KGB to submit comprehensive reports on the technical aspects of their trip, including descriptions of installations visited, research being conducted and the status of particular projects. They must also submit reports concerning Americans contacted for possible future use by the KGB.

Students—As to the students, many of the Soviet exchange students attending colleges and universities in the United States are utilized as Agents by the KGB. Having the responsibility of obtaining any information of intelligence interest, they photograph (or deliver to their KGB superiors for photographing) documents and scientific papers to which they have access as students.

Of the Soviet students in the United States for the school term beginning in the fall of 1964, over 20 percent were suspected of being agents with specific KGB assignments or officers of the Soviet intelligence services.

Press representatives—Press cover is tailored for the intelligence work of the Soviets. They are in a business in which they are expected to be where news is developing, to meet those persons having intimate knowledge, to ask questions and to seek information.

As of February 1, 1965, over half of the Soviet nationals posing as press representatives in the United States were known to be intelligence agents.

Amtorg Trading Corporation—Disguising their intelligence personnel as legitimate trade representatives has long been a tactic of the Soviet intelligence services. The official cover utilized enables such personnel to travel extensively and meet many persons associated with fields of special intelligence interest.

Over half of the Soviet nationals employed by the Amtorg Trading Corporation in New York City on February 1, 1965, were known or suspected to be actually connected with the Soviet intelligence services.

United Nations—Fully exploiting their diplomatic immunity, freedom from travel restrictions and the respectability enjoyed as members of an international organization dedicated to world peace, the Soviet intelligence services have continued to increase their use of employment with the United Nations as a cover for their espionage personnel.

On July 1, 1960, there were 32 Soviet official personnel assigned to the United Nations Secretariat. By February

71

1, 1965, the number had mounted to 108, of whom half were agents or officers of the Soviet intelligence services.

(Discussion off the record.)

Mr. Hoover. Not only does the Soviet bloc take advantage of all types of cover but the flow of visitors to and from the many Soviet-bloc countries is on the increase.

For example, in the case of Hungary, only a handful of visitors arrived in the United States from that country in any given month 4 or 5 years ago. In July, 1964, we received notification of the arrival of over 1,000 visitors from Hungary alone. This not only adds to our work, but also creates a vehicle for the clandestine introduction into the United States of individuals having intelligence assignments. (*FBI Appropriation 1966*, pp. 68-69.)

DANGER? The basic concept of Communist Party operations is infiltration into all strata of American life. The Party is especially interested in penetrating all types of legitimate organizations. It is particularly eager to get as many members as possible into basic and heavy industry. This is sometimes referred to as its "concentration" or "colonization" program. In this connection, labor unions are special targets.

In time of crisis, the concealed communist puppet in the steel, coal, or rubber industry, or the automobile, airplane, atomic or similar defense plant can be of far greater value to the communist masters who pull the strings than whole divisions of armed soldiers. ("Communist 'New Look' A Study in Duplicity," *The Elks Magazine*, August, 1956 reprint, p. 3.)

We face an immense slave empire whose rulers utilize deceit and duplicity as techniques of government and diplomacy. Under those rulers the slave empire of communism is engaged in absolute and total war on the economic system of the United States. It is striving ceaselessly to capture our markets, destroy our trade, and, through infiltration and subversion, tie up our industrial development at home. ("God and Country or Communism?" *American Legion Magazine*, November 1957, reprint, p. 7.)

DAUGHTERS OF THE AMERICAN REVOLUTION. Over the years, the Daughters of the American Revolution on national, state and local levels, has been alert to this menace and outstanding in its cooperation with the FBI. You as individual members have time and again rendered assistance of the highest order to the FBI. This is another reason why I am so happy to meet with you today. More and more, the women of the country have been capably filling their rightful roles in our national life. In protecting the home, women are also protecting the security of our Nation. The Daughters of the American Revolution, long before the general public recognized the true nature of communism, was out in the forefront calling attention to this growing menace.

In taking a stand for the preservation of the American way of life, your organization became the target of vile and vicious attacks. So have all other patriotic organizations and, for that matter, every other person who has dared to raise his voice against the threat of communism. It is an established fact that whenever one has dared to expose the Communist threat he has invited upon himself the adroit and skilled talents of experts of character assassination. The Federal Bureau of Investigation has stood year after year as taunts, insults, and destructive criticism have been thrown its way. (Remarks before the Continental Congress of the National Society Daughters of the American Revolution, April 22, 1954, p. 2.)

DEACONS OF DEFENSE AND JUSTICE, INC. Another organization spawned from the racial unrest existing in the South during the past year is the Deacons of Defense and Justice, Inc. This militant Negro organization was organized in Jonesboro, La., in 1964 and incorporated under the laws of the State of Louisiana for the purpose of members defending themselves against Klan violence and to provide protection not given by local authorities. The Deacons were most prominent in the Bogalusa, La., area during much of the racial disturbance there during 1965 and worked closely with the Congress of Racial Equality and the Bogalusa Voters League. Leaders of this organization have encouraged Negroes to arm themselves and form roving patrols equipped with walkie-talkies in an effort to discourage Klan-type violence. (*FBI Appropriation, 1967, p. 53.*)

Nonetheless, the hypocrisy in what the Communists say they are for is evident. The Communists declare themselves for a lasting international peace (as long as no one stands up to Communist aggression), for peaceful coexistence (strictly on Communist terms), and for freedom for all people (to live under a Communist dictatorship). (*FBI Law Enforcement Bulletin*, October, 1961.)

DEFEATISM. A realistic appraisal of the Communist picture should not be disheartening. The Communists desire nothing more than to rule us, to make us believe that, regardless of what we do, we are lost. The inevitability of history, they say, is digging the tomb of Western civilization. This philosophy is wrong—absolutely wrong. It deadens our initiative and weakens our resolve. In fact, a clear, cool, levelheaded analysis of communism will do much to strengthen our resistance. We find that communism, though a mortal menace, carries within itself the seeds of its own destruction. Communism depends upon mass slavery, brutal utilization of manpower and the "divinity" of a guiding master for success. The spirit of man is liquidated; his moral stamina scorned as a relic of superstition.

Herein lies the basic weakness of communism—why it will falter and fail. Any philosophy which denies the validity of ethical standards is doomed. The achievements of man are but flickering candles before the power of God. Communism, grounded in an atheistic materialism, lacks the inner moral strength to give it direction, purpose and meaning. ("Foe to Freedom," *The Elks Magazine*, October, 1950, reprint, p. 4.)

DEFEATIST. Our freedoms were not won by defeatists—fair-weather patriots who crawl into hiding at the first sign of danger. (*FBI Law Enforcement Bulletin*, April 1962, p. 19.)

DEFINED. Communism, most simply defined, is terror—brutal terror over the minds, souls and bodies of men and women. The individual is but a petal to be plucked from the stem of life and then tossed aside to wither and die. The State is omnipotent, defining the opinions, conduct and actions of the people. Behind the State stands a ruling clique, all-powerful, responsible only to itself. Communism is age-old tyranny, painted with twentieth century slogans and catchwords. ("Foe To Freedom," *op. cit.*, p. 2.)

What is communism? It is a system of thought and action originated by Marx and Engels, developed by Lenin, and continued by Stalin and Khrushchev. That system embodies, among other things: A materialistic explanation of man and the universe; a materialistic interpretation of history centering about the class struggle; abolition of the non-Communist state; a revolutionary theory and a flexible course of action by which to abolish freedom of enterprise; a code of action based not on morals but on utility—the end justifies the means; the abolition of all religions; and, finally, a worldwide Communist revolution leading to a worldwide Communist society.

What is the end result of this system of thought and action? It is the reduction of man from a spiritual creature to the level of a high-grade animal whose sole reason for being is to copulate and die. ("God and Country or Communism?," *The American Legion Magazine,* November 1957, p. 55.)

DEMONIC. This rejection of God gives communism a demonic aspect—transforming it into a fanatical, Satanic, brutal phenomenon. Morality is not determined by ethical standards grounded in an Absolute, but in the expedient interpretations of the Party—meaning, in actual practice, the whims and desires of the ruling clique or Party leader. This leads to the terrifying doctrine that "the end justifies the means." Proof of the cynical ruthlessness of such morality is the following description by long-time American revolutionaries: "With him the end justifies the means. Whether his tactics be 'legal' and 'moral,' or not, does not concern him, so long as they are effective. He knows that the laws as well as the current code of morals, are made by his mortal enemies . . . . Consequently, he ignores them in so far as he is able and it suits his purposes. He proposes to develop, regardless of capitalist conceptions of 'legality,' 'fairness,' 'right,' etc., a greater power than his capitalist enemies. . . ." ("The Communist Menace: Red Goals and Christian Ideals," *Christianity Today,* October 10, 24, November 7, 1960, reprint, pp. 1-2.)

DEMONSTRATIONS. In the internal security field, Mr. Hoover stated: "Members of the Communist Party, USA, and their supporters continued to constitute a major disruptive influence on the national scene during the fiscal year 1965. Concentrating particularly on youth, Communists launched widespread propaganda compaigns designed to enlist support for a determined and vicious attack on American foreign policies and to foment confusion and create disorder in regard to the Nation's efforts to resolve the racial situation." Mr. Hoover made it quite clear that for the most part the racial and student demonstrations which erupted throughout the Nation during the past year were neither instigated nor controlled by Communists; however, he emphasized: "Communists used the opportunities presented to infiltrate many of the demonstrations and exploit them to their benefit in line with their own objectives. Communists today, in this country, are confident that they are on the verge of swelling their ranks and are optimistic about their chances to expand their influence on the national scene in the coming year." (*FBI Release,* July 14, 1965, p. 3.)

DIPLOMATIC—SPIES. A former Soviet intelligence officer has estimated that from 70 to 80 percent of the Russian officials stationed in the United States have an intelligence assignment. This may range from a careful review of hundreds of daily newspapers and other publications to the acquisition through any means of technical information on military and industrial equipment and installations, either classified or unclassified. Penetration of various Government agencies as well as anti-Communist organizations also is a major goal of Communist bloc officials.

Never in the history of the world has espionage been emphasized as it is today by the Communist nations. In addition to the use of official representatives for intelligence purposes, Communist bloc powers are training professional undercover spies—men like Rudolf Ivanovich Abel—to carry on clandestine operations. Likewise, Communist officials are constantly seeking contacts with Americans, contacts they can exploit. (SISS, "The Current Communist Threat," October, 1962, p. 1.)

DISSENT, WHAT KIND? Actually, graduating seniors should have no questions as to the greatness of our way of life. But as we know, some do have questions. We do not and

76

should not isolate and shield them from theories and ideologies which we believe to be contrary to the best interests of our country. As growing boys and girls, they have been exposed to the dubious theme running through much of entertainment, movies, television, radio, literature, arts, and theater which often depicts our orderly processes as inept, incompetent, and out of step with the times. This trend comes close to undermining the concepts and ideals on which our Nation was founded; and even in those instances when the age-old battle of right versus wrong is presented, right, though usually victorious, is often tainted.

Students as well as other Americans recognize and accept the longstanding custom in our society of satirizing public officialdom. The mere fact that this practice has become a part of the American scene is a tribute to our freedoms. Obviously, no one seriously suggests that all Congressmen, judges, prosecutors, law enforcement officers, city officials, and other authorities are jelly-brained nincompoops as frequently featured. While some may question the degree of such jest, none can question the privilege to do so.

The real danger lies in the more subtle, low-keyed, so-called objective, and serious castigation of principles involving our way of life. This is no complaint against the inherent rights of public criticism and freedom of expression. My objection is against the wholesale defilement and universal down-grading of our treasured freedoms and institutions—the time-tested attributes of democracy which are manifested in a representative government ruled by law.

A well-known editor and columnist some months ago, speaking on this topic, stated, "I am tired of seeing America debased in the eyes of foreigners. And I am genuinely disturbed that to the idealistic youth in many countries the fraud of communism appears synonymous with morality, while we, the chief repository of real freedom, are regarded as being in the last stages of decay."

Let us cast aside those who spread distrust and ridicule of our heritage. Let us extol the virtues of our noble traditions. And let us, by example rather than words, instill in the hearts of American youth the true pride and joy known to those who can proclaim, "I am an American." (*Congressional Record,* June 8, 1964, p. A3058.)

DO? What can we do? And what should be our course of action? The best antidote to communism is vigorous, intelligent, old-fashioned Americanism with eternal vigilance. I do not favor any course of action which would give the Communists cause to portray and pity themselves as martyrs. I do favor unrelenting prosecution wherever they are found to be violating our country's laws.

As Americans, our most effective defense is a workable democracy that guarantees and preserves our cherished freedoms.

I would have no fear if more Americans possessed the zeal, the fervor, the persistence, and the industry to learn about this menace of Red Fascism. (HCUA, *Menace of Communism*, March 26, 1947, p. 11.)

The first step in the fight to preserve the American way of life is the exposure of the true aims of communism and then a contrast of them with our American way of life. ("How To Fight Communism," *Newsweek*, June 9, 1947, reprint, p. 2.)

If there were to be a slogan in the fight against communism it should convey this thought: Uncover, expose, and spotlight their activities. Once this is done, the American people will do the rest—quarantine them from effectively weakening our country. (*Ibid.* p. 4.)

Western democracy must utilize its vast reservoirs of moral and spiritual strength—the sparks which set the souls of men afire and light the dark path ahead. We can do the job and do it in the American way. There is no need, whatsoever, for an abridgement of civil liberties or the creation of a national police system. The answer to the Communist menace is a thoroughly alert and aroused citizenry, cognizant of the evils of Marxism-Leninism, and ready at all times to work for the promotion of democratic principles. ("Foe To Freedom," *The Elks Magazine*, October, 1950, reprint, p. 5.)

The formula which has proved best in combating crime can also be applied to communism. Vigorous prosecution, wherever and whenever the Communist violates the law, is the first step. Applied in the American way, the fairness of our judicial process stands as a lesson for the world to see, and the courts have become the means of exposing the

Communist objective for what it is—a fifth column in America. Truly, the Trojan horse of antiquity has become the Trojan snake of today.

Communism can be defeated by the truth—and only the truth. Vigilante attacks, irrational tirades, forceful suppression are instruments which increase and do not decrease the menace. Such acts result only in making martyrs of the Communists.

The American people today, more than ever before, through a process of education have seen the true purposes of the Communist conspiracy. The public trials of the Communist leaders, the results of congressional inquiries, and the effective job done by an aroused American press have educated the average right-thinking American to recognize communism for what it is.

Further education is necessary if a well-lighted path must cut through the fog of confusion, misunderstanding, and indecision.

Communist strength is based on hypocrisy, duplicity, and sham. Too often, the ordinary American cannot strip the deceiving cloak of communism away from its framework and recognize it for what it is. The answer lies in education. An intelligent, well-informed public opinion, sensitive and conscious of the evils of communism and dedicated to the preservation of the sanctity of our democratic tradition, can pale the mockery of communism to extinction. (*Pathfinder,* November 5, 1952, *Congressional Record,* January 26, 1953, reprint, p. 3.)

What we need to do most about the concealed Communists is to be alert to the threat which they represent and aware of their undercover tactics. It is not necessary for anyone to become unduly suspicious of his neighbors. On the other hand, great caution should be exercised by anyone who thinks he has detected a concealed Communist. False accusations and careless insinuations can do more to destroy our way of life than to preserve it. Anyone who obtains evidence of what he believes to be subversive behavior on the part of another person should not jump to conclusions, but should at once turn over his evidence to the FBI. ("Communists Are After Our Minds," *American Magazine,* October, 1954, reprint, p. 4.)

I have always felt that an alert, informed citizenry is our most potent weapon against communism. The vast majority of Americans are patriotic, loyal citizens. They abhor treachery, deceit and any forces which would deprive us of our freedom and democratic liberties, and will not long tolerate the perpetuation of such evils. Through the schools, churches, press, and radio, the public should be given the facts about communism. Not through demagogy or appeal to their prejudices and fears, but through a clear, factual, truthful presentation, the public should continue to be informed of the real purposes, objectives, loyalties, and methods of operation of the Communist Party. Because Communist strategy is based on deceit and its true motives are concealed, communism cannot flourish under the spotlight of truth. The more fully it becomes exposed to the public eye, the more limited becomes its area of effective operations and the more restricted the number of people who will be duped into serving its evil purposes.

Along with informing the public of the truth concerning communism, and publicly exposing it as the foreign-inspired conspiracy that it is, another effective method of fighting communism is by prosecuting Communists for violations of federal law. ("Where Do We Stand Today With Communism in the Unitel States?," *Congressional Record,* March 1, 1954, p. 2296.)

The defense of the cherished freedoms secured and handed down to us by our forefathers is the responsibility of each American. Knowledge of the enemy, alertness to the danger, and everyday patriotism are the brick and mortar with which we can build an impregnable fortress against communism. Only the intelligent efforts of all Americans can prevent the decay of public apathy from laying open our Nation to the Red menace. (*FBI Law Enforcement Bulletin*, March, 1960, p. 1.)

To counter Communist reasoning we must have a basic understanding of Communist concepts and practices, plus a thorough understanding and appreciation of our own principles, traditions, and objectives. It is vitally important that we know what we stand for and why. This will, of course, give us the dedication and drive we need to counter the Communist challenge in the battle for the minds of men.

To counter Communist actions requires rational, calm, constructive, and creative national and international action of our own directed against the root causes of communism, which include ignorance, poverty, disease, economic dislocation, social injustices, racial discrimination, religious anemia, educational deficiencies, and corruption—political, labor, and business. (*FBI 1965 Appropriation*, p. 44.)

DO—ABROAD. Americans, both military and civilian, who are working in or visiting foreign nations can play an important role in the struggle against communism. Every citizen abroad is, in a very real sense, a full-time "ambassador" not only of our Nation but also of the democratic way of life. An understanding of and a respect for the rights of others are fundamental to our concept of individual freedom. This also applies in our dealings with citizens of other nations regardless of their educational attainments, social status, or economic level. By exercising his individual freedom in a responsible manner without violating the rights of others, every American traveling abroad can serve as a forceful example of how democracy works. The American abroad, by his conduct, can sow positive and constructive ideas which one day may help to produce a harvest on which the Free World can grow stronger. ("Communist Illusion and Democratic Reality," December, 1959, p. 7.)

DO—BE RESPONSIBLE. Attributing every adversity to communism is not only irrational, but contributes to hysteria and fosters groundless fears. Communism is, indeed, our paramount adversary, and it leans on its credo of invincibility and a concept of historical inevitability to accomplish its ends. The way to fight it is to study it, understand it, and discover what can be done about it. This cannot be achieved by dawdling at the spring of knowledge; it can only be accomplished by dipping deeply into thoughtful, reliable, and authoritative sources of information. (*FBI Law Enforcement Bulletin*, April, 1961, reprint, p. 1.)

DO—CHRISTIAN. 1. *Know what you believe as a Christian.*

2. *Attend church and Sunday school regularly.* Make worship and the study of God's Word a part of your daily life.

3. *Be a personal witness for your faith.*

81

4. *Take seriously the Christian mission of love, justice, and truth, which is the inner heart of the Gospel's teachings.*

5. *Live the optimism and hope which are inherent in the Christian faith.* ("Storming the Skies: Christianity Encounters Communism," *Christianity Today,* December 21, 1962, p. 5.)

DO—COMMUNITY. Individual initiative and originality, geared to local action, are the wellsprings by which living democracy is continuously nourished. These examples illustrate how, in the very practice of democracy, the moral strength of our Nation is constantly replenished. Programs such as these, infused with a renewed sense of dedication, should be expanded, coordinated, and continued on a long-range basis.

In a democracy, the importance of local communities cannot be overemphasized. It is there that social understanding and growth take root. It is there that education, business, labor, and religion take on form and substance to influence, nourish, vitalize, and give direction to our national life. It is in our local communities that cogent, penetrative thinking should be done now to re-evaluate the position of this Nation in the present world crisis. From this constructive effort can come a decisive contribution to formulating and carrying out a coordinated, comprehensive, affirmative global strategy which will insure the supremacy of freedom over all types of totalitarianism. ("Communist Illusion and Democratic Reality," December, 1959, p. 7.)

DO—FAITH IMPORTANT. A demonstrated faith in this heritage of democracy, rooted as it is in the Judeo-Christian tradition, is our mightiest weapon in the struggle for the minds of men. Our military might, political structure, economic resources, while effective, will not by themselves insure the victory of freedom over communism. These weapons must be reinforced by each citizen's experienced and abiding awareness of the intrinsic superiority of his society. From this awareness will develop a revitalized determination, not only to continue our resistance to communism, but, more important still, to make our living democracy a force of moral and spiritual persuasion which will fire the imagination of the entire world. (*Ibid.,* p 7.)

DO—INDIVIDUAL. Every loyal American citizen can and should join in the fight against the Communist menace. These are some of the things each person can do:

1. Learn the facts about communism—its history and objectives, its program and techniques in this country. The better informed one becomes, the more rapidly he can detect Communist influences and the more intelligently he can fight communism.

2. Through such media as the press and radio, keep up with Russia's stand on matters of foreign policy. The Communist Party in America will take the same position, and the Party line will fluctuate as Soviet foreign policy changes. Sudden reversals in Soviet policy will cause members of the Party to make sudden similar reversals in their pronouncements, which is one of the best ways to spot Communists.

3. Become familiar with the names of organizations publicly cited as Communist fronts, and refuse to join such groups, to sponsor their causes or to contribute to their fund drives.

4. Be alert to Communist tactics in unions and other organizations. Out-maneuver them. Keep them under control and in the minority at all times and attempt to eliminate or neutralize their effectiveness. Openly oppose their efforts to promulgate pro-Communist activities or resolutions.

5. Keep Communists out of official positions in schools, churches, and other institutions where they can poison the minds and influence actions of youth.

6. Exercise your privilege to vote and keep Communists and their sympathizers out of public office.

7. Develop an intelligent, participating interest in civic affairs and programs for social improvement. Don't let Communists claim a monopoly in such matters or move in and direct established programs.

8. Report to the FBI immediately any pertinent information relating to subversive activities.

9. Conduct no private investigations of suspicious persons or organizations, but leave that to trained investigators who are authorized to perform such investigations. Do not become involved in the Communist movement for whatever worthwhile motives without first discussing the matter thor-

oughly with the FBI and establishing a cooperative relationship.

10. Learn as much as possible about America—its history, government, culture, laws and heritage of freedom; and make the practice of democracy its own bulwark against subversion. Speak up for America and work for America. ("Where Do We Stand Today With Communism in the United States?" *Congressional Record,* March 1, 1954, p. 2297.)

DO—KNOWLEDGE NEEDED. Our free society is so far superior, both spiritually and materially, to communist totalitarianism that, until recently, we assumed that our citizens did not need any specialized knowledge or training to withstand Communist psychological pressures. This somewhat naive presumption was abruptly dispelled during the Korean War. In military combat on the battlefield, the men of our fighting forces acquitted themselves admirably. Unfortunately, however, in the individual, personal, ideological conflict with their Communist captors, some American prisoners of war capitulated. The majority of those who collaborated with the Chinese Communists were unable to resist Communist indoctrination by practitioners skilled in the technique of the Big Lie. ("Communist Illusion and Democratic Reality," December, 1959, p. 3.)

DO—LECTURES. In the State of Florida, for example, the Bar Association developed a lecture program on the theme of the advantages of democracy over communism. These lectures are given to high school students throughout the state by specially trained practicing attorneys. The speakers explain how our Government operates, what must be done to keep it functioning effectively, and why it is superior to the Soviet system. All of the lectures given under this program stress the duty of each citizen to interest himself actively in public affairs. The American Bar Association, in cooperation with the American Heritage Foundation, annually observes Law Day with ceremonies which contrast the Rule of Law in our country with the rule of fear in Communist nations. (*Ibid,* p. 6.)

DO—POSITIVE. The Communists are agreed that the revolution will not come until the precipitation of a "great crisis" such as a general strike, a war which could be turned into civil strife, or a great economic depression.

Our cue is to make democracy work so that the Communists will never have their "great crisis." ("How To Fight Communism," *Newsweek*, June 9, 1947, reprint, p. 2.)

DO—RELIGIOUS PEOPLE. Men and women in the field of religion must play a more vital role. Communism is fanatically opposed to religion. Communists reject belief in God, morals derived from religious principles, and the immortality of the soul. A Communist theoretician said flatly:

"It is our duty to do even more than we have done to make the anti-religious movement, not only in the U.S.S.R., but in the capitalist countries as well, a movement of vast millions. . . ." ("How to Beat Communism," *The Lion*, October 1957, reprint, p. 3.)

DO—RETURN TO FUNDAMENTALS. Faith can come only from spiritual sources. We need to drink again at the wells from which the Founding Fathers drank. We need to return to the fundamentals which our fathers knew. We need to steep ourselves in the idealism from whence sprang the seeds of our constitutional form of government—to read again the immortal documents, the books and memoirs of the men whose faith in God and in posterity gave us our heritage of freedom. Our youth must understand that faith is essential to the continuance of freedom.

The battle we are presently engaged in is a struggle between the spiritual and the material. The proponents of atheistic materialism are determined to wipe the Judaic-Christian principles of morality, on which Western civilization is founded, from the face of the earth. The strength we bring to this struggle is dependent upon one thing: our individual understanding of the enemy we face. ("Communist 'New Look' A Study in Duplicity," *The Elks Magazine*, August, 1956, reprint, p. 4.)

DO—SPIRITUAL. We can defeat this atheistic enemy by drawing upon our spiritual resources.

The future, to a large extent, will be determined by what we as Christians have to say and do. Those who are ministers of the gospel can help determine this fateful decision:

Shall it be a world of Communist domination or Christian rededication?

A God-centered nation, ever humble before the majesty of the Divine Creator, can keep alive freedom, justice, and mercy. This is the heritage of America. (*Congressional Record*, February 2, 1961, p. A703.)

DO—YOUTH. Local activity can have far-reaching effects. A group of graduate and undergraduate students decided to capitalize on the Communist-inspired Seventh World Youth Festival held in Vienna in 1959. For a year prior to the Festival, they visited college campuses searching for students who could effectively represent the United States and who were willing to attend. They distributed pamphlets outlining the Communist background of this and previous festivals, as well as booklets of facts and figures on issues which Communist propaganda has been exploiting. This group also conducted briefing sessions for the anti-Communists who planned to attend. News accounts of the Festival highlighted how the anti-Communist American delegates stole the Communists' thunder as a result of their ability to correct the misconceptions and distortions of American society which have always characterized these festivals. ("Communist Illusion and Democratic Reality," December, 1959, pp. 6-7.)

DuBOIS CLUBS. A primary task of the students who attended this school was the recruitment of minority youth for the Party's year-old front group, the W.E.B. DuBois Clubs of America. During the summer of 1965, this organization launched an ambitious program aimed at bolstering its Midwest region which had been beset by factional disputes, lack of organization, and adverse publicity. Participants in this program spoke of this "summer project" in glowing terms at a conference of national coordinators of the DuBois Clubs held over the Labor Day weekend in Chicago. (*FBI 1967 Appropriation*, p. 44.)

DUPES. To me, one of the most unbelievable and unexplainable phenomena in the fight on communism is the manner in which otherwise respectable, seemingly intelligent persons, perhaps unknowingly, aid the Communist cause more effectively than the Communists themselves. The pseudo-liberal can be more destructive than the known Communist

86

because of the esteem which his cloak of respectability invites. ("Remarks before the Continental Congress of the National Society Daughters of the American Revolution," April 22, 1954, p. 2.)

DUTIES. In a democracy, all men have duties as well as rights. We are proud of the privileges which free government provides—freedom of speech, worship, and the press. They are the very essence of our way of life. Yet every citizen must be cognizant that these rights become meaningful only when he is willing to perform his duties of citizenship. If we as a Nation forget our obligations to be good citizens, we shall forfeit the historic liberties of America.

To men of religious faith, the responsibilities of citizenship are of deep and continuing concern. From religion comes the principles of tolerance and brotherhood. As servants of God, men and women know their obligations to their fellow man. They want their community to be a better place in which to live. They are ready to go the "extra mile," to lend the "helping hand." ("Remarks of J. Edgar Hoover upon acceptance of the National Interfaith Award from the Washington Interfaith Committee," June 9, 1959, p. 4.)

DUTY: It was Abraham Lincoln who, during a time of grave peril, told the American people, "Let us have faith that right makes right, and in that faith let us to the end dare to do our duty as we understand it." The words of our martyred President still ring true today. ("Faith or Fear," *Congressional Record*, June 28, 1960, p. 13653.)

EDUCATION FAILURES. The subversive knows well the value of fully exploiting these vital fields. It is clearly by design, rather than by accident, that communist propaganda surfaces from time to time in our institutions of advanced learning.

We have failed in our educational processes to inculcate the basic element of American history, our philosophy of government and our moral and spiritual foundations. It is time to make our history and traditions glow and throb. We have heard about America with our ears, but not with our hearts. ("America—Freedom's Champion," October 18, 1960, p. 7.)

EFFECTIVE—WHY. The most important reason for their continued effectiveness in many areas, however, is attributable to Party discipline and their fanatical adherence to it. ("The Communists Are After Our Minds," *American Magazine,* October 1954, reprint, p. 4.)

One reason lies in the fact that they are assisted by a host of sympathizers and fellow travelers. It has long been their boast that for every Party member they control at least 10 other persons who are ready, able, and willing to do the Party's work. (*Ibid,* p. 4.)

Another reason for the effectiveness of the Communists is that they are well financed. (*Ibid,* p. 3.)

ENEMIES OF THE REPUBLIC. Daniel Webster knew the heavy price America had paid for her liberty. And he knew also the disintegrating effect of self-indulgence, neglect of duty and public lethargy in a nation of free men.

These lethal influences are at work, constantly undermining the sense of personal responsibility and self-discipline so essential to our Nation's welfare. They form a common denominator with the aggressive enemies of our Republic in assaulting the cause of decency and justice across the length and breadth of the land.

Who are these enemies of our Republic? They are the crime syndicates, the narcotics peddlers, the labor racketeers, the unscrupulous businessmen, the corrupt politicians and all others who blatantly defy the laws of the land.

They are the hatemongers and the false liberals who would subvert our Constitution and undermine our democratic processes in furtherance of their selfish ends.

They are the Communists and other subversive elements who wave false banners of legitimacy and patriotism while relentlessly plotting to destroy our heritage of freedom. ("Keys to Freedom," November 16, 1963, pp. 4-5.)

ENEMIES. Who are these enemies of our Republic? They are the crime syndicates, the narcotics peddlers, the labor racketeers, the unscrupulous businessmen, the corrupt politicians and all others who blatantly defy the laws of the land.

They are the hatemongers and the false liberals who would subvert our Constitution and undermine our democratic processes in furtherance of their selfish ends.

They are the Communists and other subversive elements who wave false banners of legitimacy and patriotism while relentlessly plotting to destroy our heritage of freedom. (*Congressional Record*, Nov. 27, 1963, p. A7293.)

ENEMY—GREATEST. We Americans—180 years after our declaration of independence—are face to face with a tyranny more monstrous, more devious, less understood and more deadly than any which has threatened civilization heretofore. ("Communist 'New Look' A Study in Duplicity," *The Elks Magazine*, August, 1956, reprint, p. 3.)

ESPIONAGE. The host of Soviet and satellite officials in the United States, 70 to 80 percent of whom are estimated by reliable sources as having some type of espionage assignment, are today feverishly attempting to obtain this country's secrets. The long list of Soviet officials declared persona non grata by this Government, following their exposure by the FBI as espionage Agents, bears testimony to their flagrant abuse of diplomatic status.

In June, 1960, our State Department estimated that Russian and Chinese Communist bloc countries have some 300,000 trained spies serving throughout the world, and commented that "there has never been a government in history which has placed heavier emphasis on espionage" than present-day Russia.

Standing side by side with these specialists in internal intrigue are those home-grown traitors who call themselves members of the Communist Party, USA, and readily admit that their purpose is and always has been the communizing of America. These fanatical disciples of Marxism are eagerly worming their way into such fertile fields of endeavor as youth, labor, education and racial minorities. ("America— Freedom's Champion," October 18, 1969, pp. 4-5.)

Among the results of prosecution for espionage violations during the year was an 8-year prison sentence imposed on Arthur Rogers Roddey, a former Government employee. FBI Agents, while making a search of Roddey's house with his consent, found about 200 classified documents. Indicted on six counts of espionage, 4 counts of fraud against the Government, and two counts of theft of Government property, Roddey pleaded guilty to one count of espionage and was.

sentenced on March 22, 1961. (*FBI Annual Report, Fiscal Year 1961*, p. 24.)

Additionally, our overall security operations have demanded unusually heavy assignments of manpower to investigative and surveillance programs directed against internal threats of communism, espionage, subversion and Communist front and Communist-infiltrated organizations. The extent of their vast scope may be found in the fact that 91,844 security matters were referred to our attention for investigation during the last fiscal year.

Supplementing the continued intense espionage activities against the United States by Soviet Russia and her satellites are the operations of elements in our country interested in the Cuban revolutionary movement. These developments have been responsible for a substantial increase in many phases of our security work. (*FBI 1962 Appropriation*, p. 15.)

ESPIONAGE—CHANNELS. In involving the great bulk of their official personnel in intelligence activity in one way or another, the Soviets utilize to the fullest extent possible any and all official means such as the United Nations, trade delegations, and the like, as transmission belts to carry additional intelligence personnel into this country. Here are some examples to illustrate this fact.

Mr. Hoover. East-West Exchange Program—The numerous Soviet scientific delegations which arrive in the United States to tour U.S. universities and scientific establishments invariably have among their members Soviet scientists who have been given special assignments by the KGB. It is established Soviet policy that among such groups are one or more full-time KGB officers who are in charge of the delegations.

Upon returning, Soviet scientists who have visited the United States under the exchange program are required by the KGB to submit comprehensive reports on the technical aspects of their trip, including descriptions of installations visited, research being conducted and the status of particular projects. They must also submit reports concerning Americans contacted for possible future use by the KGB.

Students—As to the students, many of the Soviet exchange students attending colleges and universities in the

United States are utilized as agents by the KGB. Having the responsibility of obtaining any information of intelligence interest, they photograph (or deliver to their KGB superiors for photographing) documents and scientific papers to which they have access as students.

Of the Soviet students in the United States for the school term beginning in the fall of 1964, over 20 percent were suspected of being agents with specific KGB assignments or officers of the Soviet intelligence services.

Press representatives—Press cover is tailored for the intelligence work of the Soviets. They are in a business in which they are expected to be where news is developing, to meet those persons having intimate knowledge, to ask questions and seek information.

As of February 1, 1965, over half of the Soviet nationals posing as press representatives in the United States were known to be intelligence agents.

Amtorg Trading Corporation—Disguising their intelligence personnel as legitimate trade representatives has long been a tactic of the Soviet intelligence services. The official cover utilized enables such personnel to travel extensively and meet many persons associated with fields of special intelligence interest.

Over half of the Soviet nationals employed by the Amtorg Trading Corporation in New York City on February 1, 1965, were known or suspected to be actually connected with the Soviet intelligence services.

United Nations—Fully exploiting their diplomatic immunity, freedom from travel restrictions and the respectability enjoyed as members of an international organization dedicated to world peace, the Soviet intelligence services have continued to increase their use of employment with the United Nations as a cover for their espionage personnel.

On July 1, 1960, there were 32 Soviet official personnel assigned to the United Nations Secretariat. By February 1, 1965, the number had mounted to 108, of whom half were agents or officers of the Soviet intelligence services.

(Discussion off the record.)

Mr. Hoover. Not only does the Soviet bloc take advantage of all types of cover but the flow of visitors to and from the many Soviet-bloc countries is on the increase.

91

For example, in the case of Hungary, only a handful of visitors arrived in the United States from that country in any given month four or five years ago. In July 1964, we received notification of the arrival of over 1,000 visitors from Hungary alone. This not only adds to our work, but also creates a vehicle for the clandestine introduction into the United States of individuals having intelligence assignments. (*FBI Appropriation 1966,* pp. 67-69.)

ESPIONAGE—DIPLOMATS. The personnel assigned to Soviet-bloc official establishments in the United States has steadily risen over the year. Consequently, there has been a corresponding strengthening of foreign-directed intelligence activities, since many of these officials are in reality trained espionage and intelligence agents. (*FBI Appropriation 1962,* p. 50.)

The number of official representatives of Communist-bloc nations assigned in the United States varies from time to time, but at any given moment there are several hundred of them. In their official capacity, these representatives serve in diplomatic establishments, United Nations delegations and various missions to this country. Many of them, however, are engaged in some type of intelligence activity, much of which is outside the scope of their recognized official duties.

A former Soviet intelligence officer has estimated that from 70 to 80 per cent of the Russian officials stationed in the United States have an intelligence assignment. This may range from a careful review of hundreds of daily newspapers and other publications to the acquisition through any means of technical information on military and industrial equipment and installations, either classified or unclassified. Penetration of various Government agencies as well as anti-Communist organizations also is a major goal of Communist-bloc officials.

Never in the history of the world has espionage been emphasized as it is today by the Communist nations. In addition to the use of official representatives for intelligence purposes, Communist-bloc powers are training professional undercover spies—men like Rudolf Ivanovich Abel—to carry on clandestine operations. (*FBI Annual Report, Fiscal Year 1962,* pp. 25-27.)

As of January 1, 1964, there were 744 Soviet bloc official personnel in this country. They were accompanied by 1,099 dependents, some of whom have intelligence assignments. (*FBI 1965 Appropriation*, p. 45.)

ESPIONAGE—FUNDS. Mr. Hoover. The Soviet bloc espionage drive against this Nation is backed by a virtual army of intelligence personnel and unlimited operational funds. A former officer of the KGB (Soviet Committee of State Security) estimated that the foreign intelligence directorate of the KGB had several thousand employees, including legal and illegal agents and trainees. He said that the head of the foreign intelligence directorate had indicated that "Soviet intelligence" (apparently referring only to the foreign intelligence directorate) spent about $1½ billion a year.

The FBI is utilizing every resource at its command to meet the threat posed by this army of spies. Because of our aggressive investigative activity, the Soviet intelligence services consider the United States as the most difficult country in which to carry on clandestine espionage operations. (*Ibid*, pp. 49-50.)

ESPIONAGE—INDUSTRIAL. Through subterfuge, deceit, and deliberate circumvention of regulations, the Soviet-bloc officials stationed in the United States have systematically developed one of the best industrial spying systems in the world. One defector has stated that the ease with which data is obtained in the United States has eliminated much of the hazardous and time-consuming clandestine operations which otherwise would be necessary. Another has estimated that the Soviet military attache's office in the United States is able to obtain legally 95 per cent of the material useful for its intelligence objectives and that the Polish military intelligence secures more technical data in the United States than in all of the other countries in the world.

During the period January 1, 1959, to February 1, 1961, Soviet officials attended approximately 141 technical, scientific, or general business conventions and expositions covering such fields as aeronautics, electronics, plastics development, radio, rocketry, and related items of strategic significance. (*FBI Appropriation 1962*, pp. 50-51.)

Mr. Lipscomb. I would like to discuss for just a moment a couple of questions on Soviet espionage activities. The Soviet Union has trading companies which exist in this country.

Mr. Hoover. Amtorg is the principal one.

Mr. Lipscomb. I believe I have come in contact just recently, through an item I have been working on, with one called Stankoimport. These trading companies are making every effort to purchase technical equipment in our country, and there are certain American business firms that are willing to trade with them. One case has just been exposed and the export license has been canceled by the Department of Commerce, for precision ball-bearing machines. I know of another instance where the Department of Commerce has granted an export license for some very technical precision machinery that among other things can manufacture aluminum V-8 motor blocks and their components. I am hopeful, at this date, that the Department of Commerce will cancel this license also after the facts are reviewed.

Is there any espionage activity here being conducted by Soviet trading agents and the trading companies?

Mr. Hoover. Yes, there is. The Soviets have maintained a large staff of officials in this country since its first recognition in 1933. These officials have been assigned to the Soviet Embassy, consulates, trade delegations, news media, United Nations, and the Amtorg Trading Corporation. It is from these installations that the intelligence activities are directed against the United States.

The Amtorg Trading Corporation, 355 Lexington Avenue, New York City, acts as buying and selling agent in the United States for approximately 25 foreign trade organizations of the Soviets. Amtorg is a New York corporation formed in 1924. Since 1949 it has been registered with the Department of Justice under the Foreign Agents Registration Act. Currently, there are 32 Soviet officials attached to Amtorg. One of the Soviet foreign trade organizations represented in the United States by Amtorg is "Stankoimport," which handles exports and imports of machine tools, metal and woodworking machinery, ball and roller bearings, and the like.

Intourist is the Soviet tourist agency with office space at Amtorg and has one representative in the United States.

Four Continent Book Corporation, 156 Fifth Avenue, New York City, handles importation and exportation of books, periodicals, and other published material. It is registered under the Foreign Agents Registration Act. One of its foreign principals is Mezhdunarodnaja Kniga (International Book), Moscow.

For the most part, the Soviet satellite nations utilize their commercial attaches for handling their trading operations.

Of course, the example you cite of the concern where the export license was suspended, I understand this resulted from attention called to it by one of the Senators as well as yourself.

Mr. Lipscomb. Is there anything we can do to call to the attention of American business the danger of this kind of trade? If Soviet Agents are making business contacts with American businessmen in such plants as precision ball bearing or these motors I was talking about, surely they have access to the plant and other things that they should not be entitled to.

Mr. Hoover. The Department of Commerce has the authority of granting export licenses and therefore has some measure of control over such matters. As you indicated, the Secretary of Commerce withdrew the export license which had been granted. It was probably granted prior to his becoming Secretary of Commerce.

Mr. Lipscomb. It was.

Mr. Hoover. Such matters are generally handled down the line and not at the secretarial level.

As to the attitude of the American businessman, a few of these individuals are unwittingly sympathetic or are inclined to fawn over the Soviets. (*Ibid*, pp. 65-67).

ESPIONAGE—NON-CLASSIFIED MATERIALS. This type of material is easily collected in numerous ways in our country. Large quantities are obtained through direct correspondence with industrial establishments, Government agencies, and the like. Other valuable data are obtained by the simple expedient of subscribing, directly or through intermediaries, to literally hundreds of American newspapers, magazines, and industrial, technical, or military publications. Taking trips about the country, and attending conferences, exhibits, conventions, and the like, are other ready means of collecting highly important intelligence information.

During the calendar year 1962, Soviet officials employed at the offices of the Soviet military, naval, and air attaches alone made 23 automobile reconnaissance trips through various sections of the United States. They covered most of the strategic areas of the country, some several times. They not only closely viewed industrial and military installations, but collected data of intelligence interest, such as maps and photographs of cities. During 1963 they made 36 such trips.

Additional trips were made by officials attached to other Soviet establishments.

The GRU (Soviet Military Intelligence Service) is reported to have divided the United States into geographical areas, each of which is assigned to a GRU officer who is to visit that area frequently to become aquainted with every military establishment and industrial facility. (*FBI Appropriation 1965*, p. 47.)

ESPIONAGE—SPIES. A growing problem is the extent to which the Soviet intelligence services are dispatching undercover spies into the United States. These individuals have no ostensible connection with either the official Soviet establishments or personnel in this country nor do they make any overt contacts with their foreign espionage headquarters. They are well-trained, professional intelligence officers and usually bear assumed identities and are supplied with expertly fabricated documents and unlimited funds. They enter the United States without difficulty to become assimilated into our population and, unless uncovered, eventually serve as the nucleus of an extensive clandestine espionage network. Their detection among the more than 190 million people in this country is a counterintelligence problem of great magnitude. (*FBI Appropriation 1966*, p. 69.)

ESPIONAGE TARGETS. Espionage targets of the Soviet-bloc intelligence organizations have no known limitations. Their quest for information has ranged from the seemingly ridiculous to such objectives as clearly reveal their intent of world conquest. Our investigations have disclosed not only the intensity of purpose of the Soviets but their willingness to spend unlimited funds in the achievement of their goal. (*FBI Appropriation 1962*, p. 50.)

ESPIONAGE TODAY. Reports from a host of reliable FBI sources clearly indicate no letup on the part of the Communist countries in their intelligence attacks against the United States for the purpose of penetrating our national defense interests. As all Americans know, it is the intent and objective of Russia and the other Communist countries to spread their brand of the Communist system wherever possible.

The coverage and thwarting of these foreign intelligence activities have over the years resulted in a steadily increasing workload for the FBI.

Bases for the intelligence operations of the Communist bloc continue to be their official establishments including their diplomatic establishments and their delegations to the United Nations. The intelligence services of the Communist-bloc countries continue to make full use of all of these as a cover for their operations. Many of the officials assigned to these establishments are actually intelligence officers engaged in the clandestine direction of intelligence agents and sources in our country.

In carrying out their aims we find the Communist intelligence services attempting to penetrate such key U. S. agencies as the FBI, CIA, State Department, and Department of Defense.

The official personnel of the Soviet-bloc countries openly in this country play an important role in this vast intelligence-gathering operation. The number of official personnel of the Soviet bloc here on April 1, 1969, totaled 2,537, including dependents. Some idea of the number of intelligence personnel involved can be obtained from the fact that a Soviet defector has stated that 70-80 percent of all personnel assigned to Soviet diplomatic establishments work in the intelligence field.

This chart shows the total Soviet-bloc official personnel in this country on July 1 for the years 1963 through 1968 and the current complement here on April 1, 1969. It also illustrates the fact that over the years the number has increased substantially.

Most of the official personnel of the Soviet bloc in this country are from Russia. This chart gives a breakdown by countries of the Soviet-bloc official personnel in the United States as of April 1, 1969.

In addition to the officials, there are those deep-cover intelligence agents operating in our country who have no ostensible connection with their foreign principal. Once a deep-cover agent has gained entry to our country, he easily becomes assimilated into our vast population under an assumed identity. His detection and identification at this point become a counterintelligence problem of extreme magnitude. (*FBI 1970 Appropriation,* pp. 73-74.)

EX-COMMUNISTS. The assistance which ex-Communists have given to the FBI has been invaluable. Having had their eyes opened to the true nature of the Communist conspiracy, many of them have reevaluated the privileges of American citizenship, have realized the duties inherent in such citizenship, and, through making a full disclosure to the FBI of the information they possess, have made contributions of great value to the internal security of this country. The truth of their testimony has been verified by corroborating evidence. Many ex-Communists have been tested by vigorous and searching cross-examination, and their opponents have been unable to contradict their testimony. Many of them have suffered ostracism, public rebuke, and social distrust as a result of their breaking with the Communist Party and testifying against it. All religions teach that redemption is possible for any man who sincerely repents and seeks to make amends for his errors. The sincerity of a former Communist can be judged by his willingness to stand up and be counted and by taking positive action to attempt to rectify his wrongs. I am always glad to see ex-Communists make their change of conscience and philosophy a matter of record, assume earnestly the responsibilities of good citizenship and join in the fight against the evil they formerly espoused, and I welcome the information which they can furnish. ("Where Do We Stand Today With Communism in the United States?," *Congressional Record,* March 1, 1954, p. 2297.)

EXCUSE FOR IGNORANCE? The free world has been slow to recognize the Communist approach, despite the blueprints for action which the Communists have proclaimed to all with ears to hear and eyes to read. (*U. S. News & World Report,* March 8, 1957, p. 110.)

FAITH NEEDED. We are living in an age of uncertainty— an age of awesome national peril—an age when the struggle between freedom and totalitarian enslavement is drawing toward a climax. We *now* have need of *faith as never before in our Nation's history.* We must revive within ourselves the faith of our forefathers, which enabled them to meet and overcome adversity.

Our Nation holds in trust the last hope of a free civilization. Our dedication to truth, justice and individual dignity *must not be compromised.* If we are strong enough, and care enough, and maintain our national integrity, this Nation will survive the terrible threat that presents itself today. With God's help, we will meet the challenge of survival. This is the heritage of America. ("The Faith to be Free," December 7, 1961, p. 8.)

FAMILY. Not long ago a Communist leader who the Party thought had fallen under suspicion of the FBI, was ordered to drop completely out of sight. He did so, not even telling his wife and children that he was leaving them, and emerged a few weeks later in another city with a new name and background which had been provided for him. He lived there with a woman Communist who, in turn, deserted her husband and children, on the Party's orders, to become his paramour. The fact that two homes have been wrecked to serve Party objectives means less than nothing to the ruthless individuals who direct its policies. ("The Communists are After Our Minds," *American Magazine,* October, 1954, reprint, p. 4.)

FARMERS. In considering what position the Communist Party, USA, will take during the 1960 political campaign, those in attendance at the 17th National Convention were provided with a document containing a 10-point program which the Party would support. One of these concerning farmers is ridiculous per se when examined in the light of the ultimate aim of communism. Despite the slaves in the communes of Communist China and the state-owned collective farms and farm machinery in Soviet Russia, the Communists in America have the effrontery to intone sanctimoniously that the Communist Party, USA, will support a program which will "protect the rights of the small farmers to their land and their implements."

What else could such a program be but one small, but expedient, step toward the sovietization of American farmers?

Who can conceive of farmers being allowed to own their farms and machinery in the type of society advocated by Communists whose very name connotes a social order in which all goods are held in common by a single authoritarian party? (Senate Internal Security Subcommittee, *Concerning the 17th National Convention, Communist Party U.S.A., December 10-13, 1959,* Washington: Government Printing Office, 1960, pp. 8-9.)

FASCISM. There is little choice between Fascism and Communism. Both are totalitarian, anti-democratic and godless. Both use the same means of treachery and deceit to accomplish their goal of tyranny and oppression. In our fight against Communism we have no place for the political police that have dominated Fascist and Communist countries. ("How to Fight Communism," *Newsweek,* June 9, 1947, reprint p. 2.)

FASCISM—RED. The mad march of Red fascism is a cause for concern in America. (House Committee Un-American Activities, *Menace of Communism,* Washington: Government Printing Office, March 26, 1947, p. 4.)

We were aware, however, that a brand of tyranny and fascism—Red fascism—far more treacherous than that of Hitler and Mussolini, was emerging as a powerful threat on the international scene. ("An American's Challenge," *Congressional Record,* October 10, 1962, p. A7516.)

FAIR PLAY FOR CUBA COMMITTEE. There is, of course, a great deal of intrigue involved in dealings among various Cuban factions. Even the Fair Play for Cuba Committee, one of the principal outlets for pro-Castro propaganda in this country, has become mired in a battle for control between the Communist Party, USA, and the Socialist Workers Party, a splinter Communist organization. (SISS, *Current Communist Threat,* Washington: Government Printing Office, October 1962, p. 4.)

FEAR—CAUSE FOR. I would have no fears if more Americans possessed the zeal, the fervor, the persistence, and the industry to learn about this menace of Red fascism. I do fear for the liberal and progressive who has been hoodwinked and duped into joining hands with the Communists. I confess to a real apprehension so long as Communists are able to

secure ministers of the gospel to promote their evil work
and espouse a cause that is alien to the religion of Christ
and Judiasm. I do fear so long as school boards and parents
tolerate conditions whereby Communists and fellow travelers
under the guise of academic freedom can teach our youth a
way of life that eventually will destroy the sanctity of the
home, that undermines faith in God, that causes them to
scorn respect for constituted authority and sabotage our
revered Constitution. (HCUA, *Menace of Communism*,
March 26, 1947, p. 11.)

FBI—ATTACKS ON. The Federal Bureau of Investigation
has been the target of both extremes in the civil rights issue
and I believe this shows the FBI has followed the proper
course in its handling of this most delicate issue.

Let me reaffirm that so long as I remain its Director,
the FBI will never be intimidated by the illogical criticisms
and pressures of those detractors who would have us *exceed*
some areas of our authority and grossly *neglect* others. We
will continue to carry out every assigned duty thoroughly,
promptly, impartially and *without apology to anyone*.

Self-serving individuals such as these are not a genuine
part of the civil rights movement. Nor are the brick-throw-
ing rabble, or the raucous hoodlums who have attacked the
forces of law and order and have turned orderly protests
into nightmares of violence and bloodshed. Theirs is a doctrine of hatred—defiance and anarchy—which cannot and
must not be tolerated! Their acts are of the greatest dis-
service to the civil rights cause. ("Our Heritage of Greatness," December 12, 1964, p. 7.)

FBI—CRITICISM. On the other hand, public criticism of a
law-enforcement agency, when such criticism is not based on
fact—whether made through ignorance, misinformation, or
deliberate maliciousness—is inexcusable. In any case, the
damage is definite and irreparable.

Law enforcement in a democracy is a two-way street.
An efficient agency has the confidence of the public. Only
an agency which has the confidence of the public can be efficient. Unless an agency retains the support of the public,
it cannot get necessary information, reports of violations,
evidence, and testimony so essential in the administration of

justice. Those who attempt to shatter that confidence inevitably are attacking the administration of justice—the prime function of Government. Politics, selfishness, ignorance, and misinformation are not legitimate excuses for wanton disregard of the truth. (*Congressional Record*, August 18, 1949, p. A5424.)

Mr. Cederberg. I do not want to prolong this discussion, but I have a concern that there seems to be a trend in certain columns and newspapers in the country to try to discredit the activities of the FBI, and I am alarmed about this. I hope that regardless of some of these trends you will carry on in the fashion you have done before. The record of the FBI as it has been portrayed to this Committee since I have been on it is one that is entitled to the highest commendation of all the people of our country.

Mr. Hoover, I appreciate that. I realize the brickbats come, but I judge the source from which they come. Many times criticisms come from sources and individuals who, had they not criticized us, would have caused me great concern.

Mr. Bow. I want to say, along the lines of the brickbats you get, I wonder if some do not come from the same sources that are trying to discredit the Congress in the eyes of the public?

Mr. Hoover. I think there is a definite effort to discredit the Congress.

Mr. Bow. Which effort comes from the same sources as those attacking the FBI.

Mr. Hoover. Exactly. They make similar statements about the FBI which they make about Congress.

Mr. Bow. I want to join my colleagues in saying we all sleep a little easier at night knowing you are on the job, you and your colleagues; they deserve much credit too.

Mr. Hoover. They certainly do. (*FBI Appropriation 1965*, pp. 65-66.)

FBI FUNCTIONS. The FBI has great responsibilities to the Nation. In addition to being charged "with the duty of investigating violations of the laws of the United States, collecting evidence in cases in which the United States is or may be a party in interest and performing other duties imposed . . . . by law," the FBI has been charged by Presidential

Directive dated September 6, 1939, "to take charge of investigative work in matters relating to espionage, sabotage . . . ."

In implementing this charge the President called upon all law enforcement officers to promptly "turn over to the nearest representative of the Federal Bureau of Investigation any information obtained by them relating to espionage, counter-espionage, sabotage, subversive activities . . . ."

The FBI is essentially an investigative agency. It is our duty to get the facts. We do not establish policies—that is the responsibility of higher authority. We do not make decisions as to prosecutions—that is the responsibility of the Attorney General, his assistants, and the various United States attorneys.

To the end that our responsibilities may be discharged, it is necessary not to lose sight of the fact that our chief responsibility is the duty to obtain information and to protect confidence. Thus, when a citizen furnishes information on a confidential basis his confidence must be respected. In any intelligence operation, security of information is of primary concern. I recall in the pre-war years that the FBI was criticized on the ill-founded premise that nothing was being done to meet the Nazi-Fascist-Japanism threat to our internal security. The real facts are now a matter of record. What was being done, and done successfully, could not then be discussed and publicized. When the time came to act the FBI was fully prepared to carry out its responsibilities. There was not one successful enemy-directed act of sabotage during the war and enemy espionage was kept under complete control.

In one of our espionage cases, a spy ring was kept under close surveillance for over 18 months. The arrests when made broke the backbone of the Nazi spy system in America. I shudder at what might have happened had there been a disclosure of our operations and our sources of information in the initial days of that investigation. That was the very time we were most criticized for inaction. I hope this Committee will understand our situation and I know you will readily agree that there are many questions that you might like to raise which I would for obvious reasons be unable to answer in a public hearing. (HCUA, *Menace of Communism*, March 26, 1947, pp. 1-2.)

103

By Presidential directives, legislative enactments and instructions of the Attorney General the FBI has the responsibility of investigating espionage, sabotage, subversive activities and related domestic intelligence matters and of serving as a coordinating agency for the dissemination of domestic intelligence information to other Federal agencies authorized to receive it. The FBI is a fact-finding agency and does not institute prosecutive action on the basis of its investigative findings. Information reflecting a violation of Federal law is referred to the Department of Justice for an opinion as to prosecution. Any information received which pertains to the responsibilities of some other Government agency is transmitted directly to that agency without recommendation or evaluation.

While the FBI for years has exposed the Communist conspiracy, it cannot divulge the confidential details of its files as to specific individuals. A Congressional Committee having the power of subpoena and contempt citation is able to focus public attention on specific situations. ("Where Do We Stand Today With Communism in the United States?," *Congressional Record,* March 1, 1954, p. 2297.)

There are summarized below the principal objectives and responsibilities upon the basis of which funds will be utilized by the Federal Bureau of Investigation:

1. *General criminal investigations*—The investigation of violations of Federal criminal statutes; collecting evidence in which the United States is or may be a party in interest; and performing other duties imposed by law.

Under this authority, the Federal Bureau of Investigation has investigative jurisdiction over some 160 Federal investigative matters. This authority covers all Federal statutes except those specifically assigned to another agency. Included in this group are various statutes concerned with kidnaping, extortion, bank robbery, white slavery, automobile theft, impersonation, illegal wearing of the uniform, crimes on Indian and Government reservations, theft and embezzlement of Government property, bribery, violations of the Selective Service Act, as well as those pertaining to civil rights, frauds against the Government, anti-trust matters, and others in the general criminal and civil fields of activity. Investigations to locate deserter fugitives are also conducted by the FBI upon request of the respective branches of the Armed Forces.

2. *Domestic intelligence*—The FBI's responsibilities in the domestic intelligence field are authorized under legislative enactments, Presidential directives, and instructions of the Attorney General. They include investigative jurisdiction over matters relating to espionage, counterespionage, sabotage, treason, sedition, subversion, and related internal security functions.

Various laws of the United States bring within the investigative jurisdiction of the FBI the activities of the Communist Party, USA; its members and sympathizers; Communist front groups; totalitarian organizations; as well as any other subversive individuals or groups which are alleged either to seek the overthrow of the Government of the United States by force or violence or to conspire against the rights of citizens. The FBI has primary responsibility for investigating matters of these types in the United States, Puerto Rico, and the Virgin Islands.

3. *Coordination and dissemination of security data*— By reason of various Presidential directives, the FBI has the responsibility of correlating information regarding espionage, sabotage, subversive activities and related matters on a national basis and of referring matters under the jurisdiction of any other Federal agencies in these fields to the appropriate sources. Under these Presidential directives the FBI disseminates a large volume of information to other agencies in the executive branch of the Federal Government. During the course of the Bureau's investigations, particular attention is given at all times to information indicating any Soviet-Communist hostile action. As a part of this overall program, the FBI makes name checks of its files for the various agencies of the Government. By reason of these functions, the FBI is inescapably tied in with all defense matters.

The FBI also conducts considerable research in all phases of communism and the intelligence operations of the Soviets and their satellites in order to determine the tactics of Soviet Russia and the satellite countries. Many of the various studies prepared in this field are furnished to other intelligence agencies who have, on a number of occasions, commented favorably concerning the value of these research studies in their own agencies.

The FBI has certain specialized defense functions in respect to which it operates as a member of the Interdepartmental Intelligence Conference and the U. S. Intelligence Board and other bodies created by the National Security Council. In connection with its participation in the work of such bodies, the FBI makes plans and recommendations on various problems concerned with strengthening the internal security of the Nation.

4. *Specialized security programs*—FBI responsibilities in the field of specialized security programs are largely concerned with various sensitive types of applicant and employee investigations. The bulk of the work derives from legislative enactments and Presidential directives requiring the FBI to ascertain facts pertinent to the loyalty and security risk of employees and applicants for positions in the Government service or in activities incident to which the Government has an official interest.

5. *Identification functions*—To gather, maintain, classify, and preserve identification data received from cities, States, penal institutions, Federal agencies, and private citizens. To furnish information concerning such records to duly authorized agencies of Federal, State, and local governments and institutions in the interest of law enforcement.

6. *Scientific crime detection*—To maintain a well-equipped technical laboratory as an aid in scientific crime detection. The facilities of the FBI Laboratory are made available on a cost-free basis to local law enforcement agencies as well as Federal Government circles. The FBI's scientific personnel are made available to testify in court upon the request of prosecuting officials.

7. *Uniform crime reporting*—To maintain a program of uniform crime reporting on a countrywide basis for the compilation of statistics concerning the extent of crime, arrests, convictions, and related crime data. This information is coordinated by the FBI and published in the form of four quarterly reports to demonstrate current crime trends as well as a comprehensive annual report which are furnished to all law enforcement agencies. (*FBI Appropriation 1962,* pp. 6-7.)

FBI—IMPARTIAL. Justice has nothing to do with expediency. It has nothing to do with temporary standards. We cannot, and will not, permit the FBI to be used to superimpose the aims of those who would sacrifice the very foundations on which our Government rests! I take humble pride in emphatically stating here tonight that as long as I am Director of the FBI, it will continue to maintain its high and impartial standards of investigation despite the hostile opinions of its detractors. Furthermore, the FBI will continue to be objective in its investigations and will stay within the bounds of its authorized jurisdiction regardless of pressure groups which seek to use the FBI to attain their own selfish aims to the detriment of our people as a whole. ("Time for Decision," November 24, 1964, p. 2.)

FBI—SCOPE OF AUTHORITY. The FBI's scope of authority is neither vague nor complex. Its responsibilites are clearly defined and strictly limited by Federal statutes and Presidential directives. Regardless of these specific provisions, as well as the great effort which has been made over the years to clarify the FBI's role in law enforcements, false information and misunderstandings in recent past have led to some public confusion.

Many persons—some obviously without facts and others obviously by design—have misrepresented the FBI's work and investigative activities. A few groups, if you are to believe their public comments, consider the FBI to be all powerful—in effect, a police arm of the Federal Government to be used to squelch trouble and strife any place at any time. Others persist that we overstep the bounds of our authority and that the discharge of our prescribed duties in certain areas is an invasion of the responsibilities belonging to State and local authorities.

In both instances, emotions and expediency have beclouded the true facts and issues. Time and again since becoming Director of the FBI, I have stressed the exacting limitations within which this Bureau operates. These controls have always been honored. The FBI has never overstepped its legal boundaries, nor shall it in the future. On the other hand, we have never failed to vigorously meet the obligations rightfully belonging to us without fear or favor. Suffice it to say, we do not intend to deviate from this practice.

107

Once again, for the sake of those who do not know and those who choose to ignore the extent of our responsibilities, I should like to state briefly what the FBI is, what it is not, and what it can and cannot do.

The FBI is an investigative agency. It investigates violations of certain Federal statutes. The facts it gathers are presented without recommendation or opinion to the Attorney General, his assistants, or the United States Attorneys who determine if the evidence warrants prosecution. The FBI also performs an intelligence function, particularly in the field of security, to assist this country in preserving its internal security.

The FBI is a service agency. Its facilities are available without charge to all duly constituted law enforcement agencies. These functions include Uniform Crime Reporting, the Identification Division, the FBI Laboratory, and the FBI National Academy.

The FBI is NOT a national police force. By law, the FBI cannot go into a State, county, or city and take over or assume the authority of local officials.

The FBI is NOT a protection agency. It has no authority to protect or guard anyone under any circumstances.

The FBI is NOT a clearance agency. There is no such thing as an "FBI clearance." When called upon by another Government agency to investigate an individual who is being considered for a sensitive position, the FBI presents the facts and evidence it gathers to the employing agency which must decide whether or not the person is granted a security clearance.

As long as the directorship of the FBI is entrusted to me, this Bureau shall never become a lackey to self-serving individuals or pressure groups of any persuasion. Furthermore, the FBI shall discharge its assigned responsibilities with the same dispatch and thoroughness which have characterized its activities in the past.

Let us always remember that in law enforcement, as in all other fields, there are no shortcuts to, nor temporary standards for justice. Special privilege is not a principle of due process. Let us also remember that in an objective search for truth, heat is a poor substitute for light. (*FBI Law Enforcement Bulletin,* February, 1965.)

FBI—SIZE. I personally feel the Narcotics Bureau has done a very good job under very great difficulties. It requires a large number of personnel.

There is no question the FBI could technically handle it if it were transferred to the FBI. But I am against, and have been for many years, the growth of the FBI. I think we are entirely too big today, bigger than we should be. I would have liked to see the FBI remain small; but that has been impossible because Congress has yearly enacted legislation expanding the investigative jurisdiction of the Bureau. (*FBI 1965 Appropriation,* January 29, 1964, p. 61.)

FELLOW TRAVELERS. The burden of proof should be placed upon those who consistently follow the ever-changing, twisting Party line. Fellow travelers and sympathizers can deny Party membership but they can never escape the undeniable fact that they have played into the Communist hands, thus furthering the Communist cause by playing the role of innocent, gullible or willful allies. (HCUA, *Menace of Communism,"* March 26, 1947, p. 5.)

The known, card-carrying Communist is not our sole menace. The individual whose name does not appear on party rolls but who does the party's dirty work, who acts as an apologist for the party and who rises in its defense and spearheads its campaigns in numerous fronts, is a greater menace. These are the "Communist sympathizers," "fellow travelers," and "Communist stooges." To prove their evil intent is at times difficult but they brand themselves by shifting and turning as the Party line changes to meet new situations. Whether they be innocent, gullible, or willful makes little difference, because they further the cause of Communism and weaken our American democracy. ("How To Fight Communism," *Newsweek,* June 9, 1947, reprint, p. 2.)

FIFTH AMENDMENT—NONE IN INVESTIGATION OF ASSASSINATION OF PRESIDENT KENNEDY. Immediately after the assassination on November 22, 1963, President Lyndon B. Johnson ordered the FBI to make a full inquiry into the assassination of President Kennedy. On November 24, 1963, President Johnson—as well as the Department of Justice—instructed the FBI to conduct an investigation into the shooting of Oswald. The Department specifically requested that we endeavor to determine if there was any conspiracy to deprive Oswald of his civil rights. Subsequently, on November 29, 1963, President Johnson named a 7-man Commission to objectively look into all aspects of the assassination of President Kennedy as developed by all governmental agencies. On December 13, 1963, Public Law 88-202, a joint resolution, was introduced in Congress authorizing the above Commission to compel the attendance and testimony of witnesses and the production of evidence. (*FBI Appropriation 1965*, January 29, 1964, p. 59.)

FIFTH COLUMN. The Communist Party of the United States is a fifth column if there ever was one. It is far better organized than were the Nazis in occupied countries prior to their capitulation.

They are seeking to weaken America just as they did in their era of obstruction when they were aligned with the Nazis. Their goal is the overthrow of our Government.

There is no doubt as to where a real Communist's loyalty rests. Their allegiance is to Russia, not the United States.

A top functionary of the Communist Party recently said, "A war by the United States against the USSR would be an unjust war, which is why it must be fought against, but that if it should come the Communist Party in the United States would be with Russia, and make no mistake about that."

In another section of the country another Communist leader made the following statement: "I believe that everyone should know that we are for Russia and if need be we will die for the cause. I don't mean that war with Russia is coming soon: I hope not, so that Russia will be better prepared. (HCUA, *Menace of Communism*, March 26, 1947, p. 11.)

The party is an integral part of the world Communist movement and a staunch ally of the leaders of communism in the Kremlin. It has earned favor in Moscow, both for its usefulness and for its importance as a fifth column in the Nation which must be destroyed if world communism is to become a reality. (*FBI Annual Report, Fiscal Year 1963*, p. 21.)

FOREIGN LANGUAGE GROUPS. The Party for the past 18 months has been giving special attention to foreign language groups, and has called for a sweeping self-critical examination of its work in this field. As long ago as 1945, in urging the importance of penetrating these groups, Party leaders said: "We need only mention the Polish, Italian, Yugoslav and Greek question" and in characteristic Party double talk observed that they occupied an important relationship "to the entire democratic camp and to the broader peoples movements." In other words, the Communists now seek strength from foreign groups who may have relatives in countries which Russia seeks to influence. (HCUA, *Menace of Communism,* March 26, 1947, p. 8.)

FREEDOM. These strong qualities —faith, individualism, courage, integrity, discipline, and vision—are the keys to freedom. Let us protect and defend the real meaning of America. This is the debt we owe to the brave legions of the past who laid down their lives to safeguard the great truths which guide our destiny today. (*Congressional Record,* September 16, 1964, p. A4726.)

Freedom is not the absence of discipline but the use of disciplines which will enable us to enter into our inheritance and accomplish our destiny.

When man surrenders his ideals, he dies spiritually. Only by protecting America's God-given heritage of liberty and justice for all can we preserve this Republic for generations yet to come to live in "freedom's holy light." ("Faith or Fear," *Congressional Record,* June 28, 1960, p. 13654.)

Let us live our lives so that we may proclaim to the whole world:

Individual freedom is our creed—national freedom is our heritage—world freedom is our goal. ("The Courage of Free Men," *FBI Law Enforcement Bulletin,* April, 1962, p. 20.)

FREEDOM CAN BE LOST. America can meet the challenges of the future. What we need is the firm resolve to keep faith with the vision of our Founding Fathers—a vision which has molded America in the crucible of liberty. Freedom must be conquered anew—time after time, day after day. It is not a commodity which can be laid away, so to speak, on a shelf and admired. Any nation which becomes derelict in its civic duties, which allows animosity to rule instead of brotherhood, which fails to be vigilant in national defense will die. Nothing is more corrosive of liberty than a lack of community interest.

We humbly pray God's guidance for the future. We all must be worthy servants in keeping America as a temple of freedom. ("Remarks on acceptance of the National Interfaith Award from the Washington Inter-Faith Committee, June 9, 1959," pp. 6-7.)

FREEDOM—COSTLY. The freedom we enjoy came dearly to this Nation; bought in blood, and tears and sacrifice. It has given us a truly magnificent system of justice, government, commerce, social institutions and a standard of living which is the highest ever recorded by a civilization. ("America—Freedom's Champion," October 18, 1960, p. 10.)

FREEDOM—LOSE IF. As His Eminence, Francis Cardinal Spellman, observed so profoundly nearly a decade ago, "We have no right to expect to keep our freedoms, if we ourselves do not faithfully and thankfully protect the soil and soul of America from those who have abandoned God, and for God's Commandments have substituted their own code of inhumanity, greed and violence. ("Keys to Freedom," November 16, 1963, p. 15.)

FREEDOM THREATENED. There must be in America a rebirth of the spirit of Valley Forge. The true strength of our Founding Fathers did not spring from materialistic ambitions—but from the deeper wellsprings of the spirit. For them, no sacrifice was too great in upholding the cause of freedom.

In our Nation today, the proper balance between the rights of the individual and those of society is being undermined by two major elements—communism and organized crime—two powerful and dangerous foes. We will underrate either of these enemies only at extreme peril to all we have and are. ("The Courage of Free Men," *FBI Law Enforcement Bulletin,* April, 1962, p. 4.)

FREEDOMS FOR WHICH WE FIGHT. Do our citizens fully appreciate what they are fighting for? This is the key question. This is the theme which you here at Freedoms Foundation have been so valiantly stressing. We are fighting—not to conquer, not to destroy, but to *preserve and strengthen* the integrity of free government, the dignity of man, the worth of the individual personality. We are fighting for the supremacy of law, for the rights of free speech, free assembly, free press, the right to worship God.

The basic answer to communism is moral. The fight is economic, political, social, psychological, diplomatic, strategic; but, above all, it is spiritual. It is a battle of ideas, of diametrically opposite concepts of man.

When our forefathers came to these shores, they came to develop a new political principle foreign to the lands whence they came. Here, men were to be superior to governments. That is why there can be no compromise with the Communists. They are at war with the entire cause of freedom, and the sooner every American faces this fact, the stronger our position will be. ("The Courage of Free Men," *FBI Law Enforcement Bulletin,* April, 1962, p. 19.)

FREEDOMS FOUNDATION. I am honored to accept the George Washington Award as a manifestation of your confidence in the men and women of the FBI. My associates join me in expressing heartfelt thanks for this recognition.

This hallowed ground upon which we stand today is the most meaningful spot in all America. It is most fittingly the home of the Freedoms Foundation and its vitally important mission. You are stimulating deeper appreciation of our Nation's noble past. Due, in no small measure, to your efforts, thousands of young people in our schools and colleges are developing a better understanding and taking greater pride in the priceless gift of freedom won for us by our early patriots—men of God-given strength and determination who laid the cornerstones for this great Nation. (*FBI Law Enforcement Bulletin,* "The Courage of Free Men," April, 1962, p. 3.)

FREEDOMWAYS. Domestically, the Party continued its efforts to gain the confidence of Negroes and other minority groups, constantly picturing itself as the true leader against racism. It hopes to indoctrinate more Negroes with Marxist dogma through the publication of "Freedomways," a new quarterly review of the Negro freedom movement. (*FBI Annual Report, Fiscal Year 1961,* p. 26.)

FRONTS—DECEPTIVE. Fronts like that are being used constantly in the name of all kinds of apparently worthy causes—to protect civil rights, to protest the high cost of living, to combat racial discrimination, to guard the rights of the foreign-born, and to advocate "true democracy." But, back of the scenes, Party members invariably pull the strings and manipulate the front to serve the Party's purposes. ("The Communists Are After Our Minds," *American Magazine,* October, 1954, reprint, p. 3.)

FRONTS—EFFECTIVENESS. Of all the mass techniques which the Reds are using to influence the minds of Americans, the Communist fronts are the most effective. A Communist front is any organization or movement controlled by the Party. It may be local, state-wide, or national in character; may be large or small; and may exist for years or only for a few days. But in every case the objective of the front organizers is to surround themselves with respectable non-Communists and use them to advance a Party program or spread Red Propaganda. ("The Communists Are After Our Minds," *American Magazine,* October, 1954, reprint, p. 3.)

How many American citizens have, innocently or otherwise, been involved in work connected in some manner with advancement of the Communist Party? I do not know. Communist fronts have allegedly embraced millions of Americans since the united front tactic was firmly established in 1935. (*Elks Magazine,* August, 1956, reprint, p. 3.)

FRONTS—HOW TO SET UP. In a midwestern state, for example, Party headquarters recently decided to create a new front organization. It would be called the— Committee for Peace. The first step was to contact a doctor who, though known as a non-Communist, was willing to cooperate with Communists. He was asked to supply a list of "conservative people" who might be asked to serve as sponsors.

Interestingly, of the group of sponsors whom the doctor proposed, the Party rejected one. "This person," an official said, "can't be used." That was because he had once publicly attacked the Communists, and the Party officials felt he couldn't be trusted. They feared he might see through the whole sham and denounce the front, which would be what the Reds described as a "disaster."

114

But the other proposed sponsors met with the Party's approval, and intense activity got under way. Telephones jingled, doorbells rang, handbills were distributed, announcements were sent to the press, and a mass meeting was arranged by the "committee." At the meeting, pro-Communist speakers made eloquent appeals for peace and disarmament, and implied, of course, that Americans were very foolish to be fearful of peace-loving Russia. The audience, composed mostly of non-Communists, was duly impressed, and so, no doubt, were many people who read accounts of the meeting in the local newspapers. Thus a handful of Party connivers were able to achieve a propaganda triumph by utilizing respectable citizens as their dupes. ("The Communists Are After Our Minds," *American Magazine*, October, 1954, reprint, p. 3.)

FRONTS—IDENTIFY. I feel that this Committee could render a great service to the Nation through its power of exposure in quickly spotlighting existing front organizations and those which will be created in the future.

There are easy tests to establish the real character of such organizations:

1. Does the group espouse the cause of Americanism or the cause of Soviet Russia?

2. Does the organization feature as speakers at its meetings known Communists, sympathizers or fellow travelers?

3. Does the organization shift when the Party line shifts?

4. Does the organization sponsor causes, campaigns, literature, petitions or other activities sponsored by the Party or other front organizations?

5. Is the organization used as a sounding board by or is it endorsed by Communist-controlled labor unions?

6. Does its literature follow the Communist line or is it printed by the Communist press?

7. Does the organization receive consistent favorable mention in Communist publications?

8. Does the organization represent itself to be nonpartisan yet engage in political activities and consistently advocate causes favored by the Communists?

9. Does the organization denounce American and British foreign policy while always lauding Soviet policy?

10. Does the organization utilize Communist "double talk" by referring to Soviet-dominated countries as democracies, complaining that the United States is imperialistic and constantly denouncing monopoly capital?

11. Have outstanding leaders in public life openly renounced affiliation with the organization?

12. Does the organization, if espousing liberal progressive causes, attract well-known honest patriotic liberals or does it denounce well-known liberals?

13. Does the organization have a consistent record of supporting the American viewpoint over the years?

14. Does the organization consider matters not directly related to its avowed purposes and objectives? (HCUA. *Menace of Communism*, March 26, 1947, pp. 10-11.)

FRONTS—NAMES. The first requisite for a front organization is an idealistic sounding title. Hundreds of such organizations have come into being and have gone out of existence when their true purposes have become known or exposed while others with high sounding names are continually springing up. (*Ibid.*, p. 10.)

FRONTS—NUMBER UNDER INVESTIGATION. For example, the Communists, foreign agents, and potential saboteurs operate behind a masquerade of stealth and deception. The extent of this activity is shown by the fact that the FBI has approximately 200 known, or suspected, Communist-front and Communist-infiltrated organizations under investigation. Many of these fronts are national in scope. They represent transmission belts through which the Communist Party furthers its conspiratorial designs. (*FBI 1962 Appropriation*, p. 12.)

FRONTS—PURPOSES. For the most part, front organizations assumed the character of either a mass or membership organization or a paper organization. Both solicited and used names of prominent persons. Literally hundreds of groups and organizations have either been infiltrated or organized primarily to accomplish the purposes of promoting the interests of the Soviet Union in the United States, the promotion of Soviet war and peace aims, the exploitation

116

of Negroes in the United States, work among foreign language groups, and to secure a favorable viewpoint toward the Communists in domestic, political, social, and economic issues. (HCUA, *Menace of Communism*, March 26, 1947, p. 9.)

One of the oldest Communist slogans is communism must be built with non-Communist hands. In this slogan lies the reason for the Communist Party front organizations. These fronts are designed to deceive the non-Communist mass of people into unknowingly supporting the Communist program and, in turn, furthering the cause of the Communist Party. (*Pathfinder*, November 5, 1952 in *Congressional Record*, January 26, 1953, reprint, p. 2.)

Front groups are particularly valuable to the Communist Party as a recruiting field for potential party members, as a source of funds, as a pressure group advocating a particular Communist program and as a means of disseminating Communist propaganda. They are established either by actually organizing a new group around a particular issue or by infiltrating a legitimate existing organization. Among those who participate in front groups are open Communist Party members, concealed Communists, fellow travelers and Communist sympathizers. ("Where Do We Stand Today With Communism in the United States?," *Congressional Record*, March 1, 1954, p. 2296.)

One of the Party's most effective propaganda platforms continues to be its front organizations. If America's resistance can be softened by the lies shouted from these hives of concealed communism, the Party will be in a better position to launch a frontal attack upon our Government. (HCUA, *The Great Pretense*, 1956, p. 173.)

FRONT—ROSENBERGS. In some instances they are so successful in doing so that they stir up nationwide agitation. A striking illustration of this was the "Save the Rosenbergs" campaign of 1953. The plot for this front was hatched high in the Communist Party, not with any hope or even desire of saving from execution Julius and Ethel Rosenberg, convicted atomic spies, but to serve five other Party aims:

(1) To discredit the American system of justice generally;

117

(2) To discredit the FBI, which had apprehended the Rosenbergs;

(3) To add fuel to the worldwide "Hate America" program which the Party has been fostering since 1945;

(4) To make it appear that the Rosenbergs were victims of widespread anti-Semitism in the United States, and thus obscure increasing manifestations of anti-Semitism in Russia and her satellite states; and

(5) To divert attention from the fact that the spies had worked hand in glove with diplomatic representatives of the Soviet Union.

The Communists went all out to achieve these objectives, and the results provided a tribute to their diabolical skill as organizers. By appealing to non-Communist humanitarian and religious leaders in the name of "mercy" and "justice," they prevailed upon literally hundreds of them to join their "crusade," received a vast amount of front-page publicity all over the world, and even induced 6,000 persons—comparatively few of whom were Party members— to go to Washington and picket the White House.

They failed to save the lives of the two traitors, as they knew they probably would from the start, but they succeeded in making them appear as martyrs to thousands of good people, and won an impressive propaganda victory. ("The Communists Are After Our Minds," *American Magazine,* October, 1954, reprint, p. 3.)

FRONTS—SCOPE. The Communists continue to use front organizations to further their aims. Much of their propaganda is distributed either through groups they have organized or legitimate ones they have infiltrated. Major front activity during the 1961 fiscal year was in the racial, peace, disarmament, nuclear, political and trade-union fields. (*FBI Annual Report, Fiscal Year 1961,* p. 27.)

FRONTS—VARIETY. Of course, the Communists have not deserted their usual front activities. They continue to operate organizations which promote programs relating to peace, disarmament, nuclear testing, youth, racial and nationality groups, labor unions, and other matters. Likewise, Party members have intensified their efforts to infiltrate various legitimate organizations. They are especially anxious to con-

118

trol, influence, or undermine the affairs of labor unions; peace movements; and minority, youth, veterans', women's, cultural, educational, civil rights, and similar groups. (SISS, *The Current Communist Threat*, October, 1962, p. 4.)

GOAL UNCHANGED. The Communists have never deviated from this objective. Despite the high-pressure campaign they have mounted behind Khrushchev's phrase of "peaceful coexistence," the Communists know that this is simply a propaganda slogan—one devised to further their own ends by stirring the hopes and emotions of those who seek an end to the turmoil, fear and sorrow that world communism itself created.

Actions continue to speak louder than words, and certainly the Communists have shown no indication of a sincere quest for peace.

The take-over of Cuba and effort to convert it into an island fortress against democracy; the ever-constant infiltration of Red Fascists into countries of Central and South America to create a Sovietized Latin America; the increase of espionage activities by Soviet and satellite agents in our country, particularly those who strive to penetrate our Government processes from the protection afforded them by diplomatic assignments in New York and Washington; the frantic efforts of the Communist Party, USA, to subvert our youth; and the intense drive of the Communists operating from concealed positions to wrest control of the movement for Negro rights—does all this indicate a real and sincere desire to live in "peaceful coexistence"? ("Keys to Freedom," November 16, 1963, pp. 8-9.)

GOD. At this Nation's beginning, in the very first words of the *Declaration*, a power greater than man's is acknowledged —a Supernatural Power which is the source of our existing moral codes. "Men," says the *Declaration of Independence*, "are created . . . " This presupposes a Creator—indeed, One who is acknowledged in the same breath. Here, then, is the key contradiction in the two major ideologies now clashing throughout the whole world. ("What Does The Future Hold?" *Christianity Today*, June 19, 1961, reprint, p. 1.)

This Nation was conceived under God and its progress has been under God. There could be no greater disaster

119

for our Nation than that it should deny in any respect, to even the smallest degree, the presence, the power, the guidance, the protection, the instruction of almighty God. ("Faith in Freedom," *Congressional Record*, December 5, 1963, p. A7435.)

Today, America is free and strong—a monument to the hopes and ideals of the Pilgrims. It stands as the greatest fortress of brotherhood in the history of man. Conceived under God, our country represents a people whose progress has been blessed with Divine Guidance and whose history is rich with evidence of His power and glory. We have emerged triumphant from devastating world wars. Our scientific achievements stagger the imagination. Our standard of living surpasses all expectations. Truly, the goodness and mercy of God have been with us. (*Law Enforcement Bulletin*, November 1, 1964.)

GOD—COUNTRY FOUNDED ON FAITH. This Republic was born of such faith held by the Founding Fathers in a Supreme Being and His Divine plan. It can continue to exist in Freedom only if that faith remains forthright and strong, and the voice of the people, bulwarked by intelligent and basic moral concepts, guides its destiny. Reason and patriotism are still the Republic's first line of defense in these troubled times. ("Faith or Fear," *Congressional Record*, June 28, 1960, p. 13653.)

GOD—OR TYRANTS. The Founding Fathers of our Republic were staunch patriots who put the common good and the righteous cause above all other considerations. They were men of deep religious conviction—men who knew that it is the Divine order in man which enables him to be free. William Penn recognized this vital truth nearly 300 years ago when he proclaimed:

"Those people who are not governed by God will be ruled by tyrants." ("Our Heritage of Greatness," December 12, 1964, p. 8.)

GOVERNMENT—INFILTRATION. Since July 1, 1941, the FBI has investigated 6,193 cases under the Hatch Act, which forbids membership upon the part of any Government employee in any organization advocating the overthrow of the Government of the United States.

For the purposes of investigation the Attorney General has ruled that a number of organizations in addition to the Communist Party are subversive under the Hatch Act because of Communist influence.

One hundred one federal employees were discharged as a result of our investigation, 21 resigned during the investigation, and in 75 cases administrative action was taken by the departments. A total of 1,906 individuals are no longer employed in the Government while 122 cases are presently pending consideration in the various Government agencies.

The FBI does not make recommendations, it merely reports facts and it is up to the interested Government department to make a decision. Almost invariably, of course, subjects of investigations deny affiliation with subversive groups, often despite strong evidence to the contrary.

The following is a case in point:

The FBI submitted a 57-page report to the Federal Security Agency on March 7, 1942, on Doxey Wilkerson. The investigation recorded interviews with persons who stated he was a member of the Communist Party. Following the submission of the reports we were advised by the Federal Security Agency that further investigation failed to show that Wilkerson was subversive or "disloyal to our Government." Wilkerson subequently transferred to O.P.A. and resigned on June 19, 1943. Within less than 24 hours he announced his new job as "a Communist Party organizer." He was subsequently appointed a member of the National Committee of the Communist Party. To be eligible for service in the National Committee one "must have been a member of the Party in continuous good standing for at least 4 years." (HCUA, Menace of Communism, March 26, 1947, p. 9.)

Penetration of the U. S. Government is one of the main targets. The Soviet-bloc countries make widespread efforts along this line and no segment of our Government is beyond their consideration as a penetration target.

The collection of information of military interest is, of course, the basic target in all of their espionage efforts. The efforts here range from the collection of significant maps and charts to any and all information regarding nuclear research and development, location of missile sites, radar detection and warning systems, satellites, and the like. (*FBI 1965 Appropriation*, p. 45.)

Mr. Hoover. Current evidence indicates that the Soviet-bloc intelligence services are placing added emphasis on long-range planning.

It is axiomatic to Soviet-bloc attempts to penetrate Government agencies that they strive to establish Agent nets in those key Government installations where the most complete and authentic information concerning intelligence is concentrated.

In line with this, it is known that the Soviet intelligence services have assigned primary importance to the development of sources within such agencies as the Department of State, the U.S. Information Agency, the Central Intelligence Agency, and the FBI. (*FBI 1965 Appropriation*, p. 45.)

GOVERNMENT—INFILTRATION DANGEROUS. The recent Canadian spy trials revealed the necessity of alertness in keeping Communists and sympathizers out of Government services. In fact, the high command of the Communist Party regards such assignments of sufficient importance to demand that Party members not contact fellow members in the Government, and if such Government employees are carried on Party rolls at all they are assigned an alias. Last fall a high-ranking Party leader instructed that all Party membership cards of Government employees be destroyed and that Party organizational meetings in Government circles be discontinued although informal social or union gatherings which could not be identified as Communist meetings could be continued. The dangers of permitting Communists or sympathizers to work in Government circles are too obvious to mention. (HCUA, *Menace of Communism*, March 26, 1947, p. 8.)

GROWTH. From "a spectre . . . haunting Europe" a little over 100 years ago, the Communist movement has developed during the past four decades into a predatory empire which now controls approximately one-quarter of the land area of the world and which boasts of its domination over nearly one billion people—approximately one third of the world's population. Elated by recent Soviet scientific, technological, and economic successes—and reinforced by demonstrated military might—the leaders of the world-communist movement are now attempting to deal from a position of arrogant power. ("Communist Illusion and Democratic Reality," December, 1959, p. 1.)

Today, there are Communist parties organized and operating, either legally or illegally, in 86 countries around the world. These parties have a combined membership of over 36 million. Communist parties have already gained control in 17 nations.

The Communist-bloc nations now control approximately one-fourth of the land area of the world and approximately one-third, or 1 billion, of the inhabitants on the face of the globe.

Even in non-Communist nations, there are approximately four million Communist party members dedicated to the overthrow of their existing governments.

The Communist Party of the United States is a vital link in this worldwide conspiracy. (*FBI Appropriation 1962*, March 6, 1961, p. 48.)

GUS HALL. Profaning the very meaning and spirit of the *Star Spangled Banner* by opening its sinister conclave with our National Anthem, the Communist Party, USA, convened its 17th National Convention on December 10, 1959, in a hotel in New York City's Harlem section. Four days later, the some 200 delegates representing other Communists throughout our Nation, adjourned in a state of jubilance.

And well they might feel in high spirits—because the Communist Party, USA, emerged from this convention more powerful, more unified and even more of a menace to our Republic.

Without question, the most signal achievement was the welding of a Communist Party, USA, into a solidly unified, aggressive force behind the militant, devious, and ruthless leadership of Gus Hall, ex-convict and avowed arch enemy of the American way of life.

Hall was elected general secretary of the party at the convention, and there is virtual unanimous agreement among Party powers and rank-and-file that he is the "Number One" man in the Party. As such, he now spearheads as powerful a group of dissidents and fanatic democracy-haters as America has seldom seen within its shores during peacetime.

The Communist conspiracy in America today is led by a man who has openly boasted that he was willing to take up arms and fight to overthrow our form of Government. Hall was convicted in Minneapolis, Minnesota, in 1934, in connection with a riot there when he was a member of the Young Communist League. During his trial he testified as follows:

Q. But you would prefer the Russian—you would prefer to be in Russia?

A. I prefer America with a Soviet Government.

Q. And you are willing to fight and overthrow this Government?

A. Absolutely.

Q. And you are willing to take up arms and overthrow the constituted authorities?

A. When the time comes, yes.

As a hot-blooded young Communist in the late 1930's, Hall was arrested in Ohio and charged with the possession and use of explosives. He subsequently pleaded guilty to a lesser charge of malicious destruction of property and was fined $500.

The election of the fiery Hall to lead a strongly knit Communist Party which has and always will have as its chief objective the communizing of America should certainly shake even the most apathetic American from his lethargy, especially when viewed in the light of this hardened Communist's own statements. During radio and television interviews at the convention, Hall blandly stated that the American public "definitely" has underestimated the size and influence of the Communist Party, USA. He added that the Communists in this country should make even greater strides toward increasing its already growing number of members. He boasted that the Party "is growing in industry and youth" due mainly to the change in political climate.

Assuredly, there is a significant lesson for every American in this display of machinations, propaganda, and opportunism which is communism itself at work within our borders. The 17th National Convention of the Communist Party, USA, was a revealing 4-day miniature prevue of what our Nation would become if those who aspire to become commissars of a Soviet America should ever fulfill their evil ambitions. It is apparent that, more than ever before, each American must maintain vigilant watchfulness toward this Trojan Horse in our midst.

The 17th National Convention is being hailed by the Communists themselves as a great milestone in the Party's history in the United States.

These gains, recognized as formidable ones, are regarded by the Party faithful as their chief accomplishments:

1. Promotion of Gus Hall, strongly pro-Russian and an energetic, aggressive leader, to the No. 1 position in the Party;

2. Uniting the membership solidly behind the newly-elected leadership, making the Party a hard-hitting, mobile weapon against the free American Government;

3. Exploiting the current international political climate in an effort to make Russian policies more acceptable to American public opinion. This involves an attempt to exploit Soviet Premier Nikita S. Khrushchev's visit to the United States as a means of furthering its own schemes for bringing about a Soviet America;

4. Implemented a number of concrete programs aimed at increasing Party membership and Party influence in America. Such programs include increased emphasis on Party recruiting, training of leaders, collection of funds, stepping up of Party propaganda, and infiltration efforts into non-Communist organizations such as labor unions, Negro groups, national minorities, etc.

The newly-elected "boss" of the Communist Party, USA, Gus Hall, vaulted to the top post of the Party through a combination of fortuitous circumstances and artful plotting. He has long been disgruntled at what he believed to be soft, ineffectual leadership in the Party—but his ambitions have been hidden by the shadow of Eugene Dennis, national chairman and previously acknowledged leader of the Party. As the date of the convention approached, Dennis still was top man in the Party although there was indication that Hall had nurtured a "dump Dennis" campaign to the point where Dennis' position was indeed a tenuous one. Then came the news that Dennis would be unable to attend the convention—that he had suffered a slight stroke and that someone else would have to give the keynote address.

The scheming, opportunistic Hall rose to the occasion and delivered the address. He saw his ambition start to crystallize. Today he is communism's champion in the United States—a powerful, deceitful, dangerous foe of Americanism.

What sort of a man is Gus Hall? We in the FBI know him as a fanatical practitioner of Karl Marx's tenet that "the end justifies the means"; a coldly calculating Communist conniver who changes tactics as easily as he changed his name many years ago. He was born Arvo Halberg in 1910 at Virginia, Minnesota, the son of Matt and Susanna Halberg, both of whom later became charter members of the Communist Party. As a result of his early background of having been born into communism, many of his followers regard him as literally a man of destiny who can breathe new life into the Party.

Hall joined the Party in 1927 and went to Russia in 1931 to attend the Lenin School where students were taught, among other things, sabotage and guerrilla warfare techniques. After returning to this country in 1933, he became active in the Young Communist League as an organizer and in 1938 entered into full-time Party work as a section organizer. As a Russian-taught disciple of Leninistic communism, Hall worked hard and rose swiftly into positions of increasing power. He was elected to the Party's national committee in 1945 and became a national board member in 1947. In 1950, he was appointed national secretary, a move necessitated by the imprisonment of Eugene Dennis, who was then general secretary and who was found guilty of conspiring to violate the Smith Act of 1940.

Then, faced with confinement himself after being convicted for violation of the same act, Hall jumped $20,000 bond and became a fugitive. He dyed his blond hair, eyebrows, and eyelashes dark brown, shaved off his mustache, and shed 40 pounds in an unsuccessful effort to evade apprehension. Arrested by the FBI in 1951, Hall was sentenced to 3 years for contempt of court, making a total of 8 years when added to the 5-year sentence imposed for conspiracy to violate the Smith Act.

Conditionally released from prison in March 1957, Hall, after his probationary period ended on April 5, 1959, immediately resumed his nefarious aim of infecting America with communism.

This, then, is the man—ex-convict, propagandist, unabashed emissary of evil, and rabid advocate of a Soviet United States. (SISS, *Concerning the 17th National Convention, Communist Party, U. S. A.,* December 10-13, 1959, 1960, pp. 1-3.)

HANDOUTS. Regrettably, too many Americans no longer care about religious ideals and heritage. To some, our country is a fantasyland filled with complimentary handouts of rights and freedoms without obligations. With patent indifference, they shirk the mere suggestion of individual responsibility. Their purpose in life is lost in moral lethargy, self-indulgence, and neglect of duty. (*Law Enforcement Bulletin,* November 1, 1964, p. 1.)

HATE DESTRUCTIVE. These elements have hurled a critical challenge at the law enforcement profession and other forces for decency across the Nation. The person who would bomb a school, desecrate a house of worship, or spread the doctrine of hate toward his fellow man constitutes a real threat to our American way of life. He lives in a vacuum of moral degeneracy. His crimes are so outrageous it is unthinkable that anyone except the extreme "lunatic fringe" could rationalize or condone them.

Invariably, these hate mongers attempt to drape themselves in a cloak of patriotism, but their real objective is to destroy the very American ideals which they claim to uphold. They preach "mobocracy"—disrespect for the law, for our Constitution, and disregard for the welfare of others. ("Faith or Fear," *Congressional Record,* June 28, 1960, p. 13654.)

HATERS. That is why the cause of communism is well served by the hate mongers, the lunatic fringe and other rabble who preach a doctrine of malice and intolerance toward their fellow man.

These venomous fanatics, whether they are extremists of the left or the right, are carriers of a highly infectious disease. They clutter the streets—and the mails—with their slanderous obscenities, urging impressionable teen-agers and unstable adults to acts of hate, terror and intimidation. They have brought forth the bombs and ignited the flames that have killed decent Americans and even innocent children

127

and destroyed churches and other temples of worship. They are a national disgrace.

Invariably, these merchants of hate attempt to drape themselves in a cloak of patriotism. But their real objective is to profiteer and capitalize upon ignorance, prejudice and bigotry while destroying the very ideals which they claim to uphold. ("Faith in Freedom," *Congressional Record,* December 5, 1963, p. A7435.)

HISTORIC MISSION. The phrase "Historic Mission" has a sinister meaning. To the uninformed person it bespeaks tradition, but to the Communist, using his own words, it is "achieving the dictatorship of the proletariat; . . . . to throw off the yoke of imperialism and establish the proletarian dictatorship; . . . to raise these revolutionary forces to the surface and hurl them like a devastating avalanche upon the united forces of bourgeois reaction, frenzied at the presentiment of their rapidly approaching doom."

In recent years, the Communists have been very cautious about using such phrases as "force and violence," nevertheless, it is the subject of much discussion in their schools and in Party caucus where they readily admit that the only way in which they can defeat the present ruling class is by world revolution.

The Communist, once he is fully trained and indoctrinated, realizes that he can create his order in the United States only by "bloody revolution." (HCUA, *Menace of Communism,* March 26, 1947, p. 3.)

HOLLYWOOD. The American Communists launched a furtive attack on Hollywood in 1935 by the issuance of a directive calling for a concentration in Hollywood. The orders called for action on two fronts: (1) An effort to infiltrate the labor unions; (2) To infiltrate the so-called intellectual and creative fields. (HCUA, *Menace of Communism,* March 26, 1947, p. 7.)

HOME—VALUE. I am honored to discuss with this outstanding group of "career" women a matter of pressing urgency to every home in America. I say "career" women because I feel there are no careers so important as those of homemaker and mother. (*FBI Law Enforcement Bulletin,* November 9, 1956, reprint, January, 1957, p. 1.)

HOOVER—ATTACKS ON. The KGB—the Soviet Committee of State Security—is waging an attack against U. S. agencies. The nefarious schemes of the Soviets, through their "Disinformation Department," were exposed in a report prepared by the Central Intelligence Agency in 1965. Details of the Agency's study were printed in the "Congressional Record" of September 28, 1965. The study revealed that the FBI as an organization and I as its Director are priority targets for attacks.

The study disclosed that the overall objective of the Soviet attacks is to discredit U. S. agencies here and abroad and the study emphasized that a preferred instrument used by the Soviets in their attacks is the forged document.

Typical of the smear tactics used in such efforts was the circulation of letters in South America in the summer of 1964. My name was forged on letters which were designed to make it appear that the FBI and the CIA had something to do with the Brazilian revolution of April 1964. The intricacies of that Soviet scheme became further apparent when we determined that my signature had been forged from a letter stolen by the Cubans in Havana in 1960.

More recently, beginning in January 1966, scurrilous anonymous mailings prepared in Moscow by the KGB and sent to its branch in New York City have been mailed to various members of Congress and other prominent Government officials and citizens. A letter supposedly signed by me is a crude forgery. Comparison of all these letters disclosed they had all been prepared by the same person. Further comparison with other letters circulated in the past in this and other countries by the Soviet "Disinformation Department," a part of the Soviet KGB, prove without a doubt that this is a Soviet scheme, amounting to character assassination both scurrilous and putrid.

The head of the New York residency of the KGB is a member of the Soviet Mission to the United Nations and as such he is immune to arrest and prosecution.

This is but one of many instances in which attaches to the United Nations from the Soviet bloc have doubled as intelligence and espionage agents.

I might say over 100 personnel engaged in espionage activities are attached to the KGB in New York City. (*1967 FBI Appropriation*, p. 65.)

HOUSE COMMITTEE ON UN-AMERICAN ACTIVITIES.
The aims and responsibilities of the House Committee on
Un-American Activities and the Federal Bureau of Investigation are the same—the protection of the internal security
of this Nation. The methods whereby this goal may be
accomplished differ, however.

I have always felt that the greatest contribution this
Committee could make is the public disclosure of the forces
that menace America—Communist and Fascist. That is
why the venom of the American Communist and the now
defunct German-American Bund has been directed at this
Committee as it has also been directed at the Federal Bureau
of Investigation. This Committee renders a distinct service
when it publicly reveals the diabolic machinations of sinister
figures engaged in un-American activities. (HCUA, *Menace
of Communism*, March 26, 1947, p. 1.)

There is renewed interest in Congress as manifested in
the Committee on Un-American Activities of the House of
Representatives. As this committee fulfills its obligation of
public disclosure of facts it is worthy of the support of loyal,
patriotic Americans. This committee has for its purpose
the exposure of un-American forces and as such its files
contain voluminous information which, when used with dis-
cretion, provide an excellent source of information. The
FBI, unlike this committee, must of necessity keep the contents of its files confidential. ("How To Fight Communism,"
Newsweek, June 9, 1947, reprint, p. 3.)

HYSTERIA—AVOID. There exists today in our land a vital
"rift" which the Communists are exploiting. Unfortunately,
this involves certain people across the country who engage
in reckless charges against one another. The label of "Communist" is too often indiscriminately attached to those whose
views differ from the majority. Those whose lives are not
led according to what one segment of society might decree
to be the "norm" are too frequently challenged as "Reds."

Attributing every adversity to communism is not only
irrational, but contributes to hysteria and fosters groundless
fears. Communism is, indeed, our paramount adversary, and
it leans on its credo of invincibility and a concept of historical inevitability to accomplish its ends. The way to fight
it is to study it, understand it, and discover what can be done

about it. This cannot be achieved by dawdling at the spring of knowledge; it can only be accomplished by dipping deeply into thoughtful, reliable, and authoritative sources of information. (*FBI Law Enforcement Bulletin,* April, 1961, reprint, p. 1.)

INFILTRATION. They have infiltrated every conceivable sphere of activity: youth groups; radio, television, and motion picture industries; church, school, educational and cultural groups; the press; nationality minority groups and civil and political units.

Some celebrated, self-styled pacifists and some men of wealth and prominence have sometimes been unwitting—but sometimes knowing—political shills and stooges of deceitful Communist manipulators. (*FBI Appropriation 1962,* p. 49.)

INFILTRATION—EVERY SPHERE. No field is overlooked for Communist infiltration; educational, cultural, civic, political and religious. Front groups, having no apparent association with Communists, have been cunningly herded along by Communists in this Nation to foster sympathy and support for the Soviet Union.

Some well-known, self-styled pacifists and some men of wealth and prominence, have been sometimes unwitting, but sometimes knowing, dupes of clever Communist manipulators. Their fawning over Khrushchev and his gang is revolting.

Some of these political shills for an enemy of the United States, who day by day are embarrassing our Government, may be wealthy in the world's goods but they are paupers in integrity.

Alert Americans look with frank suspicion on those articulate apologists for Soviet imperialism who are so quick to criticize our security measures and attack our elected representatives who resolutely withstand the international diplomatic blackmail practiced by the Communists. Beware of those who preach that America should never be first in anything but disarmament and demobilization!

The greatest guarantee that America will remain free is to be well prepared, as were the Minutemen of our infant Nation. (*"America—Freedom's Champion,"* October 18, 1960, pp. 5-6.)

The Communists, at this very moment, are attacking the institutions of this great Nation. They are trying to subvert our homes, our schools, our churches, and our Government. They have penetrated all walks of life. Communism is all-encompassing, squeezing the human personality into a dried pulp. ("How FBI Tracks Reds & Spies," *Pathfinder*, November 5, 1952 in *Congressional Record*, January 26, 1953, reprint, p. 2.)

INFILTRATION—ORGANIZATIONS. The Communist Party is endeavoring, in every possible way, to infiltrate non-Communist groups. Civic clubs, churches, labor unions, schools and similar patriotic American groups—these organizations are today the targets of an insidious campaign to increase Communist strength. The pressure is tremendous. The Communists are determined to advance their cause by cunning, stealth and downright dishonesty. ("Make the Communists Show Their Own Colors!" April 14, 1952, p. 1.)

INFILTRATION PURPOSES. Communists are trying to join legitimate organizations—a women's community club, a youth organization, a parents' study group. They are working hard, taking an active interest. Why? To gain control of the organization? No. The Communists are few in number, probably one, two or even three. They desire, rather, to influence policy: perhaps elect a "favorable" candidate, determine a policy decision, postpone action on an anti-Communist proposal. In this way, by being "inside" a legitimate organization, they are misguiding many unsuspecting loyal citizens into support of policies fostered by the Communists. ("Make the Communists Show Their Own Colors!," April 14, 1952, p. 1.)

INFORMANTS. As in previous years, J. Edgar Hoover paid special tribute to confidential informants. "Many of our investigative and intelligence accomplishments during 1958 were directly attributable to information furnished by FBI informants and other alert citizens. Without their assistance, our work in protecting America's internal security and in identifying and apprehending Federal offenders would be immeasurably more difficult.

Facts supplied to our Agents by confidential informants resulted in approximately 1,700 arrests in FBI cases during

1958. Other information furnished by our informants and disseminated to the authorities concerned was responsible for well over 2,000 arrests by other law enforcement agencies. Additionally, recoveries of stolen and contraband merchandise and valuables amounting to nearly $2,000,000 are traceable directly to data received from FBI informants. (*FBI Release*, December 22, 1958, p. 3.)

Good informants in the underworld are among the most valuable tools available to law enforcement in the fight against crime. Much of the information they supply might never be obtained through other sources. Not only do they provide invaluable assistance in the solution of crimes, but they frequently furnish tips about planned crimes which enable law enforcement to take preventive action.

In the 1962 fiscal year, confidential informants supplied information which led to the apprehension of 1,980 persons, 1,205 being fugitives, and the location of 523 subjects of other FBI investigations. Their aid also resulted in the recovery of $4,225,063 in money and merchandise.

Much of the information obtained from FBI informants during the year related to criminal activities under the jurisdiction of other agencies—Federal, State and local. This data was relayed to proper authorities promptly, and they have reported it led to the arrest of 2,371 persons and the recovery of $24,452,804 in money and stolen or contraband merchandise. (*FBI Annual Report, Fiscal Year 1962*, pp. 8, 10.)

INFORMANTS—ATTACKS ON. The confidential informant has become an institution and is used as a means of establishing truth. The use of the confidential informant is as old as man. In fact the first recorded use of the confidential informant is found in the Old Testament. As an institution, the confidential informant is used not only by law enforcement, but in practically every walk of life, particularly by the press and our financial institutions. In recent years, there has been a determined campaign designed to deprive law enforcement of the use of the time-tested and valued confidential informant. This campaign of vituperation is part and parcel of Communist strategy to convert the courtroom into a forum to discredit the judicial processes. For the most part, the technique of the smear has been devised by Communist lawyers, skilled in concealing foul and despicable acts behind the Fifth Amendment. They employ tactics which even the most unscrupulous underworld "mouthpiece" would frown upon as improper.

The Communist owes no allegiance to God, to his family or to his country. He owes it only to the Party and will do anything the Party commands him to do. He will lie, cheat, steal or do anything for the Communist cause.

The inroads that Communist propaganda has made in influencing law-abiding Americans, who fail to realize that criminal conspiracies are conceived behind closed doors under the cover of darkness, are disheartening. It is through the efforts of confidential informants that we have been able to expose the Communist conspiracy in the past and through them we must stake much of the future security of the United States. That is why such a vicious and sustained attack has been made against former Communists who have first-hand knowledge of the secret, diabolical purposes of the Communist Party.

Those now furthering the campaign of vituperation against witnesses say that the Communist menace is a myth created by those who testified against it. Therefore, to destroy the myth, they feel it is necessary to destroy the witnesses. They refuse to recognize the Communist enslavement of one-third of the world's people and one-fourth of the world's surface. These witnesses have been cross-examined in our courts, observed by judges and juries and they have been brought under the penetrating eye of the American press. ("Our Common Task," October 3, 1955, pp. 2-3.)

INFORMANTS—DEFINED. These persons indulge in sabotage by semantics—they stigmatize patriotic Americans with the obnoxious term "informer," when such citizens fulfill their obligations of citizenship by reporting known facts of the evil conspiracy to properly constituted authorities. It would require very little time for these critics to pick up a dictionary. Webster's unabridged volume specifically states that an "informant is one who gives information of whatever sort; an informer is one who informs against another by way of accusation or complaint. Informer is often, informant never, a term of opprobrium." ("Communist 'New

Look' A Study in Duplicity," *The Elks Magazine,* August, 1956, reprint, p. 3.)

INFORMANTS—VALUE. The members of the International Association of Chiefs of Police know how the confidential informant has contributed to law and order. We cannot minimize the hate of the underworld whether it be the underworld of hoodlums or the underworld of subversive traitors and its urgent desire also to identify and discredit the confidential informant. There needs to be a greater effort to protect those who risk their lives for the protection of society.

It is almost a daily occurrence for FBI Agents to convey information secured from confidential informants to local police which, for example, cleared up 300 burglaries in one case. In another case, 47 stolen cars were recovered and, in still another instance, a million-dollar robber was thwarted. Without this two-way street of exchange of information, many crimes would go unsolved. ("Our Common Task," October 3, 1955, p. 3.)

INTERNAL DANGER. Herbert Hoover 13 years ago succintly stated the situation—"Our greatest danger is not from invasion by foreign armies. Our dangers are that we may commit suicide from within by complaisance with evil. Or by public tolerance of scandalous behavior. Or by cynical acceptance of dishonor. These evils have defeated nations many times in human history.

"The redemption of mankind by America will depend upon our ability to cope with these evils right here at home."

As America was born out of faith in God, so it will continue in freedom only as that faith remains forthright and strong.

We must revitalize the miracle of faith that keeps men free. Therein lies our heritage of greatness. ("Our Heritage of Greatness," December 12, 1964, p. 8.)

INTERNAL DANGER—PARTY. The Communists work untiringly to change our form of government while, at the same time, they attempt to be accepted as legitimate partners in our society and to achieve respectability. Not only young people, but all Americans should be cognizant of the Party's propagandizing and should be alert to the falsities of the Communist claims. Nothing can defeat this Communist propaganda offensive more quickly than the truth. This does not mean that we must merely counter communism. We must at the same time deepen and enrich our own heritage of freedom.

Party leaders would hope that this country would consider the Party strength here to be insignificant. It would be fateful to so consider it. The Party in this country is operated by a corps of hardened, disciplined Communists who feel that Moscow represents the final goal of all mankind's hopes. The influence of the Party is far greater than its size would indicate and the small band of openly admitted Communists is bulwarked by the innumerable inactive Party members who are patiently waiting for such events as the complete defeat of the Internal Security Act of 1950. These individuals have not disclaimed the Party and, as legal restrictions are removed, many of those now sitting on the sidelines can be expected to move back into action.

The reaction of the Communist Party in this country to the recent retaliatory airstrikes in North Vietnam by U. S. Navy aircraft for mortar attacks on U. S. bases in South Vietnam is a most timely example of the unification of the Communist movement in this country. Within minutes after the attacks were announced, Arnold Johnson, the Party's public relations director, issued a press release which bitterly condemned the airstrike as "an act of brutal aggression which horrifies the world." The American people were urged to speak out and demand that the U. S. withdraw all troops from South Vietnam. Telegram campaigns were organized and protest demonstrations were urged. Other groups, such as the W. E. B. DuBois Clubs, the youth group formed by the Party, supported the Party in the protest action.

The devious hand of the Communists also appeared on the turbulent campus of the University of California at Berkeley, which has been constantly disrupted with "student demonstrations" over the past months. On February 8, 1965, about 1,300 demonstrators protested U. S. intervention in Vietnam. Speakers, condemning the United States for starting the War in Vietnam, included Herbert Aptheker, a member of the National Committee of the Communist Party, USA, and other Party members who "just happened to be there." All speakers urged their listeners to more direct action and called for a demonstration at the New Federal Building in San Francisco.

At Madison, Wisconsin, at the University of Wisconsin, a similar protest meeting held by students and faculty members was led by individual students and faculty members, some of whom have Communist backgrounds. One of these was Daniel Friedlander, who is active in the DuBois Clubs in Madison.

The major lesson to be learned from all this is that the Communists and their supporters in this country are not a weak, insignificant element on the American scene. The wave of demonstrations which erupted on a national scale immediately following news of the U.S. counterstrike against Communist forces in Vietnam demonstrates how unified, organized, and powerful an element the Communist movement in the United States is today. While many of the demonstrations were organized by legitimate, sincere pacifist groups, Communists and their supporters also organized a number of demonstrations and are attempting to exploit to their own benefit the activities of the legitimate organizations.

Mr. Hoover. In regard to espionage and counterespionage operations, we differentiate between these activities and those of the Communist Party, USA. The Communist Party, USA is made up mostly of U. S. citizens.

The subversive role of the Communist Party, USA, is but one aspect of the Communist threat to the internal security of our Nation. The other is the espionage and intelligence attacks mounted against this country by the Communist-bloc countries. Underlying both aspects of the threat to our internal security from the international Communist movement is the fact that we are competing with a totalitarian system, intent on our destruction, which operates the most extensive networks of subversion and espionage ever developed in history.

In regard to the Communist-bloc espionage attack against this country, there has been no letup whatsoever. (*FBI Appropriation 1966*, pp. 65-66.)

INTERNAL SECURITY ACT OF 1950. Party leader Hall has been on a whirlwind, whistle-stop tour of our country trying to stir up support for the Party's opposition to the

137

Internal Security Act of 1950. This law, which was recently upheld by the United States Supreme Court, would, in brief, compel registration of Party membership and disclosure of finances. Hall, with his catchy phrase, was setting the "line" for the Party in its maneuvers to thwart the law. (*FBI Law Enforcement Bulletin,* October, 1961, p. 1.)

The Supreme Court ruling of June 5, 1961, upheld the order of the Subversive Activities Control Board that the Communist Party, USA, must register under the internal Security Act of 1950 as a Communist-action organization. After a petition for a rehearing was denied by the Supreme Court, the registration order became final on October 20, 1961.

In addition to the registration provision, the law also imposes a number of sanctions upon the Party which became effective as a result of the Board's registration order becoming final on October 20, 1961. Among other things, it is unlawful for any member of the Party to held employment in any defense facility designated by the Secretary of Defense; or to apply for, or make use of, a U. S. passport.

Neither the Party as an organization, its officers, nor the individual Party members complied with the registration provisions of the act nor with any of the provisions regarding sanctions.

The Government has taken prosecutive steps against the Communist Party, USA, as an organization, against Party officers, and against Party members. Although the conviction of the Party, as an organization, for failure to register was reversed by the District of Columbia Court of Appeals on December 17, 1963, this decision is not final and the Department of Justice is considering additional legal steps.

Unless and until all of the provisions of the Internal Security Act af 1950 are held unconstitutional by the Supreme Court, and as the Department of Justice continues its prosecutive and administrative program under this act, the FBI will be called upon on a continuing basis to determine the facts necessary to establish violations and to produce necessary witnesses for testimony. (*FBI 1965 Appropriation,* p. 11.)

Shortly before I appeared before this committee last year, the Communist Party, USA had been fined $120,000 after having been found guilty on the charge of failing to register as a Communist-action organization under the provisions of the Internal Security Act of 1950. The Party took an appeal to the Court of Appeals and on December 17, 1963, the Court reversed the decision of the District Court on the grounds that the Fifth Amendment privilege against self-incrimination was available to the officers of the Party as legal justification for refusing to sign the registration forms. The court further held that the burden of proof rested with the Government to establish that "someone" was willing to sign the registration statements on the Party's behalf. The Government on January 21, 1964, petitioned the Court of Appeals to rehear the matter sitting en banc. (*FBI 1965 Appropriation*, p. 43.)

INTERNATIONAL UNION OF MINE, MILL & SMELTER WORKERS. The International Union of Mine, Mill & Smelter Workers on May 4, 1962, was declared a "Communist-infiltrated" union by the Subversive Activities Control Board under provisions of the Communist Control Act of 1954. The Union has petitioned the Board to determine that it is no longer infiltrated. (Senate Internal Security Subcommittee, *The Current Communist Threat*, October, 1962, p. 4.)

IRRESPONSIBLE ACTION WEAKENS NATION. The ingredients for Communist coups in nations which have fallen under its spell always include a populace shaken with fear, hysteria, and confusion. Above all, however, is the danger of irresponsible counteraction by citizens who lend impetus to communism through inept attempts to fight this insidious menace. (*FBI Law Enforcement Bulletin*, April, 1961, p. 1.)

JEWS—PERSECUTION. The ruthless suppression of Christian worship under the Communists is common knowledge, but it is only recently that the pitiful plight of the Jew in Russia has become known. Of course, anyone who truly has understood communism must, from the first, have recognized that it is anti-Semitic in nature. Marx, himself, stated:

"The Social emancipation of the Jew is the emancipation of society from Judaism."

This, in simple words, is an order for the liquidation of the rich and ancient culture to which Western civilization owes so great a debt. How far, through devilishly subtle methods, that liquidation has progressed is only now becoming

139

visible. Many good Americans for long years were victims of a horrible hoax. While the Communists were using Hitler's bestial treatment of the Jews as a propaganda device to masquerade as champions against discrimination, they were themselves engaged in a campaign of brutal anti-Semitism! ("How To Beat Communism," *The Lion,* October, 1957, reprint, pp. 3-4.)

JUSTICE HINDERED. When this great Nation was founded and when its guidelines were being established for future generations of Americans, George Washington proclaimed, "The administration of justice is the firmest pillar of government." What has happened to that "firm pillar" in the intervening 175 years?

Far too often, it has become weakened by impractical theorists, emotion-blinded pressure groups, warped idealists, and self-serving politicians. Misguided leniencies, including pardons, paroles and probation for unrepentant and unreformed offenders, continue to prevail in many jurisdictions— as does the use of loopholes, technicalities and delays in the law which benefit rogues at the expense of decent members of society.

Judges, in particular, must remain alert to the reprehensible tactics of those members of the bar who would play the venal game of legal charades in our courts of justice. This point was emphasized most clearly by a distinguished member of the Pennsylvania Supreme Court, Chief Justice John C. Bell, Jr., when he declared:

". . . . law-abiding citizens and communities . . possess certain fundamental inalienable rights. One of these rights is that their life and property shall be protected . . . . Justice is not a one-way street—law-abiding citizens are entitled to protection of the law and to justice just as much as (if not more so than) criminals." ("Our Heritage of Greatness," December 12, 1964, p. 3.)

KHRUSHCHEV. His Hitleresque tirades and harangues have exposed him and his cohorts to the entire world as leaders, without conscience, of an unmoral tyranny—the most godless atheism ever devised by the mind of man.

The abuse of the Red-Fascist leader of the Kremlin represents brazen vulgarity and a lack of moral principles.

140

The deceit and trickery practiced by the international gang of Communist charlatans, who loudly spout lies of "peaceful co-existence" while they blandly carry out their ceaseless campaign of open and concealed subversion, are a repugnant display of Red diplomacy. ("America—Freedom's Champion," October 18, 1960, p. 3.)

KHRUSHCHEV—VISIT. Why is the Party so optimistic for the future? Why were Gus Hall and other Communists almost gleeful in speaking of Communist possibilities in the days ahead?

The answer comes from the convention proceedings— an answer which, like a thread, runs through all the remarks, actions, and hopes of the leadership. It is: *that the recent visit of Premier Khrushchev to the United States has done much to create an atmosphere favorable to communism among Americans.* In one convention discussion, for example, it was stated that as the result of the Khrushchev visit the American people have open minds toward socialism. Hence, the Party must learn how to get socialism across to the people and break down misconceptions about the Soviet Union.

To Party leaders, Khrushchev's presence in this country has eased the way for Party activities. The Communists see the possibility of gaining still more influence in American society. Gus Hall, in his keynote speech on the convention's first day, was most sensitive to this point. He stated:

". . . the central question of this convention is: What is the role of the Party in this entirely new situation? How can it now move out into the broad stream of the people's movement? How can it break the bonds of its isolation and become more and more effectively a factor in the life of our Nation. . . ."

He then went on:

"We want to participate in, organize, and lead the broadest of united front movements—on every level—in a thousand ways, in 10,000 places, on 100,000 issues—if possible, with 180 million people." (SISS, *Concerning the 17th National Convention, Communist Party, U. S. A., December 10-13, 1959, 1960,* pp. 4-5.)

KOREAN WAR PRISONERS. A 5-year study of the conduct of American prisoners of war during the Korean conflict was made by the United States Army. This study disclosed that there was, in the morale of American prisoners of war, a breakdown which reached disturbing proportions. Almost one out of every three American prisoners of war collaborated to some degree with the Communists. This collaboration included broadcasting anti-American propaganda, writing articles praising life under communism, "confessing" to the use of germ warfare, and signing peace appeals and other Communist petitions. Our soldiers informed on one another and fraternized with the enemy. The death of some American prisoners could have been prevented if they had not been completely neglected by their fellow captives. Not one American prisoner of war succeeded in escaping. Some even chose to remain in Communist China rather than to return to the United States. That American military personnel collaborated at all is difficult to understand. Even more disturbing are the extent of the collaboration and the casual attitude of those who were guilty.

As a result of the study, President Dwight D. Eisenhower, in August 1955, promulgated for members of the Armed Forces a Code of Conduct specifying the duties and obligations of our fighting men. The report of the special committee which had recommended the adoption of this code pointedly noted:

"The uninformed P.O.W.'s were up against it. They couldn't answer arguments in favor of communism with arguments in favor of Americanism because they knew very little about their America. . . ."

The report concluded that our Armed Forces had not adequately prepared their men for the rigors of Communist indoctrination. It looked behind this failure, however, and stressed that our homes, schools, churches, and patriotic organizations must also assume greater responsibility in educating Americans in the principles which underlie our democratic way of life. The importance of such an affirmative long-range educational program is borne out by the special committee's finding that, in many cases, our fighting men were at a disadvantage because they knew less about the ideals and traditions of their own country than did their Communist interrogators.

The behavior of these prisoners of war was less an individual failure than it was an indictment of our entire

142

society which had not prepared them adequately for their head-on collision with Communist indoctrination. All Americans must share some responsibility for the conduct of these prisoners of war. More important, we must not ignore this forceful example of the impact of Communist psychological pressures. Our continued survival may well depend upon the action we take now to insure that all citizens, not only military personnel, are fortified against the continuous Communist ideological assault.

We can defeat Communist ideology and—at the same time—reinforce the structure of our own democracy by the combined process of exposure and education. ("Communist Illusion and Democratic Reality," December 1959, p. 4.)

KU KLUX KLAN. I place the fiery cross of the vicious Ku Klux Klan in the same category as the swastika of the Nazis and the godless hammer and sickle of atheistic communism. All ignore the rights of everyone to life, liberty and the pursuit of happiness.

All right-thinking citizens know that there is no place in America for vigilantes, rabble rousers, the "lunatic fringe" and those who make a profit—political or material—out of merchandising prejudice.

No problem is so acute, no crisis so severe, that terrorism can be tolerated in our society. Intimidation and mob action are not the American way—nor are they God's way—of accomplishing any objective which is truly worthwhile. ("Faith or Fear," *Congressional Record*, June 28, 1960, p. 13654.)

And I include the false liberals of the extreme left, such as the Communist Party, as well as the counterfeit patriots at the fanatic limits of the far right, such as the Ku Klux Klan, who not only take the law into their own hands on occasion but who would use the Constitution and laws of the United States to defeat the very purpose for which they were drafted—liberty and justice for all. ("Our Heritage of Greatness," December 12, 1964, p. 2.)

We must be ever alert to the activities of the Ku Klux Klan and other racist groups that would trample upon the rights of their fellow man. These cowardly jackals, who attack only the weak and the outnumbered, have earned the contempt of every genuine American. But here again, too

143

often justice is not only blind, but deaf and dumb. We saw this recently in an area of Mississippi where nine men were brought to trial in State court following a series of racial bombings. None of the defendants offered a pretext of a defense against the charges; yet, all were given suspended sentences and released on probation. Such blindness and indifference to outrageous acts of violence encourage others to defy the law.

We cannot have full citizenship for some and part citizenship for others. Nor can we apply different standards of justice to our people according to the color of their skin.

Concerted effort, understanding, logic and reason must prevail over hate, bigotry and intolerence. ("Our Heritage of Greatness," December 12, 1964, pp. 7-8.)

Racial disturbances have added greatly to our work. The FBI does not have jurisdiction in civil disturbances except in cases where subversive influences are at work or violations of civil rights or other Federal statutes within our jurisdiction are involved. We do, however, follow on the racial situation from an intelligence viewpoint and all pertinent information received concerning conditions and the organizations involved is disseminated to interested Government agencies and officials.

Indicative of our work in this area is the fact that we are currently investigating 14 Klan-type organizations having a membership of approximately 9,000 individuals. This membership represents the "hard-core" individuals who are strongly anti-Negro and opposed to the integration of the races. The largest and most dominant Klan group is the United Klans of America, Inc., Knights of Ku Klux Klan, with headquarters in Tuscaloosa, Alabama. This group is active in eight States, has an estimated membership of 4,600 individuals, and is led by Imperial Wizard Robert Shelton.

Another prominent Klan group is the White Knights of the Ku Klux Klan of Mississippi, which was organized in February 1964, and operates solely in the state of Mississippi. Its membership is estimated at 2,000 persons and it is led by Imperial Wizard Samuel Bowers.

In the state of Louisiana, the Original Knights of the Ku Klux Klan is active. Its headquarters are in Jonesboro,

Louisiana, and its membership is estimated to be 1,500. The leader of this organization is Roy E. Davis.

Another large Klan group is the United Florida Ku Klux Klan which operates in the state of Florida. It has an estimated membership of 900, and is led by Jason C. Kersey, and its headquarters is in Samsula, Florida.

During the past year there has been a marked increase in Klan membership. Investigative experience has shown that Klan activity and membership have increased in those areas in the South where civil rights groups have been most active. (*FBI Appropriation 1966*, p. 81.)

LEFT—NEW. It can be expected that most of these young people will fulfill the promise they represent to us. In so doing, they will join hands with the millions of Americans of good will who actively seek meaningful solutions to our social life. If our joint progress in this regard is impeded and deterred, much of the trouble will come from a growing band of self-styled revolutionaries who are using college campuses as a base for their destructive activities. This comparatively small group of arrogant, hard-core militants have contempt for the majority and our democratic processes. They regard themselves as the nucleus of an elite dictatorial ruling class of the future.

These extremists openly avow that their aim is to overthrow the existing order. Under the guise of academic freedom and freedom of speech, they profess to seek a dialog, when actually what they seek is a confrontation with established authority to provoke disorder. Through these confrontations, they expect to smash first our educational structure, then our economic system, and finally our government itself.

It is vitally important to recognize that these militant extremists are not simply faddists or "college kids" at play. Their cries for revolution and their advocacy of guerrilla warfare evolve out of a pathological hatred for our way of life and a determination to destroy it. The workshops they hold on sabotage and how to use it to further their objectives are grim forebodings of serious intent.

This New Left movement, as it is known, is growing both in numbers and varied forms of violence. Last spring, major disorders precipitated by the revolutionary adherents of the movement occurred on a number of college campuses.

145

In the violent uprising at Columbia University, militant students and outsiders took over several buildings and committed senseless and deliberate destruction. The incident triggered similar disturbances on other campuses. Changes may be necessary and improvements in any institution can be made, but this is not the way to do it.

Encouraged by their "success" at Columbia, the anarchists in the New Left movement are boldly spreading the word that they intend to "create two, three, many Columbias," in the manner of one of their "heroes," Che Guevara, the Cuban revolutionary who cried "create two, three, many Vietnams!"

The main thrust of the New Left movement arises from the concerted efforts of the Students for a Democratic Society. Many of its members and some of its national leaders openly profess their faith in communist concepts and their determination to "restructure" our society. One of the militant spokesmen of this group stated, for example, that "perhaps 25 universities linked to the movement would be too much for the police—for the dominant class—and we would get what we demand."

The New Left leaders plan to launch a widespread attack on educational institutions this fall. They are relying on collegiate dissidents and militants to bolster and accelerate this drive. It would be foolhardy for educators, public officials, and law enforcement officers to ignore or dismiss lightly the revolutionary terrorism invading college campuses. It is a serious threat to both the academic community and a lawful and orderly society. (*FBI Law Enforcement Bulletin,* September 1, 1968.) See also the chapter on the new left.

LIBERAL—PSEUDO. The phenomenon which I call the pseudo-liberal is something quite different. The individuals who belong to this cult are not members of the Communist Party. They even deny any sympathy with communism. But they live in a never-never land. Seemingly ignorant of the existing conspiracy, duped by Communist contacts which they are apparently incapable of recognizing, the pseudo-liberals constantly take off on intellectual flights that inevitably end on an enticing airstrip planned for them by the Communists. Even when the concealed pitfalls on that strip bring each subsequent flight to a disastrous conclusion, the experience apparently holds no lesson. The pseudo-liberals flit off eagerly again to a rarefied stratosphere, and, inevitably as before, return to the Communist hangar.

These misinformed dupes are among the persons who offer blanket opposition to all security programs now in effect and to all that are suggested. They are among the ones who demand the removal of all measures designed to eliminate security risks from Government. They add their voices to those that rant endlessly at patriotic committees of the Congress whose efforts are dedicated to exposing the conspiracy and to alerting citizens to the danger. These persons indulge in sabotage by semantics—they stigmatize patriotic Americans with the obnoxious term "informer," when such citizens fulfill their obligations of citizenship by reporting known facts of the evil conspiracy to properly constituted authorities. It would require very little time for these critics to pick up a dictionary. . . .

The persons who are so careless with the slur and smear in their use of the word informer maintain that communism is not a menace. It is, they say, simply a political party like the Republican and Democratic parties. These incredible people profess to find the tyranny of communism compatible with Christianity and synonymous with academic freedom! Our difficulties today, they proclaim, stem from a myth created out of fear and hysteria. These simple-minded souls would have you believe that this foreign-directed conspiracy which already has enslaved approximately one-third of the peoples of the earth, and is resolutely working night and day to bring us to our knees, is a myth!

The antics of these vociferous individuals create a smoke screen which helps to conceal the deadly menace of communism. The manipulators, working ceaselessly behind that screen, smile with satisfaction and characterize as "a growing understanding of communism" the failure to see their real objective. In the double-think, double-talk lexicon of communism, this "growing understanding" means simply that American citizens are failing to comprehend the deadly facts of the Communist conspiracy. ("Communist 'New Look' A Study in Duplicity," *The Elks Magazine,* August, 1956, reprint, pp. 3-4.)

"The cult of the pseudo-liberal, which is anything but liberal," said Hoover, "continues to float about in the pink-tinted atmosphere of patriotic irresponsibility" though it remains "strangely silent" when a Hungary is pillaged. ("Legion Alert as Guest Speakers Decry Public Apathy to Dangers," *The American Legion Magazine*, November, 1957, p. 32.)

It is through the "pseudo-liberals" that the Communists do some of their most destructive work. These fictitious liberals are the individuals who through insidiously slanted and sly propagandistic writings and reports oppose urgently needed internal security measures; conduct a one-sided campaign to discredit Government witnesses; present the menace of Communism as a myth of hysteria; urge that we tolerate the subversive acts of Communists because Communists are only "nonconformists"; contend that the Communist Party is a "political" movement and that it is improper to consider it a criminal conspiracy linked to a world conspiracy to overthrow our Government by force and violence.

Constructive criticism and constant evaluation of methods, procedures and accomplishments in an objective manner is the way to progress. But, the eagerness of some to attack everyone and everything related to the exposure of the Communist conspiracy in this country is hardly the mark of a true liberal. Indeed, the true liberal is opposed to everything Communism represents, for the very nature of Communism is the antithesis of liberalism. ("Our Common Task," October 3, 1955, p. 3.)

LIQUIDATION PRIORITY. Under Communist domination in America, the first campaign of liquidation would engulf the lawyers, champions of due process of law; newspapermen, whose ageless fight for freedom of expression would have no place under totalitarianism; law enforcement officers, guardians of individual rights; Governmental leaders, local, state and national; and everyone falling in the so-called "capitalist" category. Occupations and professions which the Communists term "useless and parasitic" would be abolished— clergymen, wholesalers, jobbers, real estate salesmen, stockbrokers, insurance men, advertising specialists, traveling salesmen—the list for purging is endless. No citizen would escape some form of suffering under a Communist regime. One need but to compare his own worth, his own ideals, his own religious beliefs with the atheistic doctrines of communism to determine his priority on the list of liquidation. (*Law Enforcement Bulletin,* March 1960, p. 1.)

LOSE—HOW TO. Nearly 200 years ago, Edmund Burke warned, "The only thing necessary for the triumph of evil is for good men to do nothing." How meaningful these words are today.

We have failed to meet the postwar goals which America had established for herself because the "good men" to whom Burke referred—the forces for decency in our country—have failed in many respects to live up to their duties and responsibilities.

What has happened to the time-honored precepts of hard work and fair play which influenced the American scene during the all-important formative years of this great Republic? Where is the faith in God which fortified us through our past trials? Have our national pride, our moral conscience, our sensitivity to filth and degradation, grown so weak that they no longer react to assaults upon our proud heritage of freedom?

Crime and subversion are formidable problems in the United States today because, and only because, there is a dangerous flaw in our Nation's moral armor. Self-indulgence —the principle of pleasure before duty—is practiced across the length and breadth of the land. It is undermining those attributes of personal responsibility and self-discipline which are essential to our national survival. It is creating citizens who reach maturity with a warped sense of values and an undeveloped conscience. ("An American's Challenge," *Congressional Record,* October 10, 1962, p. A7517.)

LOVE. What the world needs is love—brotherhood love. Through the eyes of brotherhood love we see the world of neighbors in need. ("Remarks on acceptance of the National Interfaith Award from the Washington Interfaith Committee," June 9, 1959, p. 6.)

MAN—NATURE. Man, says the *Declaration of Independence,* was created by God. No, says communism, man is merely a fortuitous product of the ceaseless interaction of chemical and physical elements—he has no soul. And, communism continues, nature is all—there is no God. Proletarian utility constitutes

149

the only acceptable moral code—the end justifies the means. The Ten Commandments, says communism, are wholly false as they are derived from supernatural concepts which have no basis in fact.

Today's great struggle, in simple terms, relates to the nature of God and the nature of man. Man, says one ideology, is a spiritual creature with an immortal soul. On the contrary, says the other ideology, he is a material creature in a material world. ("What Does the Future Hold?," *Christianity Today*, June 19, 1961, reprint, p. 1.)

MANAGEMENT—DO. Management can do more by looking out for the welfare of employes and getting closer to labor problems. In most disputes a satisfactory solution can be worked out if both sides will use decency and fair play as the basis for their dealings. More and more union members are awakening to the realization that Communist members owe their first allegiance to the Party. The Party line which argues that attacks against Communism are attacks on labor is a lie and the Communists know it. So do patriotic labor leaders. ("How To Fight Communism," *Newsweek*, June 9, 1947, reprint, pp. 3-4.)

MATERIALISM. And what is that philosophy? To scholars, it is known as "dialectical materialism." While all Communists are materialists, not all materialists are Communists. Scores of individuals who have never been members of the Communist organization contribute to the spread of the philosophy of materialism. In so doing they are adding generously to the strength of the Communist movement. Among these philosophic materialists are numerous educators, authors, and lecturers. These materialists deny the existence of God. They deny the existence of the soul, of immortality, and of values derived from unchanging moral principles. Reality, the materialists maintain, consists only of matter. These people, as I stated, are not Communists; yet they are preparing mental soil for the seeds of communism. Their pernicious doctrine of materialism, fed to young Americans as something new and modern, readies the minds of our youth to accept the immoral, atheistic system of thought we know as communism. ("God and Country or Communism?," *American Legion Magazine*, November 1957, p. 58).

MEDICAL PROFESSION. Concealed Communists in the medical and legal professions are also being used by the Party in its efforts to capture the mass mind. In a number of communities, Red doctors regularly dish out Communist propaganda to their patients while treating their aches and pains, and they lend the prestige of their name to Red causes. Right now, some Red doctors also are providing needed medical care for Communists hiding from the law, and performing facial surgery to alter their appearance. Red lawyers, in addition to giving legal advice to comrades in trouble, are working in a number of communities to influence the opinions of public officials, including senators, representatives, governors, and mayors. ("The Communists are After Our Minds," *American Magazine*, October, 1954, reprint, p. 3.)

MENACE. This fact, horrible but true, emerges: Communism, a brutal, godless, materialistic way of life which would ruthlessly destroy the values and ideals we cherish, has made appalling advances. Within a generation Communism has catapulted from a small, militant underground coterie into a worldwide conspiracy, already embracing one-third of the earth's population, and knocking, in most literal terms, on countless other doors. Communism is a deadly menace; a scourge which threatens the very existence of Western civilization. It has altered the orderly progress of history, deflected men's hopes for a better world—whether permanently or temporarily depends, in large measure, upon the people of America, upon you and me. We must win this battle, for the alternative to victory is the erasure of freedom, perhaps forever, from the parchment of time. ("Foe to Freedom," *The Elks Magazine*, October, 1950, reprint, p. 1.)

MIND—STRUGGLE FOR. Basic to all other aspects of this offensive, however, is the psychological struggle. This is the campaign to win the minds and loyalties of men. It explains the use by Communists—to a degree unprecedented in history —of every means of mass communication in their efforts to mold men's minds. ("Communist Illusion and Democratic Reality," December, 1959, p. 1.)

MINISTERS' ROLE IN FIGHTING COMMUNISM. If communism is to be defeated, the task must rest largely upon the theologians and the ministers of the Gospel. Communism is a false secular religion with pseudo-theological explanations of the great verities of life, such as the creation, life on earth, and the world to come. Communism is an all-encompassing system with explanations—though wrong ones—for this great universe of God. The Party offers answers—though perverted ones—for the hopes, joys, and fears of mankind.

In the final analysis, the Communist world view must be met and defeated by the Christian world view. The Christian view of God as the Creator, Sustainer, and Lord of the universe is majestically superior to the *ersatz* approach of dialectical materialism concocted by Marx and Lenin. The task of our clergy today is to translate this Holy Truth into the daily lives of our men and women. This truly is their responsibility as Christian clergymen.

Strong, responsible, and faithful Christians, wearing the full armor of God, are the best weapons of attack against communism and the other problems of our day. "Seek ye first the kingdom of God, and his righteousness." In this way you will be playing a vital role also in helping defend our cherished way of life. ("The Communist Menace: Red Goals and Christian Ideals," *Christianity Today*, October 10, 24, November 7, 1960 issues, reprint, p. 3.)

MINORITY GROUPS. During the 17th National Convention, much was made of the Party's responsibility of championing the causes of such groups in the United States as the Mexicans, Japanese-Americans, Puerto Ricans, and, a relatively new target, the American Indian. Again, such pseudo concern by the Party is readily made apparent by its history of exploiting any area of unrest.

As early as 1921, the Communist International laid down the following rule to be followed by foreign Communist parties affiliated with the Comintern:

"In countries whose population contains national minorities, it is the duty of the Party to devote the necessary attention to propaganda and agitation among the proletarian strata of these minorities."

The choice of the words "propaganda" and "agitation" belies any "noble" motive which those who are easily beguiled might ascribe to the international Communist conspiracy. (SISS, "Concerning the 17th National Convention, Communist Party, U.S.A., December 10-13, 1959," Washington: Government Printing Office, 1960, pp. 7-8.)

MINUTEMEN. The Minutemen organization is another group whose activities are closely followed. We have penetrated this organization and our sources keep us posted on developments. We disseminate the results of our investigations on a continuing basis to pertinent agencies of the Government, including the Secret Service.

The organization is headquartered at Norborne, Missouri, and is headed by Robert DePugh.

Minutemen claims its primary purpose is to prepare its members to overthrow the Government of the United States in the event the Government is taken over by the Communists. In January 1966, DePugh advised special Agents of the FBI that this country needs to get rid of those "parasites in Washington and draw up a new Constitution inasmuch as the old one is outmoded."

DePugh has also said that the Minutemen as an organization does not buy or store arms, but individual members maintain whatever arms and ammunition they purchase with their own personal funds "which is their constitutional right."

He has stated that his organization will stress "infiltration" of opposing groups, and turn to armed revolt only as a last resort. He has said that "we feel that with the use of intelligence, security, propaganda, and infiltration we can turn our enemies' weapons against themselves." He has stated that the Minutemen advocate "armed resistance only when it has become very apparent to all the people that Communists or Fascists have overtaken the Government and all the people themselves are willing to support an armed revolution." An excellent example of this organization's effort to store munitions is shown by the fact that in June 1965, through information furnished by the FBI, local authorities located 36 sticks of dynamite and other blasting equipment in Prince William County, Virginia. The explosives were stored by a local Minutemen unit which had been using the area as a training site.

We have long been aware of the Minutemen organization and our investigation indicates the organization is a loose federation, with each unit acting independently and lacking

153

any real central control. DePugh is the only known leader of the group and acts as its sole spokesman.

DePugh avoids the responsibility of trying to substantiate all of the things he says of the Minutemen. For example, while he has placed the membership of the organization at "more than 25,000," there is little real evidence that the Minutemen is anything more than essentially a paper organization with a membership estimated at 500. (*FBI Appropriation, 1967*, pp. 55-56.)

MORALITY. Hence, there arises the ugly manifestation of Communist "ethics"—namely, the Communist belief that morality must be subordinated to the class struggle, the inevitable conflict between communism and its opponents. What is moral? Anything which serves to destroy the enemy and promote communism. Lenin was most explicit: "Morality is that which serves to destroy the old exploiting society and to unite all the toilers around the proletariat, which is creating a new Communist society."

Communist morality, of course, is rooted in total rejection of a belief in God and in the values of the Christian moral code. Supernatural concepts and divine revelation play no role in communism. "We repudiate all morality that is taken outside of human, class concepts," Lenin proclaimed. "We, of course, say that we do not believe in God, and that we know perfectly well that the clergy, the landlords, and the bourgeoisie spoke in the name of God in order to pursue their own exploiters' interests." ("The Communist Menace: Red Goals and Christian Ideals," *Christianity Today*, October 10, 24, November 7, 1960, issues, reprint, p. 1.)

MOVIES. The Party is content and highly pleased if it is possible to have inserted in a picture a line, a scene, a sequence, conveying the Communist lesson and, more particularly, if they can keep out anti-Communist lessons. (HCUA, *Menace of Communism*, March 26, 1947, p. 7.)

NAIVE—WHY? Mr. Director, I just wonder if you can give any explanation as to why so many organizations that are basically sound and dedicated to doing what is right—and I do not hesitate to name one of them, the National Council of Churches—why are some of the hierarchy of these organiza-

154

tions so naive to the threat posed by communism in this country?

Mr. Hoover. Mr. Congressman, I think it is due to the fact they have not fully informed themselves as to what the facts are. Many people have the idea that communism is not a serious threat because the movement is numerically small in this country. Its numerical strength is one thing but we must judge it by its fanatical, dedicated, and disciplined membership. Most non-Communists are not disciplined, fanatical believers in the theory and practice of American democracy as are the Communists in communism. That is a reason why some of these people err in their thinking.

Such erroneous thinking often results in a great deal of harm, particularly in many organizations where the practice is followed of having the rank-and-file elect delegates to represent them at conventions without exhibiting a sufficient degree of alertness and interest to determine the beliefs of their chosen representatives. As a result, these representatives commit large groups of the rank-and-file to a course of action which in reality is contrary to their true feeling and beliefs. As I pointed out previously in my testimony, apathy also plays a strong part in creating a prevailing atmosphere of indifference to this threat. (House Appropriations Committee, *Departments of State and Justice*, 1962, pp. 439-440.)

NAME CALLING. They capitalize upon ill-founded charges, associating known honest progressive liberals with left-wing causes. I have always entertained the view that there are few appellations more degrading than "Communist" and hence it should be reserved for those justly deserving the degradation. (HCUA, *Menace of Communism*, March 26, 1947, p. 6.)

Knowing what communism really is and how it operates will also help us to avoid the danger of confusing communism with legitimate dissent on controversial issues. Communism feeds on social ferment. On both the local and national levels, the Communist Party, USA, is continually exploiting social, economic, and political grievances for its own tactical purposes. For this reason, the "Party Line" will frequently coincide with the views of many non-Communists on specific issues. We must not, therefore, indiscriminately label as Communists those whose opinions on a particular question may, on occasion, parallel the official Party position. We must also guard against the tendency to characterize as Communists those who merely disagree with us or who advocate unorthodox or unpopular beliefs.

When anyone is erroneously branded a Communist, it not only constitutes an injustice to the individual, but also helps communism by diffusing the strength of anti-Communist forces. In combatting communism, we must beware of vigilante action. The responsibilities of citizens are to be certain of the facts and to report these facts to the proper authorities. ("Communist Illusion and Democratic Reality," December, 1959, p. 5.)

Lenin said, "The more powerful enemy can be conquered only by exerting the utmost effort, and by *necessarily*, thoroughly, carefully, attentively and skillfully taking advantge of every, even the smallest, 'rift' among the enemies . . . ."

There exists today in our land a vital "rift" which the Communists are exploiting. Unfortunately, this involves certain people across the country who engage in reckless charges against one another. The label of "Communist" is too often indiscriminately attached to those whose views differ from the majority. Those whose lives are not led accordingly to what one segment of society might decree to be the "norm" are too frequently challenged as "Reds." (*FBI Law Enforcement Bulletin,* April, 1961, reprint, p. 1.)

NATION OF ISLAM (NOI). The long established Nation of Islam, headquartered in Chicago, Ill., and which teaches violent hatred of the white race and nonallegiance to the United States, continues to be the largest black extremist group in the country. It has been somewhat overshadowed during the past year by other more vocal groups such as the Black Panther Party. (*FBI 1970 Appropriation,* April 17, 1969, p. 71). See BLACK MUSLIM.

NATIONAL STATES RIGHTS PARTY. The National States Rights Party, whose national director is Dr. Edward R. Fields, has an estimated membership of approximately 75. A principal spokesman who travels about the country spewing hate is vice chairman of the group, J. B. Stoner. This organization favors segregation of the races in schools, Armed Forces, and residential communities. (*FBI Appropriation, 1967,* p. 53.)

156

NEGROES. Another of the major aims of the 17th national convention was to reemphasize the recruitment of Negroes into the Communist Party by reembellishing the same old hackneyed phrases alleging that the Communist Party is the savior of the Negro. It is no secret that one of the bitterest disappointments of communistic efforts in this Nation has been their failure to lure our Negro citizens into the Party. Despite every type of propaganda boomed at our Nation's Negro citizens, they have never succumbed to the Party's saccharine promises of a Communist Utopia. This generation and generations to come for many years owe a tremendous debt to our Negro citizens who have consistently refused to surrender their freedom for the tyranny of communism.

Behind the Communists' scheme of recruiting Negroes is deceit as there is in every one of their designs. The Reds are not so interested in the Negro as they are in using him to further Communist goals. This is clearly shown by instructions issued by the Communist Party, USA, to its members as early as 1925:

"The aim of our Party in our work among the Negro masses is to create a powerful proletarian movement which will fight and lead the struggle of the Negro race against exploitation and oppression in every form and which will be a militant part of the revolutionary movement of the whole American working class, to strengthen the American revolutionary movement by bringing into it the . . . Negro workers and farmers in the United States to broaden the struggles of the American Negro workers and farmers, connect them with the struggles of the national minorities and colonial peoples of all the world and thereby further the cause of the world revolution and the dictatorship of the proletariat."

The Negro resolution adopted by the convention discarded the Party's historic position advocating "self-determination," meaning that Negroes should be given the right to form a separate nation in the Southern States. Stalin had defined "self-determination" in these words:

". . . the right of the oppressed peoples of the dependent countries and colonies to complete secession, as the right of nations to independent existence as states."

The 1959 convention resolution hence represents a Party admission that its position concerning Negroes is bankrupt.

157

Time itself has shown that the Party is not interested in the welfare of the Negro, but only in using him as a tool to advance Party interests. (SISS, *Concerning the 17th National Convention, Communist Party, U.S.A., December 10-13, 1959*, 1960, p. 7.)

Throughout the 1963 fiscal year the Communist Party, USA, circulated tons of propaganda on the race issue. This pictured the Party as the great champion of Negroes and other minority groups. Actually, the Party is not the least bit concerned with helping the Negro or any other minority — it merely hopes to ensnare those persons who are naive enough to accept the Communists for their claims instead of their deeds. (*FBI Annual Report, Fiscal Year 1963*, p. 25.)

Today, the Communists are engaged in a vigorous campaign to divide and weaken America from within. Foremost in this campaign are the Party's efforts to exploit misunderstandings and capitalize upon areas of dissension and unrest wherever they exist. This is especially true in the intense civil rights movement, for America's 20 million Negroes and all others engaged in this struggle are a major target for Communist propaganda and subversion.

It would be absurd to suggest that the aspirations of Negroes for equality are Communist inspired. This is demonstrably not true. But what is demonstrable is that some individuals and groups exploit the tension for purposes not confined to the equality of human rights under the Constitution of the United States. The crusade should not become a vehicle for political radicalism or organized violence.

Devotion to race must not supercede devotion to established institutions.

It would be useful if responsible Negro leaders themselves could make it clear to all who follow them that their interest is solely in racial equality. ("Faith in Freedom," *Congressional Record*, December 5, 1963, p. A7435.)

Turning to the subject of Communist interest in Negro activities, the approximate 20 million Negroes in the United States today constitute the largest and most important racial target of the Communist Party, USA. The infiltration, exploitation, and control of the Negro population has long been a Party goal and is one of its principal goals today.

In this drive, Negroes have, over the years, been subjected to intensive and extensive Communist agitation and propaganda. The Communist Party has always depicted itself to Negroes as the champion of social protest and the leader in the struggle for racial equality. But the truth of the matter is that the Communist Party is not motivated by any honest desire to better the status or condition of the Negro in this country, but strives only to exploit what are often legitimate Negro complaints and grievances for the advancement of Communist objectives. Controversial or potentially controversial racial issues are deliberately and avidly seized upon by Communists for the fullest possible exploitation. Racial incidents are magnified and dramatized by Communists in an effort to generate racial tensions. As a result, such campaigns are actually utilized as a steppingstone to extend Communist influence among the Negroes.

Communists, through their worldwide Communist propaganda apparatus, transmit propaganda regarding selected instances of racial inequity and injustice to every part of the world. They do not confine themselves to facts but resort to distortion, exaggeration, and the big lie.

Communists thus capitalize on the adverse propaganda effect that reports of discrimination and oppression in the United States can produce in the eyes of the rest of the world, particularly among the African and Asian peoples; that is, the idea that this country is against equal rights for all races.

The Communist Party is attempting to use the Negro movement, as it does everything else, to promote its own interest rather than the welfare of those to whom it directs its agitation and propaganda. It may collect funds ostensibly in behalf of Negro activities, hold discussions on civil rights at all levels, and increase its coverage of Negro affairs in its publications, but behind all of this effort is its clear-cut primary interest in promoting communism.

The Party is continually searching for new avenues in order to expand its influence among the Negroes. In particular, it has sought ways and means to exploit the militant forces of the Negro civil rights movement.

The number of Communist Party recruits which may be attracted from the large Negro racial group in this Nation is not the important thing. The old Communist principle still

159

holds: "Communism must be built with non-Communist hands."

We know that Communist influence does exist in the Negro movement and it is this influence which is vitally important. It can be the means through which large masses are caused to lose perspective on the issues involved and, without realizing it, succumb to the Party's propaganda lures. (*FBI 1965 Appropriation*, pp. 40, 41.)

OSWALD. When testifying before the Warren Commission on May 14, 1964, I stated that a State Department report indicated Lee Harvey Oswald was a "thoroughly safe risk."

Such statement was based upon a Foreign Service dispatch from the American Embassy in Moscow to the Department of State, Washington, D.C., dispatch No. 29 dated July 11, 1961. This dispatch set forth a summary of Oswald's visit to the American Embassy, Moscow, U.S.S.R., on July 8, 1961, at which time Oswald requested to return to the United States with his wife. The dispatch contains the following paragraph relating to Oswald as noted by the American Embassy interviewing official, Mr. Richard Snyder:

"Twenty months of the realities of life in the Soviet Union have clearly had a maturing effect on Oswald. He stated frankly that he had learned a hard lesson the hard way and that he had been completely relieved of his illusions about the Soviet Union at the same time he had acquired a new understanding and appreciation of the United States and the meaning of freedom. Much of the arrogance and bravado which characterized him on his first visit to the Embassy appears to have left him. He stated that he is in contact with his mother and brother in the United States. He stated that he had about 200 rubles and that he and his wife would save more for the eventual costs of traveling to the United States."

Further indication that the State Department did not consider Oswald a risk is shown by the fact that the State Department renewed Oswald's passport for a return to the United States and gave him a loan in the sum of $435.71 to finance his and his family's trip to the United States.

Additional evidence that the State Department did not consider Oswald a risk is shown by the fact that when Oswald requested a new passport for travel abroad on June 24, 1963, wherein he indicated he planned to stay abroad for from 3 months to one year and to visit England, France, Germany, Holland, Russia, Finland, Italy, and Poland, the State Department saw fit to issue him a passport for such travel on the following day, June 25, 1963. Obviously the State Department did not consider Oswald a risk in issuing him a passport on this occasion. (*FBI Appropriation 1966,* p. 24.)

PARTY — DANGER. Despite the party's public record of treachery, deceit, and inhumanity, tolerance of the danger of communism continues to grow. Today, those of us who actively oppose the subtle tactics of the Communist Party find ourselves subjected to mounting abuse and ridicule. Misguided and ill-informed persons, posing as alleged "experts" on Communist subversion, would have it believed that the party is a shattered, broken and threadbare group of harmless misfits. Nothing could be further from the truth. ("Faith or Fear," *Congressional Record,* June 28, 1960, p. 13653)

The Communist Party, USA, constitutes a grave security threat to our Nation, not only because of its subversive historical background, its antidemocratic philosophy and its insidious tactics, but also because of the particular nature of the Party itself—an organization controlled and directed by Moscow whose ultimate goal is to overthrow our form of government.

A widespread underestimation of the menace which the party presents to the internal security of the United States is just the impression the party desires to present. The ability of the party to seize upon items of discontent and to fan the sparks of civil disobedience into actual strife presents a clear and present danger. (*FBI Appropriation, 1967,* p. 49.)

PARTY FINANCES. Public and private statements by party officials in the past would seem to indicate that the party has been perennially on the verge of bankruptcy. Yet it is a fact that the party has never approached actual bankruptcy and these announcements regarding the alleged precarious financial condition of the Party appear to be designed primarily to stimulate increased contributions from its members and to lull the anti-Communist opposition into a false sense of security.

161

The Communists in this country raise money through a variety of ways to finance many of the day-to-day party operations. Membership dues constitute only a small part of the total needed to cover the yearly expenditures. The Party raises the remainder through a multitude of sources, such as fund drives, assessments, donations, and investments.

The Party is always alert for domestic developments which it can exploit to add to its operating capital. A typical example occurred in May 1963, when a Party official told the members of the Party's national board that the racial unrest in this country presented an excellent opportunity to start a fund drive to raise up to $10,000 in order to finance Communist Party activities among Negroes.

The determination of the Soviet Union to maintain the Communist Party, USA and to strengthen and direct it in such a way as to make it a continuing danger to this Nation is clearly evidenced by the fact that for the past 44 years Soviet Russia has in one way or another directed and controlled the Communist Party, USA and helped to finance it. (*FBI 1965 Appropriation,* p. 38.)

PARTY—GROWTH. Party leader Gus Hall, in the past, in placing the membership at 10,000, has declared that there are at least 100,000 "state of mind" members whom he defined as persons sympathetic to the party line and objectives. Bolstering this declaration of many persons being sympathetic to the Party is the claim of party leaders that if they can defeat the Internal Security Act of 1950 they can recruit 50,000 new members within a year.

In keeping with this, on November 15, 1965, following the Supreme Court decision which held that the membership provision of the act was unenforceable if the fifth amendment was utilized as a defense, Hall promptly indicated the decision would result in renewed growth of the Party. In substantiation of his prediction, Hall stated during a press conference in Chicago, Illinois, on December 6, 1965, that the Party was experiencing the greatest upsurge in its history, and that the Party membership had jumped to 1,000 or 2,000 above its 10,000 total of a year ago. (*FBI Appropriation, 1967,* p. 47.)

PARTY—GROWTH SUDDEN. The record clearly establishes that Communist parties have the power of swift and solid growth when the opportunity arises. When the Communist Party membership was at its peak in the United States a decade ago, it was stronger in number than the Soviet Communist Party when it seized power in Russia. In Italy, the Communist Party once dwindled to only 15,000 members and then increased to more than 2 million. In Red China, a small inconsequential party of less than 10,000 grew to more than 6,000,000. ("The Twin Enemies of Freedom," reprint. *FBI Law Enforcement Bulletin*, January 1957. p. 5.)

PARTY — INDICTMENT. On December 1, 1961, an indictment was returned against the Communist Party, USA, as an organization, for failure to register with the Attorney General under provisions of the Internal Security Act of 1950. The indictment contains 12 counts subjecting the Party to possible fines totaling $120,000. The trial has tentatively been set for February 1, 1962.

The Party's leaders, as well as its individual members, also are subject to prosecution under the Internal Security Act of 1950 for failure to register with the Attorney General. (*FBI Release*, December 28, 1961, p. 6.)

PARTY — INTERNAL DANGER. The Communist Party, USA, as an integral part of the international Communist movement, represents a beachhead of subversion within our own Nation. So long as the Communist movement threatens to impose its domination on the entire world, the Party will represent a threat to our internal security. Consciously modeled after the Communist Party of the Soviet Union, the Communist Party, USA, is today a tightly knit, hard-core group which offers its unswerving allegiance to the Soviet Union. In the showdown with the United States which the Communists insist is inevitable, there is no doubt that the Soviet Union is relying heavily on the Party as an advance detachment within our borders ready and willing to carry out any hostile act within its capability. ("Communist Illusion and Democratic Reality," December, 1959, p. 2.)

It is indeed appalling that some members of our society continue to deplore and criticize those who stress the Communist danger. What these misguided "authorities" fail to realize is that the Communist Party, USA, is an integral part of international communism. As the worldwide menace be-

163

comes more powerful, the various Communist Parties assume a more dangerous and sinister role in the countries in which they are entrenched. Public indifference to this threat is tantamount to national suicide. (*FBI Law Enforcement Bulletin*, March 1960, p. 1)

PARTY INTERNATIONAL. In his keynote speech to the convention on February 9, 1957, Eugene Dennis deplored that the Communist Party in the United States had been unaffiliated with other "Socialist Parties" throughout the world and stated that the Communist Party, USA, must work within the framework of full international solidarity.

The most important single lesson to draw from the recent convention of the Communist Party is the singular fact that all debate, changes, and action resulted from the 20th Congress of the Communist Party of the Soviet Union. (SISS, *An Analysis of the 16th Annual Convention of the Communist Party of the United States,* Washington: Government Printing Office, March 12, 1957, pp. 5-6.)

PARTY—LARGEST SUBVERSIVE ORGANIZATION. The Communist Party, USA, is the largest subversive organization in existence in our country today. As a member of the international Communist family, it poses a grave menace to our internal security for it is an acknowledged fact that the ultimate goal of international Communism is the domination and control of all nations on the face of the globe. With the United States standing as the greatest bulwark of freedom in the world, it is understandable why the Communist Party of the Soviet Union is so vitally interested in the progress being made by the Communist Party, USA—the organization which the Soviets are counting on to retain a toehold for international Communism in this land of freedom.

There has never been a time since its founding in 1919 that the Communist Party, USA, has not taken direction and guidance from the Communist Party of the Soviet Union. The line followed by the Party in the United States parallels the Moscow line with sickening consistency. Every move made by the Communists in the United States is calculated to further the ultimate aims and purposes of the Party; namely, the overthrow and destruction of our Government, by force if necessary. (*FBI Appropriation 1962*, March 6, 1961, p. 11.)

PARTY—LAWLESS. Recently, the Communist Party in the United States deliberately and flagrantly refused to comply with the United States Supreme Court decision which requires it to register as an agent of the Soviet Union with the Attorney General. Thereby, it once again has formally declared itself to be a lawless organization. No longer can its members falsely profess that the Party is a legitimate political organization. Nor can its sympathizers and fellow travelers feign innocence of the true nature of the un-American conspiracy which they support. ("The Faith to be Free," December 7, 1961, p. 17.)

PARTY—OPTIMISM. The leaders of the Communist Party, USA are optimistic about the future because of such factors, beliefs, and hoped-for events as:

(1) The expansion of Communism outside the United States to the point where there are now 40 million Communists controlling one-fourth of the world's territory and one-third of the world's 3 billion people.

This chart shows the magnitude of their influence.

(2) The military and scientific prowess of the Soviet Union.

(3) The belief that Communist appeals are far more suited than our own to the peoples of the underdeveloped nations.

(4) Hoped - for diplomatic reverses to be suffered by this country.

(5) Hoped - for withdrawals of American investments abroad followed by a depression here.

(6) The conviction that any such economic reverses will cause wide-spread dissatisfaction among our people, particularly our youth, with our way of life and a more sympathetic approach toward a new economic and political structure, Marxist in nature. (*FBI 1965 Appropriation*, January 29, 1964, p. 44.)

It would be difficult to single out any period since the passage of the Internal Security Act of 1950 in which the optimism of the Communist Party, USA, surpassed that exhibited in 1964. The most important reasons for this optimism

165

were the December 17, 1963, decision of the U.S. Court of Appeals for the District of Columbia reversing the conviction of the party for failing to register under the provisions of the Internal Security Act of 1950 and the subsequent refusal of the U.S. Supreme Court on June 8, 1964, to review that decision.

Following another ruling of the U.S. Supreme Court on June 22, 1964, which declared unconstitutional the passport provisions of the Internal Security Act of 1950, various leaders of the Communist Party in this country promptly announced their plans to travel to the Soviet Union. (*FBI Appropriation 1966*, pp. 53-54.)

PARTY—SPLINTER GROUPS. Splinter groups are those groups which have broken away from the mainstream of the Communist Party, USA, usually over interpretation or implementation of basic Communist ideology. While the teachings of Marx, Engels, and Lenin form the base for the programs of these groups, they vary as to the interpretation of these teachings and in the manner in which their objectives are to be reached. Many of these groups have shown a tendency to favor the Chinese Communist Party line as opposed to that of the Soviet Union. (*FBI Appropriation, 1967*, p. 50.)

PARTY—A WEAPON. Every Communist Party is an organizational weapon. Its strength lies in the day-to-day practical application of Communist ideology by each individual Party member. Communist theory is not merely a dogma. It is a guide to action. Every Communist unhesitatingly sacrifices his personal life to advance the cause of Communism. He is not bound by any of the traditional moral or ethical scruples. Any action—violent or peaceful, lawful or unlawful, moral or immoral, open or covert—which will promote Communist goals, automatically becomes justified. His every tactic is guided by the principle that he is actively at war with the entire non-Communist world and that this conflict is not restricted to the political, social, and economic fields, but invades every phase of human endeavor. Thus, much of the ultimate strength of Communism lies in its flexible ideology translated into organized action by the rigid discipline and militant dedication with which every Communist is imbued. ("Communist Illusion and Democratic Reality," December, 1959, pp. 2-3.)

166

PARTY—U.S. The reason is clear: The Communist Party is not simply *un*-American; it is *anti*-American in every conflict of issues between Washington and Moscow. Its members are not simply *pro*-Soviet; they are deliberately and intentionally an *active part* of the inflexible Soviet empire. ("Our Heritage of Greatness," December 12, 1964, p. 6.)

PARTY LINE—DEFINED. In communism, however, the Party line plays a highly significant and specific role — a vital part in the Party's program for the revolutionary overthrow of our form of government. We, as Americans, should know more about the Party line. What is it? How is it formed? How does it operate? As citizens we should know how to understand and interpret the Party line — realizing that it is a hypocritical and deceitful technique to hoodwink and beguile us. The great danger today is that the constant reiteration of the Party line by Communists—day after day— may cause their demands to be accepted as valid and truthful.

The Party line, in fact, is the sum total of all Party demands at any given time. These demands, whether they are local, national, or international in nature, are designed to promote the Communist revolution. However vehemently the Communists may campaign for the various proposals which compose the Party line, they are not genuinely interested in "reforms" or improving our society. For the Party, reforms are useful only to the extent to which they advance the ultimate revolution. The Party regards reforms as temporary, transitional adjustments which can be achieved during a period when the Party has not yet attained sufficient strength to risk direct revolutionary action. (SISS, *The Communist Party Line*, September 23, 1961, p. 1.)

PARTY LINE—IMMEDIATE DEMANDS AND THEIR PURPOSES. In its never-ending struggle for power, the Communist Party, USA, uses a wide variety of tactics, all designed, in one way or another, to strengthen the Party's influence and, at the same time, to divide, weaken, and confuse the anti-Communist opposition.

A favorite—and frequently effective—Communist tactic is the policy of "partial" or "immediate" demands. These are the short-term or temporary demands which the Communists advance in order to create favorable conditions for future

167

revolutionary action. The pages of the Worker, Political Affairs, Mainstream, and other Communist publications are filled with these demands. The public speeches and statements of Party leaders are largely based on them. Indeed, these demands play a vital role in the Communist Party line at any given time.

The immediate demands which the Communists advance vary greatly in scope and objective. They may be local, regional, national, or international in range. They may be of interest to a large majority of the population or only to a limited minority group. They may involve economic, social, political, or cultural issues, and they may vary in significance from a proposal relating to world peace to a demand for improved low-cost housing in a specific slum area. There is probably no significant section of the American public—regardless of age, race, social standing, occupation, or political orientation—whose interests have not coincided, on occasion, with one or more of the Communists' immediate demands.

In itself, each of the immediate demands proposed by the Party may be entirely legitimate, or even popular, in nature, representing the desire for a limited and specific reform within the framework of our present system of government. Very frequently, these demands do not originate with the Communists at all but in wholly non-Communist segments of the population.

It goes without saying, of course, that the immediate demands put forward by the Party at any given time must be in close accord with the fundamental strategy of the world Communist movement during that particular period. Thus, while many partial demands are almost perennial planks in the party's platform—higher wages, lower taxes, et cetera— a considerable number of them are extremely short lived. This is particularly true of those demands which deal with international affairs and which, therefore, must follow every shift in Soviet foreign policy.

The Communists derive a number of advantages from their immediate-demands tactic. Urging specific reforms in which many non - Communists are legitimately interested helps the Communists to identify themselves with the "masses" and to foster the image that the Party is a progressive, enlightened, humanitarian organization which is acting in the best interests of the American people. At the same time the Communists are afforded the chance to pose as the "champions" of the poor and the oppressed, and, whenever the occasion requires, offer tangible "evidence" of their working-class "leadership."

The immediate-demands tactic also serves as a convenient disguise behind which the Party can carry on its ceaseless agitation against our free economy. More important still, the immediate-demands tactic enables the Party to subtly instill a feeling of "class-consciousness" among employees, to promote a general feeling of unrest and discontent among large sections of the population—in the words of the Communists themselves, to "radicalize" and to "politicalize" the masses. At the same time, Communists appeal to employers to do business with Communist nations.

For this reason, the Party's strenuous campaign for immediate demands is never allowed to subside. As soon as one set of demands is met, the Communists immediately propose new and stronger demands calculated to provoke a new controversy and to act as a new source of social friction and unrest. The substitution of fresh demands for those which have been satisfied or outmoded in one way or another continues in a never-ending cycle with the aim of gradually convincing the "masses" of the need for a revolutionary transformation of society.

In addition, the immediate-demands tactic provides Party members with frequent opportunities to work among the "masses" to gain valuable experience in agitating, organizing social discontent, and guiding large numbers of people in the "class struggle." The fight for specific reforms enables the Party to test its leadership, discipline, and organizational ability in practical situations. In effect, the struggle for immedate demands serves as a small-scale model of, and a dress rehearsal for, future revolutionary action, thereby affording the Communist "vanguard" invaluable experience.

The cumulative aim of the Party's immediate - demands tactic, therefore, is to condition the entire social climate for eventual revolutionary action. If these tactics are successful, the Communists will have been accepted as the leaders of the "masses" who, in turn, will be led to believe that there is a need for a drastic transformation of the entire social sys-

169

tem; and non-Communist opposition will have been weakened and divided to the point of hopeless confusion. In short, the Party will have successfully laid the groundwork for launching the actual revolution.

This is the real meaning of the Communist Party line, which promises all things to all men. It is skillfully designed to appeal to people from every walk of life, and, at the same time, to confuse the public by blending proposals ostensibly sponsored by the Communists with those of legitimate organizations.

The uninformed citizen is thus doubly misled. He may accept the Party line at its face value, without realizing that it is just another Communist tactic, and erroneously conclude that the Party is a legitimate political group which is sincerely interested in promoting these issues. Or, he may make the equally dangerous assumption that anyone who advocates proposals similar to those which make up the Party line is automatically a Communist.

Because Communism thrives on turmoil, the Party is continuously attempting to exploit all grievances — real or imagined—for its own tactical purposes. It is, therefore, almost inevitable that, on many issues, the Party line will coincide with the position of many non-Communists. The danger of indiscriminately alleging that someone is a Communist merely because his views on a particular issue happen to parallel the official Party position is obvious. The confusion which is thereby created helps the Communists by diffusing the forces of their opponents.

Unfortunately, there are those who make the very mistake the Communists are so careful to avoid. These individual concentrate on the negative rather than on the positive. They are merely against communism without being for any positive measures to eliminate the social, political, and economic frictions which the Communists are so adroit at exploiting.

These persons would do well to recall a recent lesson from history. Both Hitler and Mussolini were against communism. However, it was by what they stood for, not against, that history has judged them. (SISS, *The Communist Party Line*, September 23, 1961, pp. 4-6.)

170

During the 1963 fiscal year, Communist spokesmen have stressed such domestic issues as the civil rights struggle; the abolition of all internal security programs and Congressional committees investigating communism; and the reduction of military spending with the funds diverted to social welfare projects. They never fail to lay claim to being the staunchest and most effective defenders of the Bill of Rights.

Their major aim is to convey the impression that Communists are loyal citizens of the United States who merely hold politcal views which differ from those currently prevailing. They deny any direction from abroad and allege they seek change only through legal means. (*FBI Annual Report, Fiscal Year 1963*, p. 22.)

PARTY LINE—MAY PARALLEL THE LEGITIMATE. Any action taken by the Communist Party, USA, is aimed at perpetuating the Party and weakening the governmental, economic, social and moral structure of the United States—all in the interest of advancing world communism. Regrettably, many non-Communists have been duped into helping. This is not to imply that an American is aiding the Communists merely because he finds himself on the same side of some issue as the Party. Since the Party takes a stand on most issues, it would be difficult for anyone to avoid being on the same side as the Communists occasionally. Motives separate loyal Americans from the Communists on these occasions. It behooves all Americans to remember that the right to disagree is a basic privilege of free men, and honest dissent should not be condemned as Communist inspired. (*FBI Annual Report, Fiscal Year 1963*, p. 25.)

PARTY LINE—ORIGIN. In the field of international relations, the Party line can be summed up as "made in Moscow." Completely exonerating the Soviet Union, the Party attempts to place the blame for all international tension on the United States. The Berlin situation, according to the Party, is a "crisis artificially created by Washington" in order to justify increased military spending and to stampede the American public into a war hysteria. It is the "aggressions and intrigues" of the United States which are allegedly making it impossible to arrange for a cease-fire in Laos. Cuba is cited as a flagrant example of "American imperialism," and the

171

United States, in the Party's eyes, is responsible for the murder of Patrice Lumumba and other "African patriots" because it created the conditions which led to these events.

"Wall Street," a traditional Communist whipping boy, is accused of reviving Hitlerism and militarism in Western Germany as a prelude to using West German military forces as possible "mercenary troops" for war against the Soviet Union. The U.S. policies of refusing to grant diplomatic recognition to Communist China and of opposing its admission to the United Nations are derided as "ridiculous." The military dictatorship which recently seized power in South Korea, allegedly with American support, is accused of using the issue of anti-communism to destroy democracy in that nation.

In contrast, the Soviet Union is hailed as being "extremely patient" in its efforts to resolve all international tensions peacefully. The Vienna meeting between Soviet Premier N. S. Khrushchev and President John F. Kennedy is cited as a typical example of the desire of the Soviet Union to negotiate all outstanding differences between the two nations.

Thus, while the Party, in line with the current Soviet peaceful co-existence strategy, describes the preservation of world peace as "the supreme task of our period," it is evident that this peace could be achieved only by complete capitulation to every Soviet demand. (SISS, *The Communist Party Line*, 1961, pp.1-2).

PARTY LINE—REFORMS. Encouraged by recent court decisions which the Party considers major victories in its efforts to nullify the Internal Security Act of 1950, and convinced that a large segment of the population is ready to accept some form of socialism as a cure for domestic problems, such as civil rights and poverty, the Party has streamlined its structure in preparation for operating more openly. Through its stepped-up programs, the Party, of course, hopes that numerous Americans will become lulled by the mass of highsounding Communist propaganda and eventually lose perspective of the issues involved and gravitate to the Party. (*FBI Appropriation 1966*, p. 61.)

PARTY LINE—SOMETHING FOR ALL. There is little of significance occurring in the United States in which the Communist Party, USA, does not take an interest. The Party is opposed to taxes, yet it favors greater Government spending, especially for welfare projects. It advocates that "big business" pay a greater share of the cost of Government, and in almost the same breath proposes that the Government take over most major industries. It is against unemployment and high prices; for equal rights and higher wages. In short, it advocates something of interest to everyone. (*FBI Annual Report, Fiscal Year 1963*, pp. 23, 25.)

PARTY LINE — TRANSMISSION. The Communist Party, USA continually makes strenuous efforts to increase and expand the distribution and consumption of its literature. James Allen, a member of the Party's national committee, remarked at a meeting of the Party's New York staff in May 1964, that sales of Party publications had increased seven percent nationwide.

This increase is important since the Communists consider their press and publications to be the most important and effective vehicle for agitation and propaganda. Through the dissemination of newspapers, books, pamphlets, leaflets, and other printed matter, the Party indoctrinates its members and sympathizers and is able to reach and propagandize the non-Communist masses.

The major Communist bookstores operating in the United States at this time are the Jefferson Bookshop in New York City; New World Book Fair, Philadelphia; New Era Bookshop, Baltimore; Global Books, Detroit; Modern Bookstore, Chicago; Mary's Bookshop, Milwaukee; International Books, San Francisco; and the Progressive Bookshop, Los Angeles. (*FBI Appropriation 1966*, p. 57.)

PARTY POLITICAL? I feel that once public opinion is thoroughly aroused as it is today, the fight against Communism is well on its way. Victory will be assured once Communists are identified and exposed, because the public will take the first step of quarantining them so they can do no harm. Communism, in reality, is not a political Party. It is a way of life—an evil and malignant way of life. It reveals a condition akin to disease that spreads like an epidemic and like

173

an epidemic a quarantine is necessary to keep it from infecting the Nation. (HCUA, *Menace of Communism*, March 26, 1947, p. 12.)

There is some sentiment that a Communist has as much right to a government job as a Democrat or a Republican, because the Communists claim to be a political party. In reality, they are a part of an international criminal conspiracy. They are no more a political party than was the German-American Bund. ("How to Fight Communism," *Newsweek*, June 9, 1947, reprint.)

The 1957 convention was cloaked with secrecy despite Party claims that it was ". . . being covered by the largest battery of newspapermen in the Party's history." The newsmen were not admitted to witness the convention proceedings but were briefed by the Party's spokesman, Simon W. Gerson, who has been a member of the Party since 1932. Gerson very adroitly slanted the accounts of the convention to make the Communist Party take on its best possible appearance to the Public.

The Communists boasted of having "impartial observers" cover the convention. However, most of these so-called impartial observers were handpicked before the convention started and were reportedly headed by A. J. Muste, who has long fronted for Communists and who recently circulated an amnesty petition calling for the release of Communist leaders convicted under the Smith Act. Muste's report on the convention was biased, as could be expected. On the other hand, another observer, whom the Party did not hand pick and who was more objective, Carl Rachlin of the American Civil Liberties Union, has stated that the arguments for democracy within the Party were "merely tactical and designed to fool the public," and that rank-and-file dissatisfaction with the Soviet Union "will never change the Party's course."

A realistic appraisal came from a reporter for *Christian Science Monitor* who said that even though the convention had debate and votes, these were "only to pull the wool over the eyes of innocents and dupes. It was one of the great fakes of our time." (SISS, *An Analysis of the Sixteenth Annual Convention of the Communist Party of the United States*, March 12, 1957, pp. 2-3.)

The Communist Party professes to be a legitimate political organization on the American scene; however, its leadership reins are firmly held by rabidly pro-Soviet elements, and the Party's ultimate objective remains the overthrow and destruction of our Government by force and violence. (*FBI Release*, December 22, 1958, p. 4.)

Despite a Supreme Court ruling on June 5, 1961, upholding the Subversive Activities Control Board's findings that the Communist Party, USA, is a Communist-action organization which is directed and controlled by the Soviet Union, Party leaders continue to claim that they represent a legitimate political group.

While openly asserting that it will not comply with the order to register with the Attorney General as required by the Internal Security Act of 1950, the Party petitioned for a rehearing of the Supreme Court's decision. This petition had not been acted upon at the close of the year.

Setting the stage for Party defiance of the Court's ruling and the order of the Subversive Activities Control Board, Gus Hall, General Secretary of the Communist Party, USA, declared on June 8, 1961:

"It (the Internal Security Act of 1950) is a monstrous law and a monstrous decision. It asks the Communist Party to commit suicide and I can say very bluntly that we will not cooperate with any such precedent."

One needs only to review some of the activities of leading Communists in this country during the past year to see how close the ties are between the Communist Party, USA, and the Soviet Union. Many Party leaders traveled to Russia and the satellite nations, returning with glowing accounts of the wonders of communism. Elizabeth Gurley Flynn, National Chairman of the Party, returned from an 8-month tour of Soviet-bloc countries in December 1960, and wrote in a Communist newspaper:

"How I hated to leave that delightful city (Moscow) and all my new friends! But all good things must end and I was leaving Socialism and returning to capitalism, with a heavy heart." (*FBI Annual Report, Fiscal Year 1961*, pp. 24-26.)

According to press reports, the body of the aged Communist lay in state in the Hall of Columns in Moscow's Trade Union House. . . .

A reasonable person could conclude only one thing: a servant was being rewarded. William Z. Foster, who followed every devious twist of the Communist Party line, who devoted his life to the advancement of totalitarian communism, who predicted in the dedication of a book that his great-grandson would live in a Communist United States, and who at the time of his death was under indictment for a crime which, in essence, charged him with conspiring to teach and advocate the destruction of our free Government, was receiving the award for his lifelong labors.

The picture presented by the press of brutal totalitarian dictators mourning the demise of a man who spent his lifetime working against every principle on which our Republic is founded should be remembered. That picture should be called to mind when apologists for communism seek to persuade the uninformed that the Communist Party is "just another political party like the Democratic and Republican Parties."

The Communist Party is not "just another political party." It does not accept or abide by democratic processes. And Communists are not liberals. They are not progressives. They are not social reformers. Above all, Communists are not American, despite their use of every Aesopian trick in in the book to trap the unwary into accepting a doctrine of absolutism falsely labeled "American."

Communism represents everything abhorrent to the American ideal. ("Communism and the Knowledge to Combat It," *Congressional Record*, January 26, 1962, reprint.)

PARTY—PROSECUTION. From 1949 to 1956, 104 leaders of the Communist Party, USA were convicted of conspiracy to organize as the CPUSA a group of persons who teach and advocate the violent overthrow of the U.S. Government and of conspiracy to teach and advocate such violent overthrow.

The U.S. Supreme Court on June 7, 1957, held in one case that since the CPUSA was organized in 1945, any indictment returned subsequent to 1948 which charged the defendants with organizing the CPUSA was void under the statute of limitations. The decision further held that the Government had failed to establish that the teaching and advocating of violent overthrow of the Government by the defendants

176

went beyond the "abstract theory" stage and actually "incited to action."

As a result of this Supreme Court decision, most of the defendants who had been convicted for conspiracy to violate the act were either acquitted or ordered retried. The indictments against the defendants who were ordered retried were subsequently dismissed at the request of the Government since available evidence did not meet the standards set by the court relative to "incitement to action." The last outstanding indictment against six former functionaries of the Party at Denver, Colorado, was dismissed on November 12, 1964. In June 1962, the Smith Act was amended to clarify the term "organize" but the act continues to be ineffective because of the second part of the Supreme Court decision pertaining to "inciting to action." Legislation aimed at circumventing the "incitement to action" aspect of the decision has been introduced in several sessions of Congress but has not been enacted.

MEMBERSHIP CASES

In addition to the 104 conspiracy convictions, five other Party leaders were convicted for violating the membership provision of the Act.

On June 5, 1961, U.S. Supreme Court decisions held that, to sustain a conviction under the membership provision of the Act, the Government must not only prove that the defendant is an "active" and "knowing" member of an organization, which advocates the violent overthrow of the Government, but must also prove specific intent by the defendant to accomplish the aims of the organization as speedily as the circumstances will permit.

As a result of these decisions, one convicted member, who served 15 months, had his 6-year sentence commuted; another conviction was reversed by an appellate court; the indictments against two others were dismissed at the request of the Government; and the remaining conviction was reversed on another ground and the indictment dismissed at the request of the Government. Outstanding indictments against nine others, including seven defendants in the first conspiracy trial, were also dismissed.

PROSECUTIONS UNDER THE INTERNAL SECURITY ACT OF 1950— PROSECUTION OF PARTY AS AN ORGANIZATION

On June 5, 1961, after more than 10 years of hearings and judicial review, the U.S. Supreme Court upheld the constitutionality of the registration provision of the Act.

The registration order of the Subversive Activities Control Board became final on October 20, 1961, but the November 20, 1961, deadline for the Party as an organization to register with the Attorney General passed without compliance—as did the deadline of November 30, 1961, for the officers of the Party and the December 20, 1961, deadline for individual members.

On December 17, 1962, the Party was found guilty under a 12-count indictment charging it with failure to register as a Communist-action organization. The maximum fine of $120,000 was imposed. This was appealed and on December 17, 1963, the Court of Appeals reversed the lower court on the ground that the Fifth Amendment privilege against self-incrimination was available to the officers of the Party as legal justification for refusing to sign the registration forms. The court of Appeals also held that the burden of proof rested with the Government to establish that "someone" was willing to sign the registration forms on behalf of the Party, and if such a "volunteer" could not be produced, the indictment should be dismissed.

On January 21, 1964, the Government filed a petition requesting that the Court of Appeals hear the matter sitting en banc. The court on February 21, 1964, denied the petition and on June 8, 1964, the U.S. Supreme Court denied a Government petition to review the Court of Appeals decision. On February 25, 1965, the Federal grand jury, Washington, D. C., reindicted the Party for failure to register. Retrial of this case is set for October 1965.

PROSECUTION OF OFFICERS

On March 15, 1962, individual indictments were returned against Party leaders, Gus Hall and the late Benjamin J. Davis, Jr., charging them with failure to register for the Party and with failure to file the registration statement. On September 25, 1963, the district court ordered the trials consolidated and then postponed hearings on motions to dismiss

178

and setting a trial date pending a final decision in the registration case against the Party as an organization. On August 22, 1964, Davis died of cancer and on October 9, 1964, the government moved to dismiss the indictment against him.

PROSECUTION OF PARTY MEMBERS

Since May 31, 1962, the Attorney General has petitioned the Subversive Activities Control Board to order 25 members of the Party's national committee and 19 additional Party officials on a lower level to register as Party members under the Act. The Board has ordered 37 to register and the remaining seven cases are under consideration by the Board.

Two membership registration cases have been consolidated for purposes of appeal. On April 23, 1964, the Court of Appeals upheld the registration order of the Board. This was appealed on July 13, 1964, to the Supreme Court.

PASSPORT SANCTION

Under the section of the Act proscribing members of the Party from applying for, using, or attempting to use a U.S. passport, the Secretary of State, after hearings before a State Department Passport Board, ordered the passports of the late Elizabeth Gurley Flynn and of Herbert Aptheker revoked. These individuals filed a civil action to enjoin the passport revocation.

The Court of Appeals upheld the Government's action but the U.S. Supreme Court on June 22, 1964, held that that portion of the Act relating to the passport sanction was unconstitutional; that the right to travel is protected by the due process clause of the Fifth Amendment; and that the passport sanction "sweeps too broadly and indiscriminately over this liberty."

As a result, there is no restriction on the issuance of passports to the Party and the Department has declined prosecution on approximately 75 cases which had been referred as possible violations under the passport sanction. Two indictments previously obtained will undoubtedly be dismissed.

As a further result of this decision, several leading Communist Party officials have obtained U.S. passports for foreign travel. Most of them proceeded directly to the Soviet Union.

Another section of the Act prohibits the employment and the like of a Party member in a defense facility designated by the Secretary of Defense. The Bureau referred approximately 30 cases to the Department as possibile violations.

On May 21, 1963, Eugene Frank Robel, of Seattle, Washington, was indicted under this section. Robel returned to his job following his release on bond. Further prosecutive steps have not been taken, it being noted that recent court decisions such as the Supreme Court decision on the passport sanction will have a bearing on whether or not the *Robel* case ever goes to trial. (*FBI 1966 Appropriation*, pp. 62-64.)

PARTY—PURGE TO STRENGTHEN. The Party is seeking to further spread the propaganda that factionalism is rife. Actually, the Party is in the process of purging its right-wing element and further subordinating itself to Moscow. The ultimate goal is a highly disciplined party, free of dissident elements, which with unswerving loyalty will carry out the objectives of international communism. The Party today is consolidating its position and new leadership is emerging which is more stern and undeviating in its Soviet loyalty. ("Our Mutual Challenge," November 4, 1957, p. 3.)

PARTY—SECRET. "It is not what you know, but what you show!" With that catchy admonition, Gus Hall, general secretary of the Communist Party, USA, recently warned Party members to destroy incriminating documents which might be used in prosecutions against them. (*Law Enforcement Bulletin*, October 1961.)

Hall's phrase, "It is not what you know, but what you show!" is more than just an admonition. It is also a devastating description of all the elements of the current Communist Party line, for the Party knows that the real purpose of its line must be deceitfully covered up with what it "shows" the American people. (*Law Enforcement Bulletin*, October, 1961.)

PARTY SIZE. The numerical strength of the Party's enrolled membership is insignificant. But it is well known that there are many actual members who because of their position are not carried on Party rolls.

New York leads in the number of enrolled Party members (30,000), followed by California (8,553); Illinois (6,500); Ohio (3,838); Oregon (3,654); Washington (2,752); New Jersey (2,487) and Michigan (2,135). The Daily Worker boasts of 74,000 members on the rolls.

What is important is the claim of the Communists themselves that for every Party member there are ten others ready, willing, and able to do the Party's work. Herein lies the greatest menace of Communism. For these are the people who infiltrate and corrupt various spheres of American life. So rather than the size of the Communist Party the way to weigh its true importance is by testing its influence, its ability to infiltrate.

The size of the Party is relatively unimportant because of the enthusiasm and iron-clad discipline under which they operate. In this connection, it might be of interest to observe that in 1917 when the Communists overthrew the Russian Government there was one Communist for every 2,277 persons in Russia. In the United States today there is one Communist for every 1,814 persons in the country.

One who accepts the aims, principles, and the program of the Party, who attends meetings, who reads the Party press and literature, who pays dues and who is active on behalf of the Party "shall be considered a member." The open, avowed Communist who carries a card and pays dues is no different from a security standpoint than the person who does the Party's work but pays no dues, carries no card and is not on the Party rolls. In fact, the latter is a greater menace because of his opportunity to w o r k in stealth. (HCUA, *Menace of Communism*, Washington, G. P. O., March 26, 1947, p. 5.)

It must be remembered that there are actually six levels to the Communist Party. In the first instance, you have the professional Communist who was referred to in other years as the card-carrying member of the Party. Secondly, there is the concealed Communist. Then there are the sympathizer, the fellow-traveler, the innocent who has been duped by the Communists, and, finally, there is the opportunist. ("Communist Threat in the U. S." *U. S. News & World Report*, March 30, 1951, p. 34.)

Communist membership is declining. Not that fewer Communists are in operation. Indeed not. They simply, for security reasons, are not enrolling. They are still here —as dangerous as ever before. Their strength lies not in numbers, but in cunning and fanaticism. They have a hard core of disciplined membership—with this nucleus they are enticing non-Communists to support their endeavors. ("Make the Communists Show Their Own Colors!" April 14, 1952, p. 2.)

But the party's actual strength never can be measured in terms of members because thousands of "bleeding hearts," pseudoliberals, sympathizers and "dupes" always stand ready to lend their aid when their services are needed. ("The Twin Enemies of Freedom," November 9, 1956 in *Law Enforcement Bulletin*, January, 1957, reprint, p. 5.)

The Party's influence in the United States is much greater than its membership. Gus Hall has boasted a Party membership of around 10,000 with another 100,000 "state-of-mind" members—people he describes as sympathetic to the Party, its line and objectives. A number of Government officials and others who have been inundated with communist-inspired communications are fully aware that Communist influence far exceeds Party membership.

Often the Party is able to extend its influence through the use of front groups it creates or through legitimate organizations it can infiltrate. There a number of organizations in existence in the United States today with appealing names which were conceived by the Communist Party, USA, and operate solely for its benefit.

Another indication of the extent of the Party's influence is its ability to constantly raise funds. Around one half of the Party's $100,000 goal for the defense of Hall and Davis had been reached by the end of 1963 fiscal year. (*FBI Annual Report, Fiscal Year 1963*, p. 25.)

Party leader Gus Hall continues to publicly state that the current Party membership is about 10,000 with no membership lists being maintained. This does not include those many individuals who dropped open party affiliation to avoid prosecution and the like. Many of these individuals remain convinced Marxists and are working as hard outside the Party today to advance the cause of communism as they would if they were still active in the day-to-day activities of the Party. Nor does this include the tens of thousands the Party claims as "state-of-mind" members. Thousands more who supported the Party in the past still remain equally dedicated and still are relied upon by the Party today to support its current intensified campaign operating through the array of newly created front organizations. (*FBI 1965 Appropriation,* January 29, 1964, p. 42.)

Leaders of the Communist Party, USA, continue to publicly place the party membership in this country at 10,000, as, for example, in May 1964, when Albert Lima, leader of the Party's northern California district, used this figure when speaking before an audience of approximately 3,000 at College of San Mateo, San Mateo, California.

There are, of course, thousands of other individuals who are not actual members but stand ready to aid the hard-core membership. Party leader Gus Hall himself at a press conference on October 26, 1964, placed the membership at approximately 10,000 with 90,000 close sympathizers. The latter group, according to Hall, comes under the Communist Party influence and is growing to the Party's satisfaction.

Encouraged by recent court decisions which the Party considers major victories in its efforts to nullify the Internal Security Act of 1950, and convinced that a large segment of the population is ready to accept some form of socialism as a cure for domestic problems, such as civil rights and poverty, the Party has streamlined its structure in preparation for operating more openly. Through its stepped-up programs, the Party, of course, hopes that numerous Americans will become lulled by the mass of high-sounding Communist propaganda and eventually lose perspective of the issues involved and gravitate to the Party. (*FBI 1966 Appropriation,* pp. 60-61.)

As late as April 1968, Gus Hall claimed that the party had 14,000 dues paying members and some 100,000 supporters. (*FBI 1970 Appropriation,* April 17, 1969, p. 65.)

PARTY SIZE NOT TRUE MEASURE. Nonetheless, in one union with nearly 100,000 members, 500 Party members were able to control the union. Another union with 8,500 members sought to free itself from Communist control but failed despite the fact that there were less than 200 Party members in the union.

In one instance a single Communist by clever manipulation at a union convention was able to dictate resolutions adopted by the convention. ("How to Fight Communism," *Newsweek*, June 9, 1947, reprint.)

PARTY SUBMISSION. To be always "right," that is, to be doing exactly what the Party approves of at that moment, is an extremely difficult—and hazardous—job. The Party line shifts, day by day, according to the prevailing wind. Today East is East; tomorrow East is West; the day after tomorrow East is South. Why? Because the Party says so. If the citizen happens to say something today, unaware that the Party line has shifted during the night, he will find himself, most embarrassingly, out upon an ideological limb. Then he must either, most humbly and obediently, climb back on the main trunk or find the limb sawed off underneath him by the "protectors of the state"—the very men who yesterday were his bosom friends. ("Foe to Freedom," *The Elks Magazine*, October, 1950, reprint, p. 2.)

PARTY—SUBSERVIENT TO USSR. The failure of the convention to take a stand on the Soviet rape of Hungary and anti-Semitism in Russia proves the hypocrisy of the American Communists' alleged declaration of independence and indicates that the American Communists, in fact, have not broken with the Soviet Union. Incidentally, these are facts which the Party's spokesman, Mr. Gerson, did not report to the daily press. (SISS, *An Analysis of the Sixteenth Annual Convention of the Communist Party of the United States*, March 12, 1957, p. 8.)

Particularly significant in this regard were the actions of the delegation of Party officials from this country who attended the 22nd Congress of the Soviet Communist Party in Moscow this fall. Not only did the American delegates pledge full support to Nikita Khrushchev in the disagreement between the Russians and their Albanian and Chinese comrades, but three of them appeared on a Moscow television program to give the Soviet people a distorted impression of conditions in the United States. (*FBI Release*, December 28, 1961, p. 5.)

The Cuban crisis in October 1962, is a good example. The full strength of the Party's propaganda arsenal—editorials, leaflets, letters, telegrams, speeches, slogans and the like —was used to condemn the actions taken by the United States Government and to praise the "peace policy" of Soviet Premier Khrushchev. The Party spokesman applied the same theme to this situation that they have used so often through the years—the United States is the citadel of imperialism and the Soviet Union is the champion of world peace.

In the ideological dispute between the Kremlin and the Chinese Communists, the Communist Party, USA, has remained loyal to the Soviet position. The Party issued a statement on January 10, 1963, in support of the Soviet Union in its rift with Communist China.

Another example of the close ties between the Communist Party, USA, and the Soviet Union was the attendance of Gus Hall and four other Party officials as honored guests at a reception given by the Soviet delegation to the United Nations. The affair was held on November 7, 1962, to commemorate the 44th anniversary of the Russian Revolution.

The American branch of the world Communist movement never deviates from the international policies decided in Russia. Soviet propaganda on peaceful co-existence, disarmament, increased East-West trade, economic competition and the like is constantly echoed by Communist spokesmen in the United States. (*FBI Annual Report, Fiscal Year 1963*, pp. 22-23.)

COMMUNIST PARTY—U.S.A.—1968

Although activities of old line Communist organizations in the United States have been overshadowed by the militancy of the New Left and racial disorders, the threat of Communism has certainly not diminished. It flows from the Communist Party—U.S.A. with its blind obedience to the Soviet Union and from the various splinter groups such as the Progressive Labor Party, the pro-Peking group I mentioned earlier which, in addition to stepped-up efforts to extend its influence on college campuses, has made a concerted effort to take over the national leadership of the Students for a Democratic Society, the militant, pro-Marxist, anarchistic, campus-based New Left group; the Socialist Workers Party;

185

the Workers World Party; and their affiliates. These organizations seek to transform this country into a Communist state but differ on the plans to be followed.

The turbulence generated by the New Left stimulated all these organizations into moving toward increased militancy themselves. Seizing any pretext as the foundation for a protest demonstration, leaders of these organizations seek to proliferate each demonstration into a massive confrontation with the authorities to generate disrespect for law and order.

A typical example occurred in connection with the coalition group participating in picketing against establishments of the French Government in the United States in July 1968. In the Berkeley, Calif., area this coalition was led by an official of the Socialist Workers Party and included members of the Socialist Workers Party; the Young Socialist Alliance, the Youth group of the Socialist Workers Party; Spartacist, a Trotskyite group; and others. The aggressive action taken by this group necessitated a curfew in Berkeley in order to quell the disturbance.

The growing militancy of the old-line Communist organizations was also demonstrated at the Eighth National Convention of the Young Socialist Alliance held November 28, through December 1, 1968, at Chicago, Ill. The Young Socialist Alliance is the youth and training section of the Socialist Workers Party, a militantly revolutionary party based upon the theories of Marx, Engels, and Lenin as interpreted by Leon Trotsky. Among the nearly 800 in attendance were seven enlisted men from the U.S. Army and several members of the Students for a Democratic Society, as well as individuals from Canada, Mexico, France, and West Germany. Members of the Black Panther Party, a militant black nationalist group, were among the speakers at the convention.

One speaker described those in attendance as being the vanguard of the young students and workers who are called upon to bring the liberating ideas of socialism to the American people. Another speaker appealed to the group to increase their efforts to reach the GIs, to invite them to participate in demonstrations, as a group of 100,000 GI's can make the revolution. At the time of the convention, Young Socialist

Alliance members were reported to be located in 101 colleges or universities, 32 high schools, and five junior high schools.

While all the splinter organizations have their roots in the Communist movement, it is essential that it be clearly understood that there are ideological differences between them and that all these organizations are not part of the Communist Party—U.S.A. Most of these Communist splinter organizations follow the interpretation of Marxism-Leninism espoused by the late Leon Trotsky or Communist China.

The Communist Party—U.S.A., on the other hand, represents that part of the international Communist movement in the United States which is pro-Soviet. As a result, we find the Communist Party—U.S.A., following the line established by the Communist Party of the Soviet Union regardless of the effect that such action will have on the party's acceptance in the United States. Thus, during the past year we had party leader Gus Hall holding a press conference in Budapest, Hungary, in February 1968, where he declared that United States "imperialism" was the central issue uniting the 67 Communist and workers parties gathered in Budapest for a consultative meeting. It was also at this time that Hall stated the meeting had unanimously approved a proposal by the U.S. delegation that it send a message of sympathy and support to North Vietnam for its valiant stand against "American aggression."

The matter of unanimous support for the party line and other issues, such as the position the party should take as to black power and the fast-growing New Left movement brought about growing factionalism within the Communist Party—U.S.A., during 1968.

There were a number of party functionaries who were critical of the invasion and occupation of Czechoslovakia by Soviet troops and tanks. The position the party should take in regard to the activities of the New Left is also a matter of much discussion but in recognition of the New Left's role in attracting dissident youth, the party will relinquish some of its activity on college campuses to the New Left in order to concentrate on industry. In March 1969, the Communist Party — U.S.A. held a West Coast Youth Conference to revamp its youth organization, the W. E. B. DuBois Clubs of America. Since the membership of the DuBois Clubs has now declined

187

to less than 100, it was deemed necessary to change the concept of the organization from a massive - type organization to a young Communist organization, but it would still remain under the DuBois label. The loss of student members to the more active organizations of the New Left was indicated by the fact that working-class youth represented about 75 percent of those in attendance at the conference while students represented only 25 percent. In former years the ratio had been reversed.

Because of the factionalism over the issues mentioned above, the special convention of the party which was held in New York City from July 4 through July 7, 1968, was something less than a resounding success for Gus Hall and his supporters in the national leadership. It now appears that the 19th national convention scheduled for the period April 30 through May 4, 1969, will have similar results.

Despite the internal strife besetting it, however, the party makes it clear that while it may disagree with the means to destroy our form of government, it has never deviated from its objective of achieving a communized America.

COMMUNIST PARTY—U.S.A. AND THE BLACK POWER CONCEPT

This is evident in a pamphlet, "Black Power and Liberation—A Communist View," published by the party in December 1967. In it, Claude Lightfoot, chairman of the party's National Negro Commission, wrote that the party's opposition to guerrilla warfare by Negroes in the United States is not based on the rejection of violence. On the contrary, he emphasized that it is a matter of timing. In other words, in line with the historical Communist approach to rebellion, it is wrong to rebel unless one can be assured the time is right, and at this time the party judges the time to be inappropriate.

During 1968 we continued to see the formation of new black extremist organizations, some of which advocate outright anarchy, insurrection, rebellion, and overthrow of the U.S. Government and openly advocate "black power."

The emergence of a militant black power concept in the civil rights movement, particularly on the part of extremist groups, has placed the Communist Party—U.S.A. in a quandary. There is a strong pro-black power current among the lower echelon rank-and-file members of the party and the

188

Negro composition of the party leans toward the black power prophets.

The Communist Party—U.S.A. is confronted with the dilemma of losing hold and influence over the more militant Negro youth within the party because of the attractiveness of the reckless propaganda of black power advocates. Stokely Carmichael and H. Rap Brown, for example, openly espouse the extreme positions of Fidel Castro, the late Ernesto "Che" Guevara, Mao Tse-tung, and the American varieties of irresponsible exponents of violence. The Communist Party—U.S.A. claims to disagree with these extreme positions at this particular time but conciliates with them for fear of being isolated from this sector of youth. It conciliates so much, in fact, that it is hard to determine whether the Communist Party is really for or against black power.

In February 1969 the party's Commission on Black Liberation (formerly the National Negro Commission) adopted a series of motions representing a decided shift from the advocacy of political action to deal with the racial issues to an acceptance of violence and guerrilla warfare as advocated by the violence-prone Black Panther Party which I will discuss later. The commission passed motions to accept the Black Panther Party program, to work as closely with the Black Panthers as the Black Panthers will permit, and to join the Black Panthers if this can be done. These motions were opposed by veteran Communist Party members and further battles concerning these issues can be expected within the party.

MORE PARTY OPEN ACTIVITY

Ever since its 18th national convention in June 1966 the party in this country has been moving more into open activities, running candidates for political office and attempting to improve its image with stepped-up public relations efforts through its publications. All this provides the party with many opportunities to propagandize the American people. While on a trip through the United States, in 1968, Gus Hall stated that through speaking appearances on television, on radio, and in person he was able to reach an estimated 50 million people.

In addition to continuing to publish the twice-weekly newspaper *The Worker*, party leaders worked hard during

1968 to accumulate finances and staff for a new daily publication, the *Daily World,* which began publication 5 days a week in July 1968. Publication of *The Worker* was then discontinued.

SPEAKING APPEARANCES ON COLLEGE CAMPUSES

Also, during the academic year 1967-68, the Communist Party—U.S.A. continued its program of having party leaders appear on college campuses as speakers, 48 such appearances having been made during that school year. This is a small decrease when compared with appearances during previous years. As I pointed out earlier, this is in line with the Party's relinquishment of some of its activity on the campuses to the New Left in order to concentrate on industry. (*FBI, 1970 Appropriation,* April 17, 1969, pp. 61-64.)

PARTY—YOUTH. Also, the youth of our Nation are being singled out for special attention. The Party's chief hope for rapid growth and approval rests on its efforts to entice restless young men and women into its ranks, and the communists already have good cause to be optimistic. Their campaign to blanket college and university campuses with communist speakers—a program which has been accepted with palliative indifference by many persons—is a resounding success in the eyes of the Party. (*FBI Law Enforcement Bulletin,* Oct. 1, 1966.)

PASSPORTS. There have been numerous instances of misuse of passports by American Communists since the Supreme Court decision of June 16, 1958, holding that Congress had not delegated authority to the Secretary of State to deny passports to subversives. Since the decision, there have been a number of well-known Communists who have traveled abroad to Russia and who have made public attacks against the United States while abroad. There have been numerous bills proposed in Congress to allow the Secretary of State to deny passports to subversives.

I noted in the paper the other day there has been a modernizing of the procedures for getting a passport in this country and to expedite their issuance. If anyone has the idea of collecting passports for ulterior motives, it should be easier to do so. (*FBI 1962 Appropriation,* March 6, 1961, p. 62.)

The passport sanction requirement of the Internal Security Act of 1950 makes it a punishable offense for any member of the Communist Party, USA, to apply for, use or attempt to use a U. S. passport. As of the close of the fiscal year, there had been no criminal prosecutions under the passport sanction. The Department of State, however, had revoked passports held by Communist Party leaders Elizabeth Gurley Flynn and Herbert Eugene Aptheker. This action was taken on the basis of information furnished by the FBI. Civil proceedings instituted by Flynn and Aptheker to enjoin the Secretary of State from revoking their passports were heard by a 3-judge panel of the U. S. District Court at Washington, D. C., on July 13, 1963, and the constitutionality of the revocation action was upheld. However, the United States Supreme Court on June 22, 1964, reversed this decision, ruling that the pertinent section of the Internal Security Act of 1950 was unconstitutional on its face and as applied to Flynn and Aptheker. (*FBI Annual Report, Fiscal Year 1964*, pp. 23-24.)

PASSPORTS—USE. A most recent prosecution which involved the misuse of American passports by Paul Carl Meyer illustrates the ready willingness of the Soviets to utilize misguided individuals to penetrate our shores. Meyer, in November 1962, acquired 15 passports of American citizens in the Chicago area by a fraudulent scheme. Meyer thereafter traveled throughout Europe and, when in Berlin in February 1963, established contact with the Soviets in East Germany who expressed intense interest in the passports in Meyer's possession. Meyer was induced by the Soviets to sell them the passports. Possibly, Soviet interest in these passports was based on their desire to alter them to enable surreptitious entries to be made into the United States by agents in their service.

On February 3, 1965, Meyer pleaded guilty in Federal court, Chicago, Illinois, to an indictment charging him with 4 counts of misuse of American passports. On February 26, 1965, he was sentenced to 2 years' imprisonment on the first of these counts and to one year each on the remaining 3 counts, these sentences to run concurrently. (*FBI 1966 Appropriation*, p. 72.)

PATRIOTISM. It is beyond my comprehension that some allegedly loyal citizens of our country should be reluctant to proclaim their devotion to our democratic ideals. It is repugnant to me that the pseudo-liberals pride themselves upon being internationalists and view the emotion of patriotism as evidence of decadence and weakness. In some circles, I regret to say, the word patriotism has become a dirty word, and belief in God old-fashioned, if not "ridiculous."

It is a great privilege to me to make known my gratitude for being a citizen of our glorious Republic. I ardently hope that the day will never come when it will be considered "super-patriotism" to have our school children, or anyone else, heartily pledge allegiance to the flag of our country, and to declare our devotion to God and country.

You and your organization have proved yourselves to be loyal Americans, yet you have been the victims of vituperation, lies and vulgar accusations which are the only weapons of the coward and the guilty. In moral and spiritual issues, there can be no neutrality. You can be proud that you have always been on the side of love of God, country, law and order.

We need more than ever to rekindle the spirit of patriotism. We have long since reached the time when loyal Americans must be willing to stand up and be counted. We are living in an era when staunch beliefs are needed to conquer the patent lies of communism and the creeping immorality of crime. It takes intelligence, rare courage and bulldog determination to fight these twin evils. (*"America—Freedom's Champion,"* October 18, 1960, pp. 2-3.)

Today, patriotism seems to be out of style. Those who express their love of country are often looked upon as paranoiac patriots or right-wing extremists.

Let me quote from an article which appeared in a recent issue of a student publication of one of our midwestern colleges. Entitled, "Nix Patriotism," this article stated, "Patriotism is an emotion that is marked by ignorance, stupidity, prejudice, autism, fear and hostility."

We can only pray that this undesirable trend which is evidenced among students in all too many of our colleges and universities can be reversed before it is too late.

This attitude can be seen in the widespread public indifference concerning the real threat of world communism. The philosophy of communism flourishes best in an environment where personal responsibility and self-discipline have been undermined by immorality, materialism and expediency.

192

Its duplicity is difficult for young Americans to comprehend. If our young citizens turn an objective, analytical searchlight on this ideology and its organizational arms, they will understand communism for what it is—a materialistic, godless dogma dedicated to world domination.

When man places himself above the law and bases his decisions on his own selfish interests, he aids the Communists' relentless efforts to destroy the ideals of our civilization. He contributes heavily to reducing life to the code of the jungle, by making it easier for communism to spread its deadly doctrines, terror and the brutalization of man. What Ignatius Loyola taught, communism seeks to destroy. ("Time for Decision," November 24, 1964, p. 5.)

In the eyes of a later-day hero, "Freedom, devotion to God and country are not things of the past. They will never become old fashioned." These words were spoken by Astronaut John H. Glenn.

America remains free because men of faith, men of individualism, men of courage, men of integrity, men of discipline, and men of vision have patrolled her most vital outposts for 187 years. (*Congressional Record*, Nov. 27, 1963, p. A7294.)

PATRIOTISM AND FLAG DESECRATION. Can there be any act more sickening and revolting than a crowd of so-called citizens desecrating and burning their country's flag? Those who resort to such moronic behavior are surely lost in the depths of depravity. Obviously, their first loyalty is not to the United States.

True, our Nation is founded on concepts and principles which encourage dissent and opposition. These are traditions we must always defend and support. But touching a torch to the flag far exceeds reasonable protest. It is a shameful act which serves no purpose but to encourage those who want our country to erupt in violence and destruction.

On this 191st anniversary of the Declaration of Independence, we might ask what causes unpatriotic outbursts and irrational protests. Why do people turn against their native land and openly support totalitarian forces whose goal is to enslave the world-forces which do not even allow token opposition from their subjects? Why do some individuals refuse to serve and defend their country? Why do they burn their draft cards and their flag?

There may be many reasons for such action, but I am fully convinced that dying patriotism is one major cause. Love of country is being deemphasized and excluded from several phases of our life. Many educators and other leaders seem to feel it is no longer necessary for boys and girls to be concerned with how our country came into being, what it stands for, and the courageous and noble deeds of our forefathers to preserve it.

Conditions are now such in some circles that an individual who professes love of his country, reverence for its flag, and belief in the principles which make our Nation great is considered a yokel. Open aversion to patriotism of any form is increasing. Even some news media take a "tongue-in-cheek" approach to persons and groups which promote and participate in patriotic endeavors. Love of one's country is treated as some kind of social disease to be tolerated, if not stamped out. Protests are made that too much patriotism leads to international conflict. I submit that the United States will never have anything to fear from its ardent and genuinely patriotic citizens. (*Congressional Record*, July 11, 1967, pp. A3466-A3467.)

PATRIOTISM NEEDED. Today, as never before, America has need for men and women who possess the moral strength and courage of our forefathers—modern-day patriots, with pride in our country and faith in freedom, unafraid to declare to anyone in the world, "I believe in liberty. I believe in justice. I will fight, if need be, to defend the dignity of man."

Too often in recent years, patriotic symbols have been shunted aside. Our national heroes have been maligned, our history distorted. Has it become a disgrace to pledge allegiance to our flag—or to sign a loyalty oath, or pay tribute to our national anthem? Is it shameful to encourage our children to memorize the stirring words of the men of '76? Is it becoming opprobrious to state "In God we trust" when proclaiming our love of country?

What we *desperately* need today is patriotism founded on a real understanding of the American ideal—a dedicated belief in our principles of freedom and a determination to perpetuate America's heritage.

The ringing words spoken in 1850 by that great patriot Daniel Webster in the Senate of the United States are as

194

meaningful today as then: "I was born an American; I will live an American; I shall die an American; and I intend to perform the duties incumbent upon me in that character to the end of my career."

These words epitomize the strength of our Republic— the determination of American patriots from Bunker Hill to the Wall of Berlin to uphold and to defend the cause of freedom ("Courage of Free Men," *FBI Law Enforcement Bulletin,* April, 1962, pp 3-4.)

PEACE? Take, for example, the issue of "peace." This topic occupies an important role today in Communist strategy. They proclaim their support for "peace," urging that "peace petitions" be signed. But the Communist "peace" is a phony peace. They utilize this word to mean a peace in which world Communism reigns supreme, a peace in which democracy submits to the overlordship of the Russian dictator. They would have America disarm, render herself powerless. Then the "Communist peace lover" would devour this Nation. ("Make the Communists Show Their Own Colors!," April 14, 1952, p. 2.)

PEACE CORPS ACT. Mr. Lipscomb. What types of new violations, for instance, would be concerned with the Peace Corps Act?

Mr. Hoover. This refers to new work accruing to the FBI as the result of Public Law 87-293, approved September 22, 1961, which provided for the Peace Corps, a new program. This Act provides that if the agency making the investigation of personnel of the Peace Corps develops data reflecting that the person being investigated is of questionable loyalty or is a questionable security risk, the investigating agency shall refer the matter to the FBI for a full field investigation. As indicated by the tabulation presented, we have received thus far as of January 1, 1964, a total of 290 cases for handling as a result of this piece of new legislation.

Mr. Lipscomb. The Disarmament and Arms Control Act shows 41 new violations.

Mr. Hoover. Public Law 87-297, approved September 26, 1961, established a U. S. Arms Control and Disarmament Agency, a new agency. Under the provisions of this Act, the Civil Service Commission—CSC—conducts the applicant in-

195

vestigations regarding personnel of the new agency, but in the event CSC determines the person investigated may be or may become a security risk, or may be of doubtful loyalty, the matter is turned over to the FBI for a full field investigation. Thus far, as of January 1, 1964, a total of 41 cases have been referred to us as a result of this new legislation. (*FBI 1965 Appropriation,* January 29, 1964, pp. 64-65.)

PEACE—LONGING FOR MAY DULL OUR JUDGMENT. I wonder if we may be permitting our sincere and deep-seated longing for a peaceful world to dull our judgment? Certainly, there are many changes taking place today in the Communist world; however, these changes are primarily a rearrangement of the Communist structure to make tyranny more adaptable to the changing conditions of our era. Make no mistake, this attitude of hailing every change inside the Soviet as a sure sign that democracy is flowering behind the Iron Curtain can be dangerous. While I have no argument with efforts to achieve a peaceful world, I do think it would be folly to ignore the fact that we are dealing with individuals whose goal is the destruction of legitimate governments. In our hungry desire for peace, we must guard against being deluded into sacrificing interests that are not ours to give away. Peace cannot be bought by a compromise with evil.

The real issue is freedom—a principle handed down to us by those serious-minded and dedicated men who made a reality of a dream of national sovereignty. It is our solemn obligation to transmit that freedom to posterity—not to barter it away because we may lack the stamina to sustain loyalty to principle. (*Congressional Record,* July 20, 1964, p. A3738)

PEACE WAR. A third and probably the most important plan is the continuation of the so-called peace offensive. Here the Communists are attempting to capitalize on the deep desire of the American people for peace. They would lay sole claim to any real efforts to achieve that goal; yet it is their Soviet masters who make the achievement of world peace so difficult. In order that we may not be misled by Communist peace propaganda, it is important that we understand the Marxist-Leninist distinction between two kinds of peace—lasting peace, obtained only after world revolution; and temporary peace, regarded as a tactical necessity as the tide of revolution ebbs and flows. In short, the peace which figures so prominently in Communist propaganda today is a temporary tactical peace designed to strengthen the Soviet Union and to stupefy its adversaries. ("Where do we Stand Today with Communism in the United States?" *Congressional Record*, March 1, 1954, p. 2297.)

PERMANENT STUDENT COMMITTEE FOR TRAVEL TO CUBA. The Permanent Student Committee for Travel to Cuba was created in the fall of 1962 as the Ad Hoc Student Committee for Travel to Cuba by a movement known as Progressive Labor. Progressive Labor is an extremely militant and leftist organization created by Mortimer Scheer and Milton Rosen. These two individuals and many of the members of Progressive Labor have been expelled from the Communist Party, USA, for disruptive activities.

This Ad Hoc Student Committee for Travel to Cuba attempted to organize a trip to Cuba in December 1962, in defiance of the State Department ban on such travel. This trip did not materialize since the Canadian Government refused clearance to a Cuban airplane which was to be used in transporting the students from Canada to Cuba.

Commencing in April 1963, the committee, with its name changed to the Permanent Student Committee for Travel to Cuba, became active in organizing students to participate in a proposed trip to Cuba in June 1963. It openly indicated that it would test the State Department ban on such travel. An indication of its success is the fact that 59 alleged "students" from 11 States departed on this trip to Cuba on June 25, 1963.

The so-called students ranged in age from 18 to 36 years. Although some were actually attending college, others have been out of college for a number of years. Some have recently graduated while some have dropped out of college and at least one is a college professor. This latter individual is Jose Maria Lima-Rivera, who is a professor at the University of Puerto Rico.

There were no known members of the Communist Party, USA, participating in the trip although many of the individuals who did participate are known to possess Marxist-Leninist views and beliefs. A number of the students were admittedly members of Progressive Labor.

These individuals departed New York City in two groups on June 25, 1963. One group traveled via British Overseas

197

Airways Corporation plane to London and thence to Paris, France. The other group traveled via KLM Royal Dutch Airlines to Amsterdam, Holland, and thence to Paris, France. The entire group then traveled to Prague, Czechoslovakia, on a chartered Czechoslovakian airplane. After a stay of several days in Prague, the group flew by Cubana Airlines to Havana, Cuba, by way of Shannon, Ireland, and Gander, Newfoundland, arriving in Havana, June 29, 1963.

While in Cuba, one member, Hector Warren Hill, died in a swimming pool accident. His body was later returned to his family in New York City.

The entire group was scheduled to leave Cuba about July 27, 1963; however, a number of delays occurred. These were explained by the Cuban Government as being due to crowded travel conditions following the July 26 celebration in Cuba and, later, as being due to the actions of the U. S. Government in pressuring other countries into refusing to allow a Cuban plane to land these students on their soil. These latter charges arose out of actions of the Canadian, Mexican, and Jamaican Governments in refusing entry to these students.

On August 24, 1963, 55 of the students departed Havana for Madrid, Spain, via an Iberia Airlines plane. Three of the group were left in Havana, reportedly due to the pregnant condition of two women and the desire of the alleged husband of one of them to remain with his wife. Of the 55 who left Havana, Barry Hoffman left the group in Bermuda and secured permission from the Government of that Country to proceed directly to New York City. Hoffman has since testified before the House Committee on Un-American Activities and has been very cooperative with Government agents. The other 54 individuals proceeded to Madrid, Spain. It was not until August 29, 1963, that 50 of these students could secure passage to New York City via Iberia Airlines. The 3 persons who had remained in Havana returned to the United States by way of Canada on October 6, 1963. Of the 4 persons who had remained in Madrid, Spain, 3 returned to the United States during October 1963. The whereabouts of the one other person is presently unknown and he presumably is still in Spain.

There is enclosed a chart which depicts the travel of these "students" from New York City to Havana, Cuba, and return to New York City in an extremely roundabout fashion in an attempt to evade the existing ban of the United States on travel to Cuba.

An informant on this trip advised that all expenses (including transportation and living expenses while in Cuba) of these "students" were paid for by the Cuban Government through the Cuban Federation of University Students. Each individual had to pay a registration fee of $10 when filing an application to go on the trip with the Permanent Student Committee for Travel to Cuba. Each individual subsequently had to pay $100 to that organization. The total of $110 was the extent of the cost to each of the individuals participating in this trip to Cuba.

On September 12, 1963, the HCUA continued its hearings into the activities of this organization and the trip to Cuba which it had begun in May 1963. Barry Hoffman, referred to above, was a very cooperative witness. Information was received that individuals from New York City traveled to Washington, D. C., for the express purpose of affording "Support" to the persons under investigation by the HCUA and to create disturbances in the audience to provoke their evictions from the hearing room. These hearings precipitated many outbursts and demonstrations by the spectators which necessitated police action in removing the demonstrators. These removals, in turn, precipitated sit-in demonstrations and street rallies and the usual allegations of police brutality.

On September 27, 1963, a Federal grand jury at New York City returned an indictment against Lee Levi Laub, Phillip Abbott Luce, Stefan Martinot, and Anatol Schlosser, charging them with conspiracy to violate section 1185 (b), title 8, United States Code, as supplemented by a State Department regulation which prohibited travel by American citizens to Cuba without a properly validated passport.

In addition, Laub, Luce, and Martinot were charged in specific counts for departing from the United States and reentering the United States without a properly validated passport. (Schlosser did not participate in the trip to Cuba but was an individual who was actively engaged in making arrangements and recruiting others for the trip.) (*FBI 1965 Appropriation*, January 29, 1964, pp. 48-49.)

PHILBRICK. Answer. I cannot go into techniques. By way of illustration of how and why pictorial records are accom-

199

plished and used, take the case of Herb Philbrick, the Boston advertising man who worked under cover for 9 years in our investigation of the Communists. A two-story brick building on Hancock Street was the blind of the West End Communist Club and a secret Communist teacher-training school.

Philbrick, posing as a Communist in undercover work, attended classes in this building.

Knowing that some day it might become important to prove that Philbrick entered and left this building in company with Communists, we recorded these comings and goings with hidden cameras. (*Pathfinder,* November 5, 1952 in *Congressional Record,* January 26, 1953, reprint.)

POSITIVE EDUCATION NEEDED. Every exposure of communism's false premises, inherent contradictions, deceitful tactics, and empty promises helps to shatter its ideological appeal and to fortify against its psychological pressures. But, in this struggle for men's minds, exposure alone is not enough. Exposure must be complemented by a long-range educational program with a dual purpose. This program must encompass, not only a penetrating study of communism, but also a thorough grounding in the basic principles of our individual freedom under law. This educational program must be designed to train people to think and to distinguish between truth and error. ("Communist Illusion and Democratic Reality," December 1959, p. 5.)

PROGRESSIVE LABOR PARTY. One of the more recently organized and one of the most militant organizations is the Progressive Labor Party. This group was created as the Progressive Labor Movement in early 1962 by individuals who had been expelled from the Communist Party, USA. At the first national convention of the Progressive Labor Movement, held in New York City, April 15-18, 1965, the name of the organization was changed to the Progressive Labor Party.

Utilizing what it considers to be ills of a capitalist society, such as unemployment, poor housing, discrimination, police brutality, un-equal educational opportunities, corruption, poverty, and the alleged indifference of trade union leaders and employers toward the workers, the Progressive Labor Party aggressively and militantly strives to enlarge its organization and develop followers for its goal, a socialist United States based on Marxist-Leninist principles.

The use of Progressive Labor Party-sponsored front groups has been another favorite tactic of this organization. One of its best known fronts has been the Student Committee for Travel to Cuba which organized successful trips to Cuba in 1963 and 1964 in defiance of the State Department ban on such travel. Based upon information developed by the FBI, the Department of Justice presented facts relative to the 1963 trip to a Federal grand jury, Eastern District of New York, Brooklyn, New York, and on September 27, 1963, indictments as to 4 individuals were returned. They were charged with conspiracy to violate section 1185 (b), title 8, United States Code, for organizing this 1963 trip of 59 individuals. Trial of these individuals has been completed and is awaiting the court's decision.

Following the 1964 trip in which 84 persons traveled to Cuba, the Department of Justice obtained indictments against 9 persons on September 22, 1964, in the Eastern District of New York, for conspiracy to organize the 1964 trip in violation of section 1185 (b), title 8, United States Code. These individuals are awaiting trial.

MAY 2 MOVEMENT

Another successful front organization of the Progressive Labor Party is the May 2 Movement which was organized in April 1964, by a group of young people who participated in the Yale Socialist Union conference on "Socialism in America." The original aim of this organization was to plan and execute a demonstration in New York City, on May 2, 1964, to demand withdrawal of United States troops from South Vietnam. Since that time, it has continued in existence and has held a number of demonstrations protesting United States action in Vietnam.

HARLEM DEFENSE COUNCIL

The Harlem Defense Council is basically the creation of Bill Epton, one of the vice presidents of the Progressive Labor Party. This organization was extremely active in the events following the outbreak of rioting in Harlem in July 1964.

As the result of his activity in connection with the Harlem rioting, Epton was arrested on August 5, 1964, on a charge of advocating criminal anarchy. This charge was dismissed on June 7, 1965, and on the same date Epton was rearrested and charged with inciting to riot, conspiracy to riot, advocacy of criminal anarchy, and conspiracy to advocate criminal anarchy. The charge of inciting to riot was subsequently dismissed but on December 20, 1965, Epton was found guilty of the other 3 charges and on January 27, 1966, he was sentenced to prison for 1 year on each count to be served concurrently.

The Progressive Labor Party and the Harlem Defense Council continue their policy of creating hate and distrust of the New York City Police Department and miss no opportunity to hurl charges of brutality and malfeasance against that department. (*FBI 1967 Appropriation,* pp. 50-51.)

PROLETARIAN PARTY OF AMERICA. The Proletarian Party of America, while not a Trotskyite organization, is a revolutionary Marxist group which was formed in 1920. Its purpose is to overthrow the Government of the United States by force and violence. (*Ibid., 1967,* p. 50.)

PROPAGANDA. Measured in terms of its subtlety, diversity, vigor, and extent, the worldwide Communist propaganda campaign must be rated a substantial one. No medium is overlooked in extolling the merits of communism while, at the same time, exploiting social, political, and economic unrest throughout the non-Communist world. Radio, television, motion pictures, and all forms of the printed word are correlated with such tactics as diplomatic measures, trade agreements, offers of economic and technical assistance, and international trade fairs to subject the Free World to a continuous propaganda barrage. Employed in close conjunction and coordination with Communist economic and political machinations, propaganda, one of the most powerful weapons in the Communist arsenal, becomes even more formidable. Woven around the themes of peaceful co-existence and peaceful competition, this campaign of psychological pressure can be expected to increase substantially in both variety and intensity in the years to come.

That the Communists regard the psychological struggle as fundamental is evident not only positively from their vast propaganda effort, but also negatively from their obsession for insulating those they have enslaved from any exposure to what are considered unorthodox—and, therefore, dangerous —influences. ("Communist Illusion and Democratic Reality," December, 1959, pp. 1-2.)

PROPAGANDA MACHINES. Communists have developed one of the greatest propaganda machines the world has ever known. They have been able to penetrate and infiltrate many respectable and reputable public opinion mediums. (HCUA, *Menace of Communism*, March 26, 1947, p. 6.)

PROPAGANDA SPEECHES. Propaganda is another field which occupies much of the Communist officials' time. In the 1962 fiscal year, for example, 193 speeches were scheduled by representatives of Communist-bloc nations. While they have actively sought speaking engagements in this country, they have ignored any suggestions that similar opportunities be offered to American representatives in Communist countries. (*FBI Annual Report, Fiscal Year 1962*, p. 27.)

PUBLICATIONS. For its size, the Communist Party, USA, has distributed more literature than any other subversive organization in this country. Through it, the Party indoctrinates and guides its members and reaches out in widespread efforts to influence the masses. Woven into all the Party's propaganda are basic Communist themes. In one way or another, it stresses the never-ending "class struggle," the necessity for destroying the capitalist system, the claimed overwhelming superiority of communism over all other social orders, and the inevitable triumph of communism in the United States and throughout the world.

I hand to the committee an exhibit which lists the main publications used by the Communist Party, USA, as propaganda media.

Mr. Rooney. We shall insert this sheet entitled "Main Publications Used by CPUSA as Propaganda Media" at this point in the record.

(The matter referred to follows:)

The Communist Party, USA, continues to use as media of propaganda the following publications which have nation-wide distribution:

1. *The Worker*, semiweekly East Coast Communist newspaper.

2. *People's World,* weekly West Coast Communist newspaper.

3. *Political Affairs,* monthly Party theoretical organ.

4. *Mainstream,* monthly Communist cultural organ. (Temporarily suspended from publication in fall 1963; due to be issued again in early 1964.)

5. *Freedomways,* quarterly Marxist Negro review.

6. *Morning Freiheit,* A Communist Yiddish daily newspaper.

7. *Communist Viewpoint,* self-described as a "Publication of the Youth Division, Communist Party, USA."

8. *La Neuva Voz* (The New Voice), Spanish-language newspaper.

9. *Labor Today,* a labor trade-union magazine.

Mr. Hoover. Virtually all of the Party's printed propaganda originates in New York City. The Party's important book-publishing firm there is International Publishers and the principal pamphlet-publishing company is New Century Publishers. From their presses flow waves of Communist propaganda in the form of new Communist books and pamphlets of all types, as well as reprints of articles from the pens of leading Communists here and abroad. (*FBI 1965 Appropriation,* January 29, 1964, pp. 38-39.)

PUBLISHING FIELD — INFILTRATION. In the publishing field, concealed Communists are not so numerous as they were a few years ago, but in some firms they still exert great influence over the printed word.

An editor, who until recently held a high editorial post in a respectable, non-Communist publishing house, provides a good illustration of this type of Red operator. An intelligent and highly educated individual, he had a wide range of contacts with writers, and played an important part in deciding what kind of reading matter his company would provide for the public. He used his strategic position to promote the Communist viewpoint.

This editor was clever enough not to reveal his Red connections or to publish the work of known Communist writers. But he featured the writings of Communist sympathizers and fellow travelers, and encouraged non-Communist authors to prepare articles favorable to Party policies. At the same time, in reviewing manuscripts, he often suggested that pro-Communist material be enlarged upon, but asked that passages unfavorable to the Party line be eliminated or toned down. His work for the Red cause was thus both offensive and defensive. He avoided any open violation of the law, but it is not possible to even speculate on the thousands of readers who were deceived or misinformed by this one Red editor. ("The Communists are After our Minds," *American Magazine*, October, 1954, reprint, pp. 2-3.)

PUERTO RICO. The Nationalist Party of Puerto Rico and other Puerto Rican groups which advocate violence in their drive for independence have been a threat to the internal security of the United States for many years. This danger has increased through the introduction of international communism into the movement and the encouragement being offered by Cuban Dictator Fidel Castro. During 1961, Castro bestowed Cuban citizenship on two Puerto Rican nationalist leaders and immediately appointed them to Cuba's permanent delegation to the United Nations. (*FBI Annual Report, Fiscal Year 1961*, p. 29.)

RACE. As citizens of a free country, we must judge people as individuals—not by race, creed or color.

Legitimate civil rights organizations must remain constantly alert to attempts by the Communists to influence their actions, take over their programs and corrupt their ranks. (*Congressional Record*, December 5, 1963, p. A7435.)

RACE DEMONSTRATIONS AND RIOTS. That Communists are not giving mere lipservice to the dictates of their masters is clearly evidenced in an examination of the many racial activities such as demonstrations, pickets, boycotts, and the like, which have taken place in the recent past. There is hardly an activity in this area that does not have a Communist element present. The degree of Communist participation and influence will, of course, vary from activity to activity but almost always there will be found the Communist at work. We also find Party leaders arrogantly proclaiming the involvment of their "slaves" to Communist dicta. In May 1965, Party leader Gus Hall proclaimed that the Communist movement is making progress in the civil rights field. In June 1965, when it became public knowledge that Communists were active in lengthy demonstrations in Chicago, Illinois, relating to a

205

school segregation protest, 2 party leaders, Claude Lightfoot and James West, issued public statements verifying the presence of Communists in these demonstrations.

The riots in Los Angeles, California, which took place during the period August 11-14, 1965, provided the Communist Party, USA, and other subversives with the means to further blacken the reputation of the United States and to attempt to fan the flame of discontent among the American people.

That the Communists had an ulterior motive in this action was clearly demonstrated in the remarks of one Party functionary who placed the entire blame for the uprising on the white people and proposed to his Party underlings that they take advantage of such riots wherever they occur since riots will eventually lead the United States to socialism. (*FBI 1967 Appropriation*, p. 46.)

RACE—MURDER. The investigation of the murder of Lt. Col. Lemuel A. Penn, which occurred while he and two others were driving along a Georgia road on July 11, 1964, en route to Washington, D. C., involved a peak assignment of 83 agents. Costs incurred in connection with this matter are estimated at $103,090.

We had the full cooperation of the Governor of Georgia as well as the State Highway Patrol. We also had a confession from a co-conspirator. The local jury, however, acquitted the defendants.

Colonel Penn was a Reserve officer and had never been connected with civil rights matters and had been an outstanding teacher in the schools in Washington, D. C. It was cold-blooded murder. (*FBI 1966 Appropriation*, p. 23.)

RACE — SIT-IN. Communist propaganda has always been quick to seize on problems of minority groups. Instances involving the Negro race have been prime targets in this barrage.

The sit-in demonstrations in the South were a made-to-order issue which the Party fully exploited to further its own ends. The Communists first showed an interest in the demonstrations in late February 1960, when James E. Jackson and Joseph North, national Communist Party functionaries, traveled to Richmond, Virginia, and wrote articles for *The Work-*

er, an East Coast Communist weekly newspaper, concerning demonstrations then in progress in Richmond.

Also during early March 1960, Daniel Rubin, national youth director of the Communist Party, USA, visited college campuses in Richmond to obtain statements from students in connection with the demonstrations.

The Communist Party strategy was not to openly advocate picketing, inasmuch as this would tend to expose its members, but rather to get behind the movement by urging college students to take the initiative.

The importance which the Communist Party, USA, has placed on these demonstrations was sharply brought into focus when Benjamin Davis, the Party's national secretary, told the Party in March 1960 that these demonstrations were considered the next best thing to "proletarian revolution." (*FBI 1962 Appropriation,* March 6, 1961, pp. 47-48.)

RACE—STRIFE.   Nowhere have the devious tactics of the Communist Party been more forcefully demonstrated than in the Party's efforts to drive a wide breach of racial misunderstanding in this country and to capitalize upon areas of dissension and unrest.

Let me emphasize that the American civil rights movement is not, and has never been, dominated by the Communists—because the overwhelming majority of civil rights leaders in this country, both Negro and white, have recognized and rejected communism as a menace to the freedoms of all. *But there are notable exceptions*—dangerous opportunists and morally corrupt charlatans who would form an alliance with any organization, regardless of its nature, to advance their own power and prestige.

We must maintain a constant vigil against these imposters, as well as against other zealots who would shortcut the orderly processes of Government and demand a mantle of special privilege under the law. ("Our Heritage of Greatness," December 12, 1964, p. 7.)

The ever-increasing evidences of racial unrest in the country during the past year have witnessed a parallel in the increased emphasis being placed by the Communist Party, USA, on the Negro question and the racial movement generally. There are clear-cut evidences that the Party has not only been "talking," but also has been directing and urging the increased participation by its adherents in the racial movement. As in any similar Party effort at infiltration, where there is participation there is influence in varying degrees.

These Party efforts, though embellished with high-sounding expressions by Party leaders, claiming a sincere interest in the Negro and his problems, are, in reality, just another of the great deceptions practiced by the Party through the years. Theirs is only a single aim; namely, the gaining of Communist objectives looking toward the ultimate goal of the spread of communism throughout the United States. The racial unrest, then, offers the Party a ready-made springboard from which it is able to project its strategy and tactics.

The past year found the Party devoting maximum attention to its efforts to influence civil rights developments. Always alert to exploit discontent and promote disorder, the Party continued to regard the civil rights issue as one facet of the class struggle within the capitalist system. With this Marxist-Leninist analysis as a guide, the Party has as an objective the use of the civil rights issue to create a Negro-labor coalition which it would dominate to advance the cause of communism in the United States. As in the words of the Party's general secretary, Gus Hall, "Jim Crow can be dealt with only by dealing with capitalism."

The Party's involvement in the racial situation is intended to also serve in the all-important task of recruitment. In early June 1964, the Party's national headquarters proposed that headquarters be opened in major cities for the purpose of holding forums. The objective, as explained by a Party functionary, is to organize special study groups to teach "socialism" and thus make it possible for the Party to recruit members from among civil rights fighters. (*FBI 1966 Appropriation*, pp. 58-59.)

RACE — TARGET. The Communists look upon students as potential sympathizers, supporters and contributors to the Party's cause. Nor are they unmindful of the rich opportunity for infiltration presented by unwary racial and nationality groups.

This is especially true of the intense civil rights movement within the United States—for America's 20 million Negroes and the countless other citizens who share their objectives in the current struggle are a priority target for Communist propaganda and exploitation. Every organization engaged in this struggle must constantly remain alert to this vital fact, for, once under communist domination, all freedoms and rights are lost.

The Communists are eager to capitalize upon all areas of misunderstanding and unrest. Their cause is the cause of Soviet Russia . . . ("Keys to Freedom," November 16, 1963, pp. 6-7.)

RADIO AND TV. Other concealed Communists are operating in a number of other publishing concerns, large and small, and still other comrades play a part in deciding what goes on the airwaves.

To cite just one case, all the programs broadcast by a big television station in a southern city are under the direction of a man with a record of Communist activities stretching back for more than 10 years. A former labor agitator in the North, and a leader in Red-front organizations and political campaigns, this individual gave up his open Party affiliations when he moved South and went to work for the television station.

To most of his fellow townsmen he appears to be a patriotic citizen. But the front he puts up is a sham. He still has secret ties with the Party, and a small Communist club comprised of local professional people meets regularly in his home. He is too cagey to put any outright Red propaganda on the air, but, like the Red editor I mentioned, he is in a position where, by the mere choice of the material he uses, and the emphasis or lack of emphasis he places on it, he can subtly shape attitudes in a large audience. ("The Communists Are After Our Minds," *American Magazine*, October, 1954, reprint, p. 3.)

REFORMS. One thing is certain. The American progress which all good citizens seek, such as old age security, houses for veterans, child assistance, and a host of others is being adopted as window dressing by the Communists to conceal their true aims and entrap gullible followers. (HCUA, *Menace of Communism*, March 26, 1947, p. 4.)

REGISTER. The order for the Party to register with the Attorney General became final on October 20, 1961. The deadline of November 20, 1961, passed without compliance, and the obligation then fell upon certain designated Party officers. The second deadline of November 30, 1961, passed, and each member of the Party then became obligated to register himself by December 20, 1961. No registration was filed.

A Federal Grand Jury in Washington, D. C., on December 1, 1961, returned a 12-count indictment charging the Communist Party, USA, with willfully and unlawfully failing to register. A motion to dismiss the indictment was filed.

Individual 6-count indictments against Gus Hall, general secretary of the Party, and Benjamin J. Davis, Jr., national secretary, were returned on March 15, 1962. Motions to dismiss these indictments were pending at the end of the 1962 fiscal year. (*FBI Annual Report*, Fiscal Year 1962, p. 29.)

RELIGION. Communism and religion—like communism and freedom—can never co-exist, for Marxism is unalterably opposed to all forms of religious beliefs. Lenin acknowledged this fact more than 50 years ago when he exhorted his followers, "We must combat religion—this is the A B C of all materialism, and consequently of Marxism." Then he declared, "The Marxist must be . . . an enemy of religion." (*Congressional Record*, December 5, 1963, p. A7434.)

RELIGION—COMMUNISM A FALSE RELIGION The real menace of communism is that it becomes a religion in itself —a religion utterly opposed to Christianity. It has no place for man's soul, for God, for heaven or hell.

Our struggle with communism is more than that of differing political systems. The struggle is essentially religious. Communism attacks all forms of religion that base themselves on belief in God. ("Communism is a False Religion." *Facts Forum News*, December 1955, p. 49.)

Religious people must realize that communism is their great enemy. The zeal of the early Christians overcame paganism in Rome, and civilized the savage gods of the northern barbarians. That same zeal could convert godless Communists. It is up to American Christians to recapture that indomitable spirit and to free the world from this menace. ("Communism is a False Religion," *Facts Forum News*, December, 1955, p. 49.)

RELIGION — IMPORTANCE. There are important lessons to be learned in the pages of American history. From Faneuil

Hall to Cape Canaveral, our greatest patriots have been men and women of deep religious conviction: Men like Thomas Jefferson, the principal author of our Declaration of Independence, who told his fellow colonists, "The God who gave us life, gave us liberty at the same time."

In the eyes of a latter-day hero, "Freedom, devotion to God and country are not things of the past. They will never become old-fashioned." These words were spoken by Astronaut John H. Glenn.

America remains free because men of *faith*, men of *individualism*, men of *courage*, men of *integrity*, men of *discipline* and men of *vision* have patrolled her most vital outposts for 187 years.

These strong qualities—Faith, Individualism, Courage, Integrity, Discipline and Vision—are the keys to freedom. ("Keys to Freedom," November 16, 1963, pp. 13-14.)

RELIGION—INFILTRATION. I confess to a real apprehension so long as Communists are able to secure ministers of the gospel to promote their evil work and espouse a cause that is alien to the religion of Christ and Judaism. (HCUA, Menace of Communism, 1947, p. 11.)

RELIGION—OPIATE. Last year, the official Soviet newspaper, *Isvestia,* openly declared, "The narcotic of religion must be combated with skill and persistence. Our ideology will never compromise with religion." These same views are shared by the Communist Party, USA, a group of fanatically pro-Soviet conspirators led by a Moscow-trained ex-convict who constitute the largest subversive organization in our Nation today. ("Faith or Fear," *Congressional Record,* June 28, 1960, p. 13653.)

REPUBLIC OF NEW AFRICA. The Republic of New Africa was formed in Detroit, Mich., March 30-31, 1968, at a conference sponsored by the Malcolm X Society. Representatives from throughout the United States were in attendance. The announced purpose of the organization is to establish a black nation within the United States composed of the States of Alabama, Georgia, Louisiana, Mississippi, and South Carolina, as well as ghetto areas in large cities.

It elected as its president-in-exile Robert F. Williams, a militant black nationalist and a fugitive from a North Carolina kidnaping charge who fled to Cuba in 1961 and then moved on to Peking, China, in 1966. He traveled to Tanzania, Africa, in May 1968 and returned to China in September 1968.

Two leaders and principal architects of the Republic of New Africa, Milton Henry, an attorney from Pontiac, Mich., and his brother, Richard Bullock Henry, a former civilian employee of the U. S. Army at Detroit, Mich., traveled to Tanzania in June 1968 for the purpose of meeting with Williams to map plans for furthering the formation of the Republic of New Africa.

In the spring of 1968, a pamphlet was distributed containing instructions on how to make explosives of various types, including Molotov cocktails, as well as ways to use these against such military vehicles as an Army tank.

This organization has attempted to buy land in Mississippi on which they hope to establish a colony which will gain control of the State by electing their people to the sheriffs' offices. Through this foothold, they will take over the entire State and then in turn the States of Louisiana, Alabama, Georgia, and South Carolina. They have established consulates in Chicago, Cincinnati, Cleveland, Dayton, Detroit, Indianapolis, Los Angeles, and New York City.

The Republic of New Africa (RNA) has established a political arm known as the Afro-American Liberation Party and a military arm known as the Black Legion. The Black Legion will consist of an overt uniformed army to protect RNA property and citizens and a covert or underground army to attack enemies of the nation.

On March 29, 1969, at the conclusion of a session of the second national convention of the RNA held in the New Bethel Baptist Church in Detroit, Mich., individuals apparently acting as bodyguards for Milton Henry opened fire on two policemen, killing one and critically wounding the other.

After the shooting began, RNA members reentered the church where some individuals fired from windows on additional police called to the scene. When the police forced their way into the church these individuals dropped their weapons and mingled with the crowd; 153 persons were arrested and police confiscated three shotguns, two rifles, and one .32 caliber handgun from inside the church. Five RNA members were wounded and hospitalized. A recorder's court judge released 151 of those arrested including some on whom a paraffin test proved they had recently fired weapons, the judge giving as the basis for release the fact that subjects were denied their constitutional rights in that the tests were performed prior to their being advised of their right to counsel. The two remaining were held on carrying concealed weapons charges with one additionally charged with assault with intent to commit murder. (FBI, 1970 Appropriation, April 17, 1969, pp. 70-71.)

REVOLUTION. The Communist, once he is fully trained and indoctrinated, realizes that he can create his order in the United States only by "bloody revolution."

Their chief textbook, "The History of the Communist Party of the Soviet Union," is used as a basis for planning their revolution. Their tactics require that to be successful they must have:

1. The will and sympathy of the people.
2. Military aid and assistance.
3. Plenty of guns and ammunition.
4. A program of extermination of the police as they are the most important enemy and are termed trained fascists.
5. Seizure of all communications, buses, railroads, radio stations and other forms of communications and transportation.

They evade the question of force and violence publicly. They hold that when Marxists speak of force and violence they will not be responsible—that force and violence will be the responsibility of their enemies. They adopt the novel premise that they do not advocate force and violence publicly but when their class resists to defend themselves then they are thus accused of using force and violence. (HCUA, Menace of Communism, 1947, p. 3.)

REVOLUTION—OURS. Let us also work for a revolution— a revolution by the spirit, not by the sword. Let there be vital forces at work in our society and not merely slogans. Let us be for America all the way; but, at the same time, let us not be taken in by those who promote hysteria by the distortion and misrepresentation of the true facts whether they be the proponents of chauvinism of the extreme right or pseudo-liberalism of the extreme left. ("The Faith to be Free," December 7, 1961, p. 7.)

REVOLUTIONARY ACTION MOVEMENT (RAM)

RAM is a black extremist organization oriented toward the Chinese Communist interpretation of Marxism-Leninism. Its leader, Max Stanford of Philadelphia, was in prison from July 1967 to May 1968, and is now a fugitive from justice in both Philadelphia, Pa., and New York City. Although RAM has not been active as an organization because of Stanford's troubles with the law, the amount of RAM literature being distributed increased after he was released from prison in May 1968. There are reports of a possible merger of RAM and the Republic of New Africa (RNA), a Detroit organization advocating the establishment of a separate black nation in five Southern States. Robert F. Williams, a fugitive from justice who fled to Cuba and then to Communist China, who now reportedly wants to return to the United States, is associated with both groups. The membership of RAM is less than 50, most of whom are in Philadelphia and New York City. (FBI, 1970 Appropriation, April 17, 1969, p. 71.) See also BLACK MUSLIM.

RIOTS. The diabolical influence of communism on youth was manifested in the anti-American student demonstrations in Tokyo. It further was in evidence this year in Communist-inspired riots in San Francisco, where students were duped into disgraceful demonstrations against a Congressional committee.

These students were stooges of a sinister technique stimulated by clever Communist propagandists who remained quietly concealed in the background. These master technicians of conspiracy had planned for some time to use California college students as a "front" for their nefarious operations. This outburst was typical of these cunning conspirators who constantly play active, behind-the-scenes roles in fomenting civic unrest in every conceivable area of our society. ("America— Freedom's Champion," October 18, 1960, p. 5.)

RIOTS — 1964. A number of charges have been made that various organizations instigated the riots in one city or another. These charges were carefully investigated. The evidence indicates that aside from the actions of minor organizations or irresponsible individuals, there was no systematic planning or organization of any of the city riots.

Following several civil rights demonstrations which received widespread publicity throughout the country earlier in 1964, one widely publicized ex-convict, the late Malcolm X Little, in March 1964, announced a broadly-based nationalist movement, the Muslim Mosque, Inc., for Negroes only. In this announcement, which was frequently repeated, Negroes were urged to abandon the doctrine of nonviolence and to organize rifle clubs "to protect their lives and property."

Shortly after the arrest in Philadelphia, Pennsylvania, on August 28, 1964, leading up to the riots there, a well-known Negro agitator, Abyssinia Hayes, a leader of a small splinter Black Nationalist group, got on the porch of a house and allegedly harangued the crowd urging them to violence against the police officers, charging that they had brutally abused the Negro woman arrested.

Another group seeking to exploit Negro unrest was the Progressive Labor Movement (PLM), a Marxist-Leninist group following the more violent Chinese Communist line. One of its organizers, Milton Rosen, is a former secretary of the New York State Communist Party, USA, (CPUSA). Following the shooting in New York on July 16, the PLM under the leadership of this individual printed and had distributed thousands of copies of a handbill containing a photograph of the police lieutenant under the headline "Wanted for Murder." At the time the handbill was distributed throughout the Harlem area a mass demonstration was announced for July 25 to demand the arrest and prosecution of the lieutenant.

Another officer of the PLM, William Epton, also a former member of the CPUSA who resigned from the Party because it was not sufficiently revolutionary, organized a number of groups in the Harlem area in New York City early in the summer. These groups, offshoots of PLM, were to be prepared to exploit incidents and were alerted to that end. Two days after the shooting above referred to, this individual harangued a street meeting in New York City announcing there was going to be a demonstration, "not necessarily peaceful," that he and his followers "were going to kill cops and judges," that "no revolution can be won by peaceful means" and that this state must be smashed "totally and completely."

Jesse Gray, a Negro who formerly was the organizer of the Harlem region of the CPUSA, achieved a widespread publicity early in 1964 through leadership of rent strikes. Three days after the shooting on July 16, this individual issued a public call for "a hundred skilled black revolutionaries who are ready to die" to correct what he called "police brutality."

Two individuals with histories of Communist affiliation Clarence Coggins and Richard Sarjeant, while not starting the riots, capitalized on them in at least two of the cities in New Jersey and tried to continue them. Coggins is chairman of the Labor Negro Vanguard Conference, a local group in New Jersey with only a few members, organized in 1961 by Coggins who, along with other of its active members, was expelled from the CPUSA in 1959, following a factional dispute. Neither Coggins nor Sarjeant appears to be more than a local and comparatively unimportant independent agitator.

The CPUSA does not appear to have officially instigated these riots though its members were observed taking part in some and its former members are leaders of the PLM, the Labor Negro Vanguard Conference and other such groups. (FBI 1966 Appropriation, pp. 42-43.)

ROSENBERG. We all know of the traitors Julius and Ethel Rosenberg, Jack Soble, of Martin and Mitchell and others who have betrayed our country. Their crimes against humanity are so unspeakable as to warrant no further mention other than to use them as examples of the perfidy against which we must be constantly alert. ("America—Freedom's Champion," October 18, 1960, p. 4.)

SAN FRANCISCO RIOTS. In May 1960, the House Committee on Un-American Activities scheduled hearings in San Francisco, California, to inquire into the activities of the northern California district of the Party. This was an opportunity which the Party had been anxiously anticipating and, when the hearing dates were announced, its machinery was thrown into high gear to infiltrate and exploit protest demonstrations and picket lines to nullify the work of this Congressional Committee.

A most significant single factor surrounding the mob demonstration was the Communist infiltration of student and youth groups engaged in protest demonstrations against this Congressional Committee. Through this infiltration, Communists revealed how it is possible for only a few Communist agitators, using mob psychology, to convert peaceful demonstrations into riots.

216

The success of the Party's strategy was vividly demonstrated by the violence which erupted at the San Francisco City Hall where the Committee hearings were held. The San Francisco debacle was not an accident. It was the result of minute and skillful planning, direction and exploitation by a handful of dedicated, fanatical, hard-core members of the Communist Party, USA. (FBI 1962 Appropriation, March 6, 1961, p. 48.)

Not to be overlooked in the organized attack that was carried out against the HCUA are organized activities that paralleled those of the Party. Much of the literature that was distributed during the campaign, for example, emanated in the name of the Citizens Committee To Preserve American Freedoms (CCPAF) and the East Bay Community Forum (EBCF). According to a Party official, both of these organizations are under control of the Communist Party.

Meanwhile, the Party had not ignored the second stage of its campaign. Plans had been formed on various ways the Party could inflame the emotions of the demonstrators. Several days before the hearings were to begin, Saul Wachter, one of the Party members subpoenaed, told Party members that HCUA would encounter "plenty of opposition" and the demonstrations would be staged against the committee. Other reports were received that Merle Brodsky and Archie Brown planned physical outbursts during the hearings so that they would be forcibly ejected and thus enabled to play on the sympathies of the students.

Officials of the Party met with and briefed various witnesses on the tactics to use in their appearances before the Committee. On May 6, 1960, for example, Mickey Lima told Party members he had met with Leibel Bergman, Andy Negro, and Vern Bown to insure that they would be hostile witnesses. Archie Brown, a veteran longshoreman and former member of the Party's national committee, also disclosed to Party members another tactic the Party planned to use in the mob. A few key Party members were to play major roles as agitators. The other Party members who were to attend had been instructed to remain in the background as much as possible to avoid becoming involved in any violence which might erupt.

As soon as the hearings began, Party members began playing their predetermined roles. The belligerent and insult-

217

ing behavior of some of the 36 uncooperative witnesses was so aggravating it became necessary to order their forcible removal from the hearing room to preserve order and decorum. Archie Brown and Merle Brodsky, acting according to plan, were sullen and contemptuous. Both directed vicious and personally insulting remarks at the members of the Committee.

An organized clique of sympathizers in the hearing room aided them in their roles. Approximately 25 percent of the spectators in the room were individuals under subpoena and their relatives, friends, attorneys, and sympathizers. This group applauded and cheered the antics of Brown and Brodsky and booed, hissed, and ridiculed the Committee at every opportunity. Archie Brown's disruptive tactics became so intense that it was necessary to forcibly remove him from the scene. This was exactly what Brown had been striving to achieve in line with his plan to evoke sympathy from the crowd.

After the luncheon recess, Brown and Brodsky went into action again. Shortly before the afternoon session was to begin, they grabbed a microphone at the front of the hearing room and demanded that all spectators outside be admitted. Their sympathizers shouted similar demands. After refusing to obey orders to be seated, Brown, Brodsky, and several others were forcibly removed, each resisting violently. Brown attempted to strike two officers, and Douglas Wachter threw a briefcase at an officer attempting to remove his father, Saul Wachter.

Brown's plan to incite the crowd was beginning to materialize. Upon his ejection from the hearing room, sympathetic cheers went up from the crowd, consisting mostly of students, gathered inside City Hall at the head of the staircase leading to the room. Both Brown and Brodsky appealed to the crowd, Brodsky encouraging and leading it in chanting "Open the doors; open the doors!"

Despite these disruptive tactics, police were able to maintain a semblance of order that first day. It was a different story on the following day. As a result of mushrooming interest generated by the activities of the first day, the crowd on the second day was much larger. A particularly noticeable aspect of the increase was the presence of additional Party members and former Party members.

Archie Brown quickly resumed his tactics of the day before once the sessions started. The crowd outside the hearing room chanted and sang songs. The songs and chants were obviously part of a well-organized plan as illustrated by the song sheets being used. Pleas for order and quiet brought only jeers.

With the tension growing, the inevitable happened. Violence flared that afternoon. One of the judges in a municipal courtroom in City Hall ordered the mob dispersed because the noise made it impossible for him to hold court. When an attempt was made to carry out the order, the crowd responded by throwing shoes and jostling the officers. An officer warned that fire hoses would have to be used if the crowd did not disperse, but the crowd, instigated by Communists who had maneuvered themselves into strategic positions, became more unruly.

One of the demonstrators provided the spark that touched off the flame of violence. Leaping a barricade that had been erected, he grabbed an officer's night stick and began beating the officer over the head. The mob surged forward as if to storm the doors, and a Police Inspector ordered the fire hose turned on. The water forced the crowd to the head of the balustrade, and the cold water had a sobering effect on the emotions of the demonstrators.

For a few minutes, relative quiet ensued. Taking advantage of the lull, police officers began to lead some of the demonstrators away, advising them that they must obey the order to disperse. Suddenly, realizing what was happening, militant individuals in the group set the pattern for renewed violence by kicking and striking the officers. In all, 68 individuals, most of whom were students, were arrested for inciting a riot and resisting arrest.

Order had been restored when Harry Bridges, president of the International Longshoremen's and Warehousemen's Union, suddenly appeared on the scene. Demanding to know what part firemen had played in the use of the fire hoses, Bridges commented that he would see if the firemen's pay could be cut. The day's activities closed with Archie Brown joining Bridges and shouting, "You tell them, Harry; they'll listen to you."

More mob violence was narrowly averted on the third day of the hearings. An attorney from Oakland, Bertram Edises, who was one of a number of attorneys the Party had obtained to represent those subpoenaed and who was to testify himself in response to a subpoena he had received, became arrogant and insulting in his appearance before the Committee. His attacks on and arguments with the Committee led to an order for his removal. The crowd, both in the hearing room and outside, had been relatively quiet and peaceful until then.

Suddenly aroused, the crowd surged threateningly toward the entrance to City Hall. Committee members were escorted by police officers out a rear exit as a cordon of uniformed officers, including motorcycle patrolmen and mounted officers, held back the angry demonstrators. The crowd, which by then consisted of about 2,000, continued to mill around the area for an hour, despite the fact that an announcement was made by loudspeaker that the HCUA staff had departed. (HCUA, Communist Target—Youth, Communist Infiltration and Agitation Tactics, 1960, pp. 6-9.)

With this setting, it is possible to reveal how the Communist Party plan of attack unfolded. It will be seen that the plan had two important objectives and unfolded in two stages to accomplish them. The first objective of the Party was to fill the scene of the hearings with demonstrators. The second was to incite them to action through the use of mob psychology.

The first stage of the Party's plan of action began to unfold after word was received on April 26, 1960, by Party officials that subpoenas had been issued for local Communists to appear for the hearings scheduled to take place May 12-14, 1960. One of the recipients of a subpoena was Douglas Wachter, an 18-year-old sophomore at the University of California. Wachter, incidentally, had attended the 17th National Convention of the Communist Party in December 1959 as an official delegate from northern California.

Party officials decided to build a major part of their plan of attack around Wachter. Immediately after receiving a subpoena, Wachter proceeded to the University of California campus to organize student demonstrators. Mickey Lima, chairman of the Northern California District of the Communist Party, instructed Roscoe Proctor, a member of the district committee, to also contact certain students at the University of California and enlist their support. Lima was assured that student support would be forthcoming from Santa Rosa Junior College in Santa Rosa, California. His contact at San Francisco State College, the son of a current member of the Sonoma County Communist Party, was equally enthusiastic in promising support. (*Ibid.,* pp. 4-5.)

We have but to look at the shameful riots in San Francisco in 1960 when college youth in that area, encouraged by Communists, acted like common hoodlums in demonstrating against a committee of the U. S. Congress engaged in public business. ("An American's Challenge," *Congressional Record,* October 10, 1962, p. A7517.)

SAN FRANCISCO RIOTS — COMMUNIST SUCCESS. The Communist Party, USA, is elated with the success it enjoyed in attempting to make a fiasco of the HCUA San Francisco hearings, which, notwithstanding these attempts at disruption, did develop valuable and needed information concerning the strategy, tactics, and activities of the Party in northern California. The Party's elation is so great, in fact, that it bears witness to the truth of the observation that such a Communist coup has not occurred in the San Francisco area in 25 years. Immediately after the affair ended, the Party's national leader, Gus Hall, congratulated the West Coast comrades for the initiative and leadership they displayed at all stages of the demonstrations.

Particularly pleasing to Party officials was the number of students involved in the demonstrations. They commented that there had not been that much "political activity" among student groups for years. Archie Brown, especially, was commended for the tremendous job he had done among the students, working with them in the corridors of City Hall and winning their sympathy.

Mickey Lima expressed his pleasure at the number of former Party members the affair had brought back into the fold. He said that individual supporters the Party had not seen or heard of in years seemed to "emerge from the woodwork" in response to the Party's campaign.

Various Party functionaries on the West Coast reported that the successful demonstrations had a noticeable effect on lukewarm Party members. One party official commented that it was a "shot in the arm" for the Party, as shown by the fact that attendance at club meetings had risen sharply.

The management of the Party's West Coast publication, *People's World,* was jubilant about the beneficial effect the

221

demonstrations had had upon a fund drive being conducted for the newspaper. The paper reportedly received letters from individuals throughout this country, as well as from others abroad, supporting the drive.

In short, the consensus in the Communist Party was that the riot was the best thing for the Party that had occurred in years. Party leaders expressed the opinion that it was especially significant that the Party had been able to enlist the support of so many people in all walks of life when the Party, itself, was publicly under attack by the HCUA. The feeling was that not only had the Party taken a major step toward its goal of abolishing the HCUA, but also it had taken a major step toward playing a greater role on the American scene. (HCUA, *Communist Target—Youth, Communist Infiltration and Agitation Tactics,* 1960, p. 9.)

SAN FRANCISCO RIOTS—WHAT WE CAN LEARN. While it must be granted that the San Francisco riot at the HCUA hearings was the best thing that had happened for the benefit of the Communist Party in years, Americans, too, can benefit from this display of Communist strategy and tactics in operation. In fact, it is impossible to stand idly by in the face of the challenge that this Communist success represents.

The Communists demonstrated in San Francisco just how powerful a weapon Communist infiltration is. They revealed how it is possible for only a few Communist agitators, using mob psychology, to turn peaceful demonstrations into riots. Their success there must serve as a warning that their infiltration efforts aimed not only at the youth and student groups, but also at our labor unions, churches, professional groups, artists, newspapers, government, and the like, can create chaos and shatter our internal security.

The Communists also demonstrated that the menace of communism is not a simple forthright threat. Instead, it is conspiracy which can be controlled only through full understanding of the true nature of the conspiracy and the ability to separate truth from propaganda. Seen in the true reporting of the facts, the San Francisco incident exposes the conspiratorial nature of the Party. Every such exposure of the tactics of communism can be used to destroy its ideological appeal and used to strengthen this Nation against the psychological pressures Communists constantly apply against every aspect of our society to weaken us.

Throughout the world today, governments are toppling with stunning rapidity. Whether large or small, the role Communists are playing in these events must not be discounted. The growing strength of our Nation over the years has not proven a deterrent to relentless efforts on the part of the Communist Party, USA, to destroy our security and prepare our Nation for a similar fate.

Looking at the riots and chaos Communists have created in other countries, many Americans point to the strength of our Nation and say "It can't happen here." The Communist success in San Francisco in May 1960 proves that it can happen here. (*Ibid.*, pp. 10-11.)

SAVIO, MARIO. Mr. Rooney. What is the background of the chap who went out there from New York City and led that riot?

Mr. Hoover. Mario Savio?

Mr. Rooney. Yes.

Mr. Hoover. Savio was born December 8, 1942, at New York City, New York. He attended Manhattan College in New York City until 1963 when he enrolled at the University of California at Berkeley.

San Francisco Police Department records show Savio was arrested March 8, 1964, during the Palo Hotel "sit-in" demonstration in San Francisco and was subsequently acquitted on a charge of disturbing the peace on May 12, 1964.

At a hearing in municipal court, Berkeley, California, for some of the defendants of the Free Speech Movement, each defendant was given an opportunity to ask questions regarding a motion to waive jury trial.

Mario Savio was asked by the judge if he understood what was meant by waiving of trial by jury. Savio answered, "I understand fully the shameless hypocrisy to which this court has been reduced." The judge asked Savio to repeat this statement which he did, more loudly and clearly. The judge held Savio in contempt of court and sentenced him to 2 days in jail, effective immediately. The defense attorneys requested postponement of the execution of sentence and the judge agreed that Savio would serve two days in jail beginning 9 A. M. March 4, 1965. (*FBI 1966 Appropriation*, p. 45.)

SECULARISM. Today, the forces of materialism are directing their most concentrated power against the very wellsprings of our strength. The forward march of secularism is visible in many areas. It is apparent in much of what we read and much of what we view. The promotion of the sensual seems to be the purpose of whole shelves of books and magazines. On every hand, deliberate pandering to the lower instincts is apparent. Innuendo permeates once wholesome publications. Movie ads and paperbacks flaunt violence and sexuality. Sex, brutality, and sadism are too often emphasized unduly on both television and movie screens. Moral degenerates spew forth a surreptitious torrent of outright obscenity in the form of films, playing cards, comic books, paperbacks, and pictures. (*"What Does the Future Hold?" Christianity Today,* June 19, 1961, reprint, p. 2.)

SELF INDULGENCE. Crime and subversion are formidable problems in the United States today because, and only because, there is a dangerous flaw in the Nation's moral armor. Self-indulgence—the principle of pleasure before duty—is undermining those attributes of personal responsibility and self-discipline which are essential to our national survival. (*"Our Heritage of Greatness,"* December 12, 1964, p. 1.)

SHERGALIS, WILLIAM J. Also during the 1963 fiscal year, William J. Shergalis was convicted for violating the Foreign Agents Registration Act. Shergalis was the copilot of a small plane allegedly shot down in March 1960, in Cuba while attempting to smuggle anti-Castro Cubans out of the country. Investigation revealed the incident was staged by Castro Agents with Shergalis' cooperation so that the United States could be charged with permitting illegal flights over Cuba. Shergalis was arrested in January 1962, when he returned to this country. He was sentenced on July 6, 1962, to a Federal correctional institution for observation for up to three months, and on November 6, 1962, was ordered placed on probation for three years. (*FBI Annual Report, Fiscal Year 1963* p. 28.)

SMEAR. They employ high-sounding, deceitful phrases, and pin the label "Redbaiter," "reactionary," or "Hitlerite" on all who reject their doctrines. Anyone who opposes the Soviet Union is a "Fascist," "imperialist" or "monopoly capitalist."

The Communist brigades of swindlers and confidence men extol democracy but when they do they are speaking of Communism and not the American brand of democracy. ("How to Fight Communism," *Newsweek,* June 9, 1947, reprint.)

SMITH ACT OF 1940. Most prosecutions of Communist Party members have come under the Smith Act of 1940. This Act prohibits the teaching and advocating of the overthrow of the United States Government by force and violence as well as membership in an organization which so teaches with knowledge of the aims of the group.

Since 1949, 104 Party leaders have been convicted on charges of conspiring to teach and advocate the overthrow of the Government and five others have been convicted under the membership provision of the Act. A Supreme Court decision in 1957, however, resulted in most of the conspiracy convictions being reversed with acquittals or retrials being ordered. Indictments against most defendants ordered retried have been dismissed. Only 29 of the convicted communists actually served prison sentences, one of whom was still in prison at the close of the 1961 fiscal year.

The Supreme Court in June, 1961, upheld the conviction of one defendant convicted under the membership provision of the Smith Act and reversed another. (*FBI Annual Report, Fiscal Year 1961,* p. 27.)

SOCIALISM. In combatting the encroachment of socialism and communist espionage, America must adhere to the laws of God and man. As a result, our fight is doubly difficult because of the communists' reckless disregard of the code of morality. ("America—Freedom's Champion," October 18, 1960, p. 4.)

We cannot defeat communism with socialism, nor with secularism, nor with pacifism, nor with appeasement or accommodation. We can only defeat communism with true Americanism. ("An American's Challenge," *Congressional Record,* October 10, 1962, p. A7518.)

SOCIALIST WORKERS PARTY. The Socialist Workers Party was the first major group to oppose the Communist Party, USA, for the right to lead an American Communist revolution. It is the largest Trotskyite organization in the United States. Factionalism within the Socialist Workers

Party itself has spawned other groups, who while following the teachings of Trotsky, differ with the Socialist Workers Party over the means to be utilized in the attainment of a workers' world and a classless society. Among such offshoots of the Socialist Workers Party are the Johnson-Forest Group, the Workers World Party, the American Committee for the Fourth International, and the Revolutionary Committee of the Fourth International. (*FBI 1967 Appropriation*, p. 50.)

SPIES AND U. S. The subversive role of the Communist Party, USA, is but one aspect of the Communist threat to the internal security of our Nation. The other is the espionage and intelligence attacks mounted against this country by the Communist-bloc countries. Underlying both aspects of the threat to our internal security from the international Communist movement is the fact that we are competing with a totalitarian system, intent on our destruction, which operates the most extensive networks of subversion and espionage ever developed in history.

In regard to the Communist-bloc espionage attack against this country, there has been no letup whatsoever. Historically, the Soviet intelligence services have appropriated the great bulk of official positions abroad, primarily using their official representation and diplomatic establishments in other countries as bases from which to carry on their espionage operations. Over the years, the number of such official personnel assigned to the United States has steadily increased.

An accompanying and growing problem is the extent to which the Soviet intelligence services are dispatching undercover spies into the United States. Unless uncovered, they will eventually serve as the nucleus of an extensive clandestine espionage network. Another problem which requires a wider coverage in our counter-intelligence work is the current emphasis being placed by the Soviet-bloc intelligence services on the utilization of bases in other countries in directing their intelligence attacks against this country.

Such factors as these indicate the need for increased coverage in this area of our operations. (*FBI 1966 Appropriation*, p. 15.) See also Espionage.

STAKES. I have the deepest faith in the future of America. Communists are driven by fanaticism, selfish ambition and an urgency to dominate and destroy all that is good. They endeavor to subvert the minds, the bodies and the souls of men. But in the end they are destined to fail because they are blind slaves of a human tyranny—not servants of God. They are puppets of a dictator, not free men and women.

Should the spirit of free men die—our Nation would no longer survive. To keep that spirit alive is the task of every true American. This means that truth must prevail in every walk of life and there must be a dedication to fight if need be to maintain that truth. The truth is that the American way of life is the hope of the world; we can have no more sacred trust than to preserve that way—of Life, Liberty and the Pursuit of Happiness.

We are fighting together for God and Country. In the end we shall win. So keep up your courage. Keep up your fight for God and Country. Millions of good Americans support you. ("Remarks before the Continental Congress of the National Society Daughters of the American Revolution," April 22, 1954, p. 4.)

STALIN—LINE CHANGE ON. The Communist leopard frequently changes his spots, but the same blood—bad blood —continuously flows through his veins.

Recently, we have witnessed another spectacular about-face in the Communist line. Joseeph Stalin, who ranked with Marx, Engels, and Lenin as an untouchable saint in the godless Soviet temple, has been exposed by his own worshippers as a power-crazed tyrant, a pathological fraud, and a cold-hearted executioner.

When Moscow broadcast this new Party line, Communists throughout the world were quick to comply. Here in the United States, the Communist Party made a new entry in its ledger: Joseph Stalin, whom it had openly proclaimed as the greatest man of his generation, was less than mortal —his feet were of clay.

To the uninformed, this is truly a remarkable development. Such drastic changes of opinion usually are developed over a long period of time. Yet, this should have been no surprise coming from a movement which has no moral principles, which lives by expediency, and which will make any move to advance the Communist cause. (HCUA, *The Great Pretense*, 1956, p. 172.)

STAND FOR SOMETHING. In the fight to preserve our Republic, it is not enough merely to be *against* crime, *against* subversion or *against* any of the other enemies which weaken the Nation's strength from within. To stand *for* the American ideal, to work *for* the cause of liberty and justice—these give true meaning to life in this great Republic.

If we are to effectively resist the eroding influence of communism, it is imperative that all citizens of this Nation exhibit in more positive ways the value and superiority of our form of Government over any foreign ideology. ("The Faith to be Free," December 7, 1961, p. 7.)

Unfortunately, some people try to resolve the problem by falling into the very error the Communists are so careful to avoid: They concentrate on the negative rather than the positive. They are *against* communism without being *for* freedom. They are *against* ignorance without being *for* education. They are *against* sin without being *for* God.

It might be well for these persons to realize that Hitler was also against communism. However, what he *stood for* is the basis of history's judgment. (*FBI Law Enforcement Bulletin*, October 1961.)

STUDENTS FOR A DEMOCRATIC SOCIETY. One of the most militant organizations now engaged in activities protesting U. S. foreign policy is a student youth group called Students for a Democratic Society. Communists are actively promoting and participating in the activities of this organization, which is self-described as a group of "liberals and radicals." This organization currently claims a membership in excess of 3,000 in over 100 chapters throughout the United States, and its members are most vocal in condemning the American way of life and our established form of Government.

This organization sponsored a march on Washington to protest U. S. action in Vietnam which took place on April 17, 1965. Communists throughout the Nation participated in this march and over 70 past or present Communist Party members from New York City alone, including

228

several national leaders, were observed among the participants.

A national convention of this organization was held at a camp near Kewadin, Michigan, in June 1965. Practically every subversive organization in the United States was represented by delegates to this convention. There were delegates from the Young Socialist Alliance, the youth and training section of the Trotskyite Socialist Workers Party, which has been designated as subversive pursuant to Executive Order 10450.

Also represented were the Communist Party, USA, and the Spartacist group, a Trotskyite splinter organization. Other delegates represented the Progressive Labor Party, a Marxist-Leninist organization following the line of Communist China, and the May 2 Movement, a front group of the Progressive Labor Party.

At this convention, a number of proposals were made to further oppose the U. S. action in Vietnam. One Students for a Democratic Society leader called for deliberate violation of the sedition statutes by Students for a Democratic Society members which it was hoped would result in mass arrests and a "political trial" of the organization. Members were urged to attempt to enter military bases to persuade soldiers that they should refuse to fight in Vietnam.

At a meeting of the national council, the governing body of the Students for a Democratic Society which was held over the 1965 Labor Day weekend, 20 of the approximately 100 participants had past or present affiliations with the Communist Party or other subversive groups. A vigorous anti-draft program was proposed at this meeting, which included plans to counsel draft-age youth on how to avoid the draft. This proposal was later submitted to the Students for a Democratic Society membership by referendum for approval but was defeated by a narrow majority.

In spite of this, Students for a Democratic Society leaders recently announced that each local chapter would make its own decisions as to whether an antidraft program would be undertaken by that particular chapter.

During the last week of December 1965, the antidraft program and the Vietnam protest movement again were subjects which dominated discussions at a national membership conference of this group held at Urbana, Illinois. Heated exchanges took place between various factions, some of which wanted to continue with a "hard line" and others wanting to retreat entirely from all protest activity in connection with the Vietnam issue. Although no foreign policy decisions resulted from this conference, the Students for a Democratic Society has continued to sponsor and participate in demonstrations throughout the United States protesting U. S. action in Vietnam.

THE PARTY AND VIETNAM

The Communist Party, USA, held a 3-day meeting of its national committee and invited guests from January 15 through January 17, 1966, in New York City. Gus Hall, general secretary of the Party, in discussing the Vietnam situation, cited the growing peace movement in this country as evidence that the people are becoming more discontented with U. S. policy toward Vietnam. He stressed the need for the Communist Party to become more active in the protest movement against U. S. policy.

Herbert Aptheker, a member of the Communist Party national committee, spoke concerning his recent visit to Hanoi with Asst. Prof. Staughton Lynd of Yale University and Thomas Hayden, a founder and an official of Students for a Democratic Society, a youth group with heavy Communist infiltration. Lynd is a former member of American Youth for Democracy, which has been designated as subversive by the Attorney General pursuant to Executive Order 10450.

Aptheker announced that he had met with the Central Committee of the Communist Party of North Vietnam. At this meeting, which was not attended by Lynd or Hayden, officials of the central committee were, according to Aptheker, "deliriously happy" that the Communist Party, USA, had established contact with the Communist Party of North Vietnam. (*FBI 1967 Appropriation*, pp. 59-60.)

STUDENTS FOR A DEMOCRATIC SOCIETY. Working hand in hand with the DuBois Clubs on the campuses are organizations such as the Students for a Democratic Society, a militant youth group which receives support from the Communist Party and which in turn supports communist objectives and tactics. Hall has characterized it, along with the DuBois Clubs, as a group which the Communist Party has "going for us." (*FBI Law Enforcement Bulletin,* October 1, 1966.)

STUDENT NONVIOLENT COORDINATING COMMITTEE. The Student Nonviolent Coordinating Committee (SNCC) under the leadership of former National Chairman Stokely Carmichael and H. Rap Brown, has developed into a full-blown all-Negro revolutionary organization.

One dominant figure at this time in the organization is James Forman. At the national conference held in Atlanta, Ga., in early June 1968, Forman was responsible for a complete reorganization of SNCC patterned after the structure of another militant black nationalist organization, the Black Panther Party. SNCC endeavored to effect a close working alliance with the Black Panther Party; however, due to the extreme militancy of the Black Panther Party, leaders of SNCC severed relations with that organization in July 1968.

James Forman has many contacts with representatives of foreign countries and has made a number of trips abroad. In April 1968, he traveled to Sweden as part of a group which met with individuals representing the North Vietnamese and the National Liberation Front of South Vietnam.

Brown has been sentenced to 5 years in prison and fined $2,000 for violation of the Federal Firearms Act. He has been indicted on a charge of assaulting and intimidating a Federal officer and obstruction of justice. Brown also has been indicted by the State of Maryland on a charge of inciting arson. He is free on bond awaiting appeal or trial on the various charges.

In August 1968, SNCC officially severed relations with Stokely Carmichael because of his "extremist ideas" and the fact that his wife, singer Miriam Makeba, exhibits "imperialistic tendencies."

Carmichael was a prime mover in the formation of the Black United Front in the District of Columbia. This group is a coalition of moderate and militant Negro leaders and organizations which Carmichael declared was organized for the purpose of black people unifying their forces against the major enemy which he said is white America.

231

Carmichael has affiliated with the Black Panther Party. At a rally of this group held at Los Angeles, Calif., on August 24, 1968, Carmichael was introduced as a leader of the Black Panther Party. His official title is that of "prime minister." Carmichael indicated a need for the black man to obtain weapons, stating black men must unite socially, economically, and militarily to avoid extermination.

Shortly after returning to the United States in December 1967 from an extensive trip abroad, Carmichael established residence in Washington, D. C., where he resided until late November 1968 when he moved to New York City. Carmichael arrived in Stockholm, Sweden, on December 29, 1968, with his wife, Miriam Makeba, who had a singing engagement in that city. Carmichael has indicated he plans to establish residence in Guinea and he did arrive in that country on February 17, 1969. (*FBI 1970 Appropriation,* April 17, 1969, pp. 68-69.)

SUBVERSIVE ACTIVITIES CONTROL BOARD. By the close of the fiscal year, the Department of Justice had petitioned the Subversive Activities Control Board to order 37 national and district functionaries of the Communist Party USA, to register as Party members under the appropriate section of the Internal Security Act of 1950. Hearings have been held in 36 of these cases and registration orders have been issued by the Board against 28 of the respondents. These findings were based on evidence developed by the FBI. Notices of appeal have been filed in 25 of these cases. On April 23, 1964, the District of Columbia Court of Appeals handed down a decision in two of the cases which had been consolidated for appeal purposes. This decision, which is binding on the remaining 23 cases in which appeals had been filed, upheld the registration orders but did not cinsider the constitutional issues. (*FBI Annual Report, Fiscal Year 1964,* p. 24.)

SUICIDE. To dismiss lightly the existence of the subversive threat in the United States is deliberately to commit national suicide. In some quarters we are surely doing just this. It would be the worst kind of folly to allow the spy and subversive immunity through technical rather than logical interpretation of the law, while they plot the destruction of our democratic form of Government. The American Communists and their dupes and fellow travelers are the skirmishing lines of the Soviet conspiracy against our Nation. (*Human Events,* October 12, 1957, reprint.)

SUPREME COURT DECISION—NOVEMBER 15, 1965. Elated with the November 15, 1965, decision of the U. S. Supreme Court, which declared the membership provision section of the Internal Security Act of 1950 unconstitutional, the Communist Party, USA, began making bold plans for the future as soon as the decision was made public.

In a press conference on November 15, 1965, Gus Hall, the Party's general secretary, declared that the Party would move immediately to get Communist candidates on election ballots and would run candidates for public office wherever possible. Hall stated that the Party would take steps for greater participation in the 1966 elections and, as part of their stepped-up activity in this regard, would issue a new program to the American people. Part of this program calls for the establishment of a new political Party which would be based on Negro, labor and "peace" groups. The program declares that the new Party is essential because the current problems facing the Nation cannot be solved under the two-party system as it is presently situated. (*FBI 1967 Appropriation,* p. 44.)

WILLIAM COTTLE TAYLOR. In regard to the increased political activity of the leaders of the Communist Party, USA, while Party leaders would rejoice over a successful campaign by a Communist, they also look to this activity to obtain other benefits. In addition to affording opportunities to assert that the Party is a legitimate political party and to lending the Party an aura of respectability, this activity provides publicity and reduces the Party's isolation from the mainstream of society. It enables them to influence vital issues of the day; to distribute propaganda; to present the Party program to the electorate; and to advance the cause of communism.

Some persons may not believe that a Communist could reach a position of responsibility in Government through the election process. They have only to consider the thousands of votes cast for William Cottle Taylor, vice chairman of the Party's southern California district, who publicly identified himself as a Communist while running in the California pri-

233

mary as an independent candidate for the Board of Supervisors of Los Angeles County. Although Taylor was defeated, he rolled up an impressive 33,576 votes, or some 13 per cent of the total vote cast for this office on June 2, 1964. (*FBI 1966 Appropriation*, p. 58.)

TEACHERS. In their unceasing efforts to shape the thinking and attitudes of what they call the "masses," the Reds have always devoted much attention to idea-molding fields, such as education, the press, radio, and television. Here, too, they are still dangerously active.

There can be no doubt that the great majority of American teachers are loyal citizens, yet a witness who formerly held a high position in the Communist Party recently testified that the Party has members at work in every kind of educational institution, from nursery schools to the universities.

For example, Communist teachers or fellow travelers are subtly persuading children aged 2 to 5 not to believe in religion, and are poisoning their minds with contempt or dislike for other "capitalistic institutions." In one of many colleges where Communists are known to have taught, there was a teacher who tried to get over to his students the idea that "Communism is the only hope of Mexico." At one of our great universities a renowned scientist recently compared Christianity unfavorably to Marxism, and stated that "Marxism has that optimism which alone can build a new world."

Being good tacticians, the Communists realize that one concealed Party member in education may be worth a dozen in less strategic fields, and some of their more successful propagandists in this area have influenced, and are influencing, the ideas of thousands of impressionable young people.

There is the case, for instance, of an ex-professor who has addressed college students all over the country. Billed as an "expert" on Russia, and reputed to have once served as an adviser to the Russian Government, the professor is introduced to students as an unprejudiced specialist on international affairs who can give them a "clear" and "unbiased" picture of conditions in that country.

When the professor starts lecturing, however, everything that he says turns out to be an apology for the Soviet Union.

234

The Soviets are misunderstood in the United States, he says. Russia is a peace-loving nation with no aggressive intentions. This country, not Russia, is the one which is wrong . . . All typical Communist propaganda!

Most students who have heard this "specialist," and the college officials who have permitted him to lecture at their institutions, think he is an honest liberal. But in the FBI we know better. We have proof that he is a concealed Communist and we know that he is under direct orders of the Communist Party, USA, which follows the Moscow line. This scholarly individual's activities have been somewhat curtailed of late, but others like him are still assailing the minds of youth with Red lies. ("The Communists are After Our Minds," *American Magazine,* October, 1954, reprint, p. 2.)

TERRORISM. The voices of temperance, logic and decency must speak out. Terrorism cannot be tolerated in a free society. Hate, terror and lawlessness are not the American way. ("Time for Decision," November 24, 1964, p. 4.)

TEST-BAN TREATY. The signing of the partial nuclear test-ban treaty was interpreted by the Communist Party, USA, as resulting from a shift in the world balance of forces in favor of communism and as a turning away from capitalism toward "socialism." Other aspects of American foreign policy which came under Party scrutiny included the involvement of American troops in South Vietnam. The Party has charged that these "imperialistic policies" have disgraced the United States before the world and endanger world peace. It has conducted an intensive campaign for the withdrawal of American forces from South Vietnam and has also demanded an end to the "unjust" American policy pursued with respect to Cuba. (*FBI Annual Report, Fiscal Year 1964,* p. 21.)

THEORY AND PRACTICE. At all times the Communists stress the relationship between theory and action. To study the Communist "masters" is to ready oneself for revolutionary action.

"We study for the sole purpose of putting into practice what we have learned. It is for the Party and for the victory of the revolution that we study."

Answer: In Christianity the action—action in building a study of the Bible is a guide to deeper Christian experience for the individual, and a better, more wholesome community.

The Party stresses the development of the "politically mature" comrade, the individual on whom it can depend to carry out its mission, the revolution.

Answer: Christians are also working for a revolution— a revolution of the spirit, not the sword. Deeply committed Christians are needed to carry on the work of the church, to uphold the Judaic-Christian faith. ("J. Edgar Hoover Warns Communism Poses Never-Ending Threat," *Los Angeles Examiner*, reprinted in *Congressional Record*, February 2, 1961, p. A703.)

TIMETABLE? The prime objective of all the public activity on the part of the Communist leaders was to create a new image for the Party—an image which connotes respectability, legitimacy as a liberal political faction and freedom from foreign dictates. Their denial of subservience to the Soviet Union, however, was clearly branded as ridiculous by the fact that several Party officials were delegates to the 22nd Congress of the Communist Party, Soviet Union, in October, 1961. Heading the delegation was Elizabeth Gurley Flynn, National Chairman of the Communist Party, USA, who, in a speech before the Congress, brazenly predicted the United States would be in the Communist orbit by 1980. (*FBI Annual Report, Fiscal Year 1962*, pp. 28-29.)

TOTAL STRUGGLE. The United States is involved in a world crisis. We did not create this crisis. The Communists in Russia began it in 1917 when they overthrew a liberal democratic government to establish their dictatorship. It was their intention then, and it has been their goal ever since, to use that revolutionary weapon to establish a world dictatorship. This is the crux of our present-day crisis. No one can predict how long the crisis will continue. We do know, however, that it has become a total struggle between two fundamentally opposed social systems. ("Communist Illusion and Democratic Reality," December, 1959, p. 1.)

TRADE. Mr. Lipscomb. It appears that some citizens are so anxious to have peaceful relations and make profits in

236

trading with the U.S.S.R. that we forget the dangers of Communist aggression, both economic and military.

Mr. Hoover. Unfortunately, that is correct. (*FBI 1962 Appropriation*, March 6, 1961, p. 67.)

Mr. Lipscomb. Mr. Director, during your excellent discussion you mentioned that the Communist Party had a goal of the extension of East-West trade. Was that the Communist Party, USA?

Mr. Hoover. Yes. They have supported the overall goal that Russia has advocated for East-West trade. In other words, this is the international Communist line.

Mr. Lipscomb. Have you ever set forth the reasons, at least in your mind, why they are pushing so hard on extension of East-West trade?

Mr. Hoover. I think there are several reasons that could be given for it. For example, the economic reason. Most of the Communist countries of the world have a propaganda program proclaiming their alleged advances in technology and in all other areas. For example, they claim their production of food for the next year will exceed the past year. Something usually happens and the production does not meet expectations. These Communist countries therefore want East-West trade where there is a market in which they can make purchases of needed goods.

From an intelligence standpoint, there is no question but that the Soviet-bloc have in mind the use of trade delegations and even exchange student groups for intelligence purposes. There is always at least one intelligence officer with trade delegations and we have found exchange students being used for intelligence work.

Mr. Lipscomb. The Communists would not push East-West trade extension unless it was to their benefit?

Mr. Hoover. That is absolutely true. They never agree to anything unless it is to their benefit and the odds are all in their favor. Very seldom are they in favor of anything advanced by the free government nations.

Mr. Lipscomb. I have heard of a rather new operation that has to do with parcels being sent to the Communist bloc where individuals buy a gift certificate or purchase a certain kind of parcel and have it sent behind the Iron Curtain. I believe I have heard the proprietor of the parcel operation in the United States is licensed by a Soviet trading company of some sort and that Soviet trading company gets a portion of the funds for these parcels.

Mr. Hoover. Yes?

Mr. Lipscomb. It is possible that the funds this Soviet trading company gains in dollars could be funneled back into Communist activities in the United States?

Mr. Hoover. Most certainly; of course, everything in Russia is controlled by the State.

(Discussion off the record.)

Mr. Lipscomb. This Communist parcel operation is one where they deal in dollars and the dollars never leave the United States. This is a convenient scheme.

Mr. Hoover. Extremely so. (*FBI 1965 Appropriation,* January 29, 1964, pp. 62-63.)

TREASON. The hand of Moscow extends across the seas into the very bosom of America. The masters of the Kremlin exercise a bitter discipline over the minds of every Party member in the United States. And behind each Party member stand ten other individuals, ready at a moment's notice to do the bidding of Moscow. This group represents a vast army of treason within our borders; a fifth column of tremendously serious potentialities. ("Foe to Freedom," *The Elks Magazine,* October 1950, p. 4.)

TRICONTINENTAL CONFERENCE. The tricontinental Conference, also referred to as the Tricontinent Conference, was held in Havana, Cuba, from January 3 to 14, 1966, with 83 African, Asian and Latin-American countries represented. Approximately 450 delegates attended, with Communist China having the largest representation next to Cuba. Western observers believe the convening of the conference was an attempt by the Soviets to gain the dominating role in the existing two-continent group known as Afro-Asian People's Solidarity Organization (AAPSO), which has been under the control of Communist China. It was believed that the Soviets felt the holding of the Conference in the Western Hemisphere and the inclusion of 20 to 30 Latin-American delegations, who historically follow the Soviet line rather than the Communist China line, would swing the balance of power to the Soviet Union. Fidel Castro, of course, considered the holding of this major Conference in Havana to be recognition of him as a world revolutionary leader.

Nothing was released at the conference concerning ideological differences arising there between the Soviets and the Communist Chinese. Various resolutions were adopted concerning anti-imperialism and anticolonialism in the Western Hemisphere, chiefly aimed at the United States. It was agreed that a committee would be formed with headquarters in Havana to coordinate "national liberation" movements on the three continents. The Soviet announcements concerning this new committee indicated a permanent-type headquarters was being established in Havana until the next Tricontinental Conference meeting in Cairo, Egypt, during 1968, while the Communist Chinese announcements showed the Havana headquarters was set up on a provisional basis only and the consensus is that the Communist Chinese will try to have a meeting of the AAPSO in 1967 in Peiping, China, at which the Communist Chinese line would be expected to prevail.

From Cuba's standpoint, the Conference was quite successful in that there were unanimous resolutions against presence of foreign military bases and troops in "oppressed" countries and Castro was able to make a big show of offering aid to Vietnam, Cambodia, and Laos. Castro castigated the U. S. "military occupation" of the Dominican Republic and projected that Columbia, Guatemala, Peru, and Venezuela were ripe for revolutionary overthrows of their Governments. The most overt action taken occurred after the Tricontinental Conference officially adjourned on January 14, 1966, when representatives from 27 of the Latin American delegations attending the conference formed the Latin American Solidarity Organization with headquarters in Havana. Present were Fidel Castro, Cuban President Dorticos, and other high Cuban officials with a Venezuelan delegate acting as chairman. The announced aims of the Organization were to prepare for a Latin-American solidarity conference in 1967, to support "liberation" movements by all means available and to firmly back "liberated" countries which may be attacked by imperialism. This group also resolved to "develop a constant campaign against the increasing policy of Yankee imperialism and its false, cynical and hypocritical propaganda used to hide its vandalistic actions in the Western Hemisphere."

While the various delegations attending the Conference were referred to as "country" delegations, thus implying that they were official delegations, only radical groups attended from Western Hemisphere countries and most of them have little or no significance in their own countries. Nevertheless, we can expect a marked increase in Cuban, Soviet, and Communist Chinese propaganda and subversion within the Western Hemisphere if a working committee is formed in Havana on a permanent basis. U. S. installations throughout Central and South America can expect to have their hands full if this group does become effective. (*FBI 1967 Appropriation*, pp. 63-64.)

TROJAN HORSE. There is purpose in this waving of olive branches and this process of "reappraisal." It is calculated to allay fear of communism in order to intensify "Operation Trojan Horse" and, through complacency, pave the way for a united front. ("Communist 'New Look' A Study in Duplicity," *The Elks Magazine*, August 1956, reprint, p. 3.)

UNDERSTAND—WHY SOME FAIL TO. Why, I have asked myself many times, is it so difficult for the average citizen to understand what communism is? Why are so many people beguiled into doing the work the Communists want done? Why have so many awakened to find themselves entangled in the Communist net? Why, indeed, is it so hard for free men and women to understand that it is impossible for communism and individual rights to coexist?

The more one ponders these questions, the more he wonders if a great stumbling block to understanding the nature of communism does not rest in our tendency to judge others by what we know of ourselves. We expect the Communist in a specific situation to react as we would react in the same situation—and we are mystified when he does not. ("A View of Reality," *General Federation Clubwoman Magazine*, May-June 1961.)

UNION. The American view of trade unionism is summed up in the words of Samuel Gompers: "To be a good trade unionist a man must first be a good American." ("How to Fight Communism," *Newsweek*, June 9, 1947, reprint.)

UNIONS—BOAST. I am convinced that the great masses of union men and women are patriotic American citizens interested chiefly in security for their families and themselves. They have no use for the American Communists but in those instances where Communists have taken control of unions, it has been because too many union men and women have been outwitted, out-maneuvered, and out-waited by Communists.

The Communists have never relied on numerical strength to dominate a labor organization. Through infiltration tactics they have in too many instances captured positions of authority. Communists have boasted that with 5 per cent of the membership the Communists, with their militancy, superior organizational ability and discipline, could control the union. (HCUA, *Menace of Communism*, March 26, 1947, p. 7.)

UNIONS—DO. If more union members took a more active role and asserted themselves it would become increasingly difficult for Communists to gain control. Patriotic union members can easily spot sympathizers and Party members in conventions and union meetings because invariably the latter strive to establish the Party line instead of serving the best interests of the union and the country. (*Ibid.*, p. 8.)

UNIONS—SOME LABOR LEADERS DUPED. I do fear so long as American labor groups are infiltrated, dominated or saturated with the virus of Communism. I do fear the palliation and weasel-worded gestures against Communism indulged in by some of our labor leaders who should know better but who have become pawns in the hands of sinister but astute manipulators for the Communist cause. (*Ibid.*, p. 12.)

UNITED FRONT. These zigzag tactics and calculated camouflage create a perfect opportunity for the Communist to build his deadly weapon—the united front.

And what, exactly, does that mean?

The united front is one of the most important of the current Communist tactics for organizing and using the mass pressure of vast numbers of deceived non-Communists to further Communist objectives. It may be applied on any level—local, state, regional, national or international. Communists begin with popular, pressing and legitimate current issues relating to unemployment, wages, hours of labor, general working conditions or similar subjects. They build a variety of organizations around these issues. They then seek to sweep

241

large numbers of laborers and the various segments of our population which can be misled into supporting veiled Communist objectives into these organizations. The objectives are gradually broadened and related to foreign as well as to domestic policies. The procedure may even develop into what it known as a "united front government." It can become a powerful weapon of a small minority Communist Party—and that Party always preserves its independent role at the very time it is manipulating huge numbers of non-Communists th way and that way in behalf of Communist designs. The united front is made to sound appealing to liberals, progressives and reformists as well as workers while at the same time it works to ultimately destroy the freedom of labor unions and all that true liberals, progressives and reformists hope to achieve. ("Communist 'New Look' A Study in Duplicity," *The Elks Magazine,* August 1956. reprint, p. 2.)

UNITED FRONT—INFLUENCE. How many American citizens have, innocently or otherwise, been involved in work connected in some manner with advancement of the Communist Party? I do not know. Communist fronts have allegedly embraced millions of Americans since the united front tactic was firmly established in 1935. ("Communist 'New Look' A Study in Duplicity," *The Elks Magazine,* August, 1956, reprint, p. 3.)

UNITED FRONT—PURPOSE. In recent months, the united front campaign, always a dangerous Communist tactic, has received even greater emphasis. Former Communists who dropped out of the Party and some who were expelled have been approached to renew their memberships. In other instances, non-Communist individuals and organizations have been approached by Party leaders under the pretext of wanting to assist in promoting a mutual objective. The Communists are confident that if they can openly cling to the coattails of reputable groups, eventually they will succeed in wearing the entire suit. (HCUA, *The Great Pretense,* 1956, p. 173.)

UNITED FRONT—VALUE. How does the united front tactic aid communism?

It divides the leadership of the Communist opposition. It confuses and weakens the great masses of people who would normally oppose communism. It splits them into differing groups, and isolates them from united leadership, thereby rendering their opposition to communism ineffectual. In the language of the professional Communist revolutionary the united front is a deadly revolutionary weapon which, if properly used, divides, splits and shatters all non-Communist mass organizations and efforts.

Once opposition is destroyed, the next step is to win the people over to the Communist Party by advocating general collaboration with broad Communist Party objectives, and by subtle indoctrination. ("Communist 'New Look' A Study in Duplicity," *The Elks Magazine,* August, 1956, reprint, p. 2.)

U. S. ATTITUDE TOWARD. In the Communist Party USA, the Soviets possess the unique advantage of commanding their own forces behind the lines of the declared enemy and of having the enemy accord such forces the status of legal participants in the quest for political power—even though many of the activities of the Communist Party, USA, are essentially treasonable. To put it bluntly, the Communist Party, USA, looks upon our Government as its enemy which it seeks to overthrow—by forceful means, if necessary. (*FBI 1966 Appropriation,* p. 54.)

Seen through the eyes of the Communists, American education is in a degenerate state; American culture, science, and religion are under the thumb of big business; and American laws are the repressive measures of desperate capitalists. Labor unions are attacked by the Communists for allegedly becoming tools of big business; promoting American "colonial rule" abroad, and joining with the professions, the Government, and the judiciary in discriminating against women in the filling of high-paying jobs. (*FBI Law Enforcement Bulletin,* October, 1961.)

U. S. TARGET NUMBER ONE. America is face to face with an ideology—atheistic Communism—which denies every ideal we uphold. The forces of this conspiracy have, in a relatively short time, expanded their rule to over a third of the world's people. And with untiring efforts they continue to unleash their weapons of terrorism, subversion and vicious propaganda in an attempt to ensnare every nation in a giant Communist web.

And make no mistake! This Nation remains Target Number One. With every tactic at its command, the Communist enemy works feverishly to weaken our country, hoping to destroy our faith in a system which upholds the worth and freedom of the individual. ("America's Ideals—Its Mark of Greatness," *The Union Central Advocate*, 1965, reprint.)

UTOPIAN ILLUSION. In the search for this "utopia," the individual Communist is transformed from a mere ideological adherent into a militant, disciplined agent whose entire life is blindly devoted to the Communist cause. This clarion call to action motivates Communists and instills in them their fervor to change the world. Yet, in their goal of a worldwide stateless, classless, godless society, the Communists are pursuing an illusion. It is an illusion because man, by nature, is meant for diversity, creativeness, freedom, change, and growth. No monolithic, static, standardized, totalitarian world-Communist society can provide the proper climate. It is also an illusion because man's origin, purpose, and destiny are intelligible—a fact which Communist theory and practice ignore. Man is not, as Communists claim, merely a fortuitous product of the ceaseless interaction of chemical and physical elements. He is endowed by his Creator with a purposeful life.

If this Communist illusion can inspire such intense energy, should not our obviously superior way of life, rooted in the realities of human nature, stimulate at least an equal measure of dedication in its adherents? The answer is yes—provided that the individual citizen realizes the specious nature of communism and is firmly grounded in and inspired by the principles and traditions of our Nation. ("Communist Illusion and Democratic Reality," December, 1959, p. 3.)

VICTORY—COMMUNISTS EXPECT. Implicit in all Communist propaganda, whether designed for domestic or foreign consumption, is the premise that the ultimate triumph of communism is inevitable because it proceeds from laws as immutable as those governing the physical sciences. Communist propaganda portrays peace, social progress, and economic prosperity as characteristic of the Communist world and claims that these make Communist nations invincible. The non-Communist world, on the other hand, is pictured as something with political instability, economic exploitation, and

244

social upheaval. By identifying the Communist world as the hero and the Free World as the villain in the drama of historical progress, Communist propaganda represents the triumph of communism, not only as an inevitability, but also as the victory of good over evil. ("Communist Illusion and Democratic Reality," December, 1959, p. 2.)

VICTORY—IF. The FBI chief expressed confidence that this Nation, as in the days of George Washington, will triumph. "The call today is for men of integrity," he said. "Democracy cannot be preserved by weak and faltering hands."

Noting a 2.5 percent increase in crime in the United States in the first 6 months of 1953, as compared with the same period a year earlier, Mr. Hoover deplored "a withering materialism that has captured the thinking of so many young people."

"The moral law cannot be violated with impunity," he asserted. "Truth is not something relative to be interpreted by every person in his own way. This is the law of the jungle. This is banishing God from our midst. This is stark betrayal of our American heritage." ("J. Edgar Hoover Cites Red Threat," *Brooklyn Tablet,* February 27, 1954, p. 9.)

VICTORY ULTIMATELY. To a people who still love freedom and who still look to a Supreme Being, their sacrifices shall not be in vain because one day the Almighty will wreak vengeance on this atheistic, terroristic tyranny. Communism runs counter to the aspirations of the human heart. The Communist way eventually will perish from this earth because it prostitutes truth, because it is heartless and cruel, because it is evil, and because it denies the existence of the omnipotent. We pray for the coming of that Day! ("The Twin Enemies of Freedom," *FBI Law Enforcement Bulletin,* January 1957, reprint, p. 5.)

VIETNAM. Tremendous pressure and criticism are being leveled against the President and the Congress to confuse and mislead the American public. Irresponsible charges of "invaders," "brutal aggression," and "sneak attacks" are used to discredit our Government in hopes it will be forced to abandon its role as defender of freedom. Some of this protest comes from legitimate peace groups and others who are opposed to the course of action being followed in Vietnam and in the Dominican Republic. However, much of the agitation is part of a diabolical scheme contrived by the Communist Party, USA (CPUSA), an integral arm of the international Communist conspiracy, the materialistic, godless ideology dedicated to ruling the world.

The CPUSA and other Communist groups are seizing this opportunity to advance their cause by false statements and half truths. Particularly, the Party is seeking to influence the youth of our country through the Communist-controlled W. E. B. DuBois Clubs and similar organizations.

The CPUSA encouraged and endorsed the student march on the Nation's Capital on April 17, 1965, protesting United States intervention in Vietnam. Although not in actual control of this demonstration, the Communists participated in the march and distributed copies of *The Worker* . . . Communist marchers from all over the country were present, and Communist leaders claimed a major role in the demonstration.

This is a typical example of the Party's widespread campaign to influence our country's foreign policies. The strategy is not new, but it is effective. The Party is working through non-communist groups and front organizations to embarrass our Government and disrupt its efforts. Communist leaders are striving to initiate other marches and demonstrations to keep their campaign of fear and terror rolling. We can expect that the Party will push for some type of nationwide action similar to "peace" strikes or work stoppages to emphasize their aims. These are methods which have served Communist causes so well since the days of Lenin.

Party leaders hope, of course, that more and more Americans will be duped and misled by these tactics. They envision a commanding wave of hostility against American policies abroad. The goal is to incite citizens to the point that they will demand American forces be withdrawn from Vietnam and other places, allowing international communism to take over and engulf more defenseless countries.

Fortunately, the strength and greatness of our Nation lie in its millions of patriotic and loyal citizens—Americans who will not swallow the Red bait of the cunning Communist emissaries; Americans who will rally behind our Government leaders at this crucial time; and Americans who are still proud to state, "I was born an American; I live an American; I shall die an American." (*FBI Law Enforcement Bulletin,* June 1, 1965.)

VIETNAM PROTESTS. Demonstrations protesting U. S. policy toward Vietnam which have been held throughout the United States during 1965 have most certainly been a factor resulting in additional demands upon our manpower because of the interest in and support of some demonstrations by some of the subversive organizations I have discussed.

Since February 1965, scarcely a day has gone by without a demonstration in some city. Particularly active have been faculty members and students from colleges and universities in all sections of this country. Demonstrations have taken the form of sit-ins, teach-ins, picket lines, speak-outs and widespread distribution of material criticizing U. S. efforts in Vietnam.

The Communist Party and other subversive groups such as the W. E. B. DuBois Clubs of America, a Communist-inspired, Marxist-oriented youth group; the Socialist Workers Party, which has been designated as subversive by the Attorney General pursuant to Executive Order 10450; its youth affiliate, the Young Socialist Alliance; the Progressive Labor Party, a pro-Chinese Marxist group and its affiliate, the May 2 Movement; and the Workers World Party, a pro-Chinese Communist splinter group, have actively supported and participated in demonstrations along with the Students for a Democratic Society, a youth group with active Communist infiltration.

There follows the highlights on five national demonstrations we have had during the past year.

STUDENT MARCH ON WASHINGTON

On April 17, 1965, a student march on Washington, sponsored by Students for a Democratic Society, attracted an estimated 15,000 participants. Included among the participants were Arnold Johnson, Communist Party, USA public relations director, and Michael Zagarell, national youth director of the party. George Meyers, a member of the national board of the party, distributed copies of *The Worker* . . . . during this demonstration. Numerous other Communist Party

247

members were observed participating. Gus Hall, general secretary of the Party, reported that the Communists participated in the march and described it as an "unforgettable event." Zagarell said "we" played a decisive role and Johnson stated "our" people were there from all over the country.

NATIONAL TEACH-INS

The Inter-university Committee for a Public Hearing on Vietnam, which is now known as the Inter-university Committee for a Public Hearing on Foreign Policy, sponsored a national teach-in on May 15, 1965, at the Sheraton-Park Hotel, Washington, D. C. This committee, which is headquartered at Ann Arbor, Michigan, is the brainchild of faculty members at the University of Michigan. Its secretary is Professor Anatol Rapoport of the university who is a self-admitted former Communist Party member.

The teach-in, which was carried by telephonic hookups to campuses throughout the United States, drew nearly 4,500 individuals to Washington, D. C. While advance publicity described the teach-in as an airing of both sides of the Vietnam issue, the actual teach-in proved to be one sided. Speakers were almost unanimous in condemning U. S. policy. Among the speakers were Professor Hans Morgenthau of the University of Chicago who stated, "if we succeed in our present policy, South Vietnam will become a colony of the United States." He contended that the United States did not have the courage to "retreat or advance too far."

Isaac Deutscher of London, England, was a featured speaker. He described himself as a Marxist who had been expelled from the Communist Party because of his opposition to Stalin. He denied that the United States was threatened by any major Communist power and said that U. S. policy had disillusioned the world.

Comments from the audience included such statements as the United States should withdraw from Vietnam; the United States needs a positive foreign policy; the United Nations should some day take precedence over national sovereignty; and Congress should have a hearing concerning American policy.

248

WASHINGTON SUMMER ACTION PROJECT

Students for a Democratic Society, joined by the W. E. B. DuBois Clubs of America; the Student Nonviolent Coordinating Committee, a civil rights group; and the Committee for Nonviolent Action, sponsored a demonstration in Washington, D. C., from August 6 through August 9, 1965, under the title "Washington Summer Action Project." This demonstration included picketing of the White House and a sit-in at the White House gate entrance, and workshops on Vietnam, the draft, Puerto Rico, and South Africa. On August 9, the demonstrators marched to the Capitol grounds for the purpose of staging a "Congress of Unrepresented People" to declare peace in Vietnam. The sponsors of the demonstration had previously announced their intention of actually occupying congressional seats; however, they were stopped at the boundary of the Capitol grounds. Numerous demonstrators were arrested when they attempted to enter the grounds. As with other demonstrations, the Communist Party and other subversive organizations supported and participated in the Washington Summer Action Project. Among the Communist Party members noted were James Jackson, a member of the Party's national committee, and Michael Zagarell, the national youth leader of the Party. Demonstrations were held throughout the United States during this period in support of the Washington Summer Action Project.

INTERNATIONAL DAYS OF PROTEST

The Vietnam Day Committee, Berkeley, California, designated October 15 and 16, 1965, as international days of protest and issued a call for groups throughout the world to join it in demonstrating on those days. Massive civil disobedience was urged on October 16.

As a result of this call to action, demonstrations were held in cities throughout the United States and in some foreign countries. These demonstrations took the form of picketing, sit-ins, teach-ins, burning of draft cards, and parades.

The Communist Party and other subversive groups once again vigorously supported and participated in these demonstrations.

In Berkeley, the demonstration started with a teach-in at the University of California. Speakers were unanimous in

249

condemning the United States and one speaker called for the impeachment of President Johnson. On the evening of October 15, approximately 8,000 demonstrators began a march from the University of California to Oakland Army Terminal, Oakland, California, where they hoped to carry their message to U. S. troops. The committee had previously called for civil disobedience at the terminal. They were frustrated when Oakland authorities refused to allow them to march through Oakland.

In New York City, the Whitehall Speak-Out Committee, an ad hoc group of the War Resisters League, sponsored a parade and a rally to protest the draft and U. S. action in Vietnam. During the rally, it was announced that Robert Thompson, a high official of the Communist Party, USA, had died and that he was a sponsor of International Days of Protest in New York City. Approximately 50 Communist Party members, including such well-known Communist Party officials as Gilbert Green, Arnold Johnson, and Mike Stein were observed participating in this demonstration. Over 20 members of the Workers World Party participated. Jack Barnes, a member of the National Committee of the Socialist Workers Party, was active during the demonstration.

Demonstrations throughout the country attracted large numbers of counter-demonstrators who were in favor of U. S. policy. In some instances, the counter-demonstrators outnumbered the demonstrators.

MARCH ON WASHINGTON FOR PEACE IN VIETNAM

The National Committee for a Sane Nuclear Policy sponsored a march on Washington for peace in Vietnam on November 27, 1965. Approximately 12,000 marchers picketed the White House carrying slogans calling for a negotiated peace in Vietnam, an end to the war in Vietnam, and the withdrawal of troops from that country. After the picketing was concluded, approximately 20,000 demonstrators gathered at the Sylvan Theater on the Washington Monument grounds to hear various speakers who were critical of U. S. action in Vietnam.

As in the past, Communist Party members, including several national functionaries, actively participated in this march. Literature was distributed by the Communist Party and other subversive organizations and Viet Cong flags were displayed by some participants. (*FBI 1967 Appropriation*, pp. 56-59.)

VIOLENCE. However, veteran newspapermen are not easily fooled, and some of Hall's answers to questions posed by the reporters quickly exposed him. For instance, Hall was asked if the Communist Party, USA, advocates the violent overthrow of the U. S. Government. Hall, convicted in Federal court for conspiring to do just that—Hall, who once openly testified that he was willing to take up arms to bring about a Soviet America, blandly said without hesitation, "No, we have never advocated this." (SISS, *Concerning the 17th National Convention, Communist Party, U.S.A.*, 1960, p. 10.)

It is the avowed purpose of the world Communist movement, of which the Communist Party, USA has always been an integral part, to destroy our free society by violent means if need be and to supplant our constitutional government by a Soviet-styled dictatorship. (*FBI 1965 Appropriation*, January 29, 1964, p. 44.)

WAR—ALWAYS. Lenin said with utter frankness, "Concessions do not mean peace with capitalism, but war on a new plane."

American Communists have not suddenly become good citizens. They are merely making war against America on a new plane. ("The Twin Enemies of Freedom," *FBI Law Enforcement Bulletin*, January 1957, reprint, p. 4.)

WAR OF IDEAS. The war between communism and the free world is not fought with bombs or other tangible weapons. It is being fought now by subversion through the medium of ideas.

It is not an accident that the greatest concentration of Communist workers has been found in three fields—education, unions, entertainment. These are the areas where ideas flourish and thinking patterns are formed. ("Faith or Fear," *Congressional Record*, June 28, 1960, p. 13653.)

WAR NOW ON. We are at war with the Communists, and the sooner each red-blooded American realizes that the better and safer we will be! Communism runs counter to all decent aspirations of the human heart. Communism destroys and

251

denies every spiritual value. Those who hate God must bring misery in their wake. They must be brutal and cruel and deceitful.

We should make it crystal clear to the Red Master of the Kremlin that we intend to win the "cold" war and at the same time impress upon him that we have the military power to prevent a "hot" war. Russia cannot stand against the United States economically, militarily or ideologically if we remain dedicated to the ideals of our Founding Fathers. (*America— Freedom's Champion,* October 18, 1960, p. 6.)

We are at war with the Communists and the sooner every red-blooded American realizes this the safer we will be! Naturally, we want to live in peace but we do not want peace at any price—we want peace with honor and integrity. And we intend to assure it for the future.

The extent of the menace posed by the philosophy of communism is clearcut and obvious. However, it is absolutely necessary that we attack and oppose it calmly, rationally, and objectively. ("The Faith To Be Free," December 7, 1961, p. 5.)

WASHINGTON'S WARNING. What was the counsel he offered? Washington warned against permanent alliance with foreign powers, partiality toward a favorite nation, big public debt, a large military establishment, and the activities of a "small but artful and enterprising minority" designed to change or control Government. He warned against any change in the Constitution by usurpation. He stressed the great need for enlightened public opinion. And, with a certainty that was unequivocal, he said: "Of all the dispositions and habits which lead to political prosperity, Religion and Morality are indispensable supports. In vain would that man claim the tributes of PATRIOTISM, who should labor to subvert these great pillars of human happiness, these firmest props of the duties of men and citizens . . . "

But can any thoughtful man ignore those two "indispensable supports" (morality and religion) of which our first President spoke?

He cannot do so without discounting the two most vital stones in the foundation of American freedom, for our freedom rests on a basis that is spiritual and idealistic—and is so acknowledged in the first words of the *Declaration of Independence.*

252

The greatness of America is spiritual in origin. The broad material achievements which we enjoy today stem largely from vision born of faith, sustained by unshakable resolution, and supported by unceasing effort. ("What Does the Future Hold?" *Christianity Today*, June 19, 1961, reprint, p. 2.)

WILLIAM WORTHY, JR. William Worthy, Jr., a writer, was convicted on August 8, 1962, for violating Government regulations regarding Cuban travel. He was sentenced to three months in prison and nine months on probation on September 17, 1962. An appeal was pending in this matter at the end of the fiscal year. (*FBI Annual Report, Fiscal Year 1963*, p. 28.)

WIN. The fight against crime and communism can be won, and it will be won with, but only with, the help of every decent American citizen. No individual in this great land of ours should underestimate the importance of his or her role.

Let us all work that there may be a rebirth of freedom under God and our Nation.

As Astronaut John H. Glenn, Jr., said, "Freedom, devotion to God and country are not things of the past. They will never become old-fashioned."

Every strong nation in history has lived by an ideal and has died when its ideals were dissipated. We can be destroyed only by our own gullibility. If we are ready, we shall neither be dead nor Red.

It is what a nation has in its heart, rather than what it has in its hand, that makes it strong. The nation which honors God is protected and strengthened by Him.

To foster the cause of liberty and justice—this is the goal of America and the goal of every Legionaire. This goal has been challenged by communism and crime. America has accepted the challenge and we must and will meet it successfully.

We are a God-loving people. This is our greatest strength. Let our national motto always be, "In God we trust." ("An American's Challenge," *Congressional Record*, October 10, 1962, p. A7518.)

In the battle against communism, as in all previous encounters with godless tyranny, the United States must win and we will win. Let Khrushchev, Castro, and Mao Tse-tung recognize there is no force more powerful than the determination of a free and righteous people.

Let us not forget that whenever we have stood firm, communism has retreated. (*Ibid.*, p. A7518.)

WIRETAPS. We have at the present time, Mr. Chairman, 64 telephone taps in operation. There has been no change in the policy which restricts their use. They are used only in matters in which the internal security of the country is involved—all of those now in operation are in this category—and in kidnaping and extortion violations where human life is in jeopardy. Further, the FBI itself does not authorize a tap. Each must be authorized in advance and in writing by the Attorney General. (*FBI 1965 Appropriation,* January 29, 1964, p. 44.)

We make use of a total of 49 telephone taps and five microphone installations in Bureau cases in the security field. All were approved in advance and in writing by the Attorney General. (*FBI 1970 Appropriation,* p. 73.)

WOMAN—COMMUNIST. This description fits only that relatively small elite corps comprising the female portion of the entire world Communist Party membership which, according to Communist reports, numbers approximately 36,000,000 individuals.

The Communist woman is a woman of fanatical dedication and purpose. Indeed, she has been changed, remade, even, in a sense, "transformed" to the extent that she has a completely different view of reality from that experienced by the woman of the free world.

Communist woman believes that she is one of a chosen class selected to transform and remake mankind. She is, with humorless, single-minded intensity of purpose, dedicated to achievement of that end. She has caught a wildly utopian dream of a perfect world of tomorrow inhabited solely by perfect creatures—all of them, of course, Communists.

I do not mean to be facetious. This dream—this idea of a perfect world with its attendant blueprint for achievement —is the bait which draws the woman of little faith to communism. It is this which enables her to subordinate all thought of individual rights for herself, and to deny entirely such rights to others. Disastrously misguided though she is, this woman fully believes that she has enlisted in a noble cause. It is this belief which enables her to accept wholeheartedly a

254

soulless, vicious, totalitarian, end-justifies-the-means doctrine, and strive to advance that doctrine with fanatic—indeed, with almost consecrated—zeal. ("A View of Reality," *General Foundation Clubwoman Magazine.* May-June, 1961.)

WORLD CONQUEST. The full implications of the Communist challenge are shocking. The ultimate Communist goal—as defined by Marx, Lenin, and other Communist leaders—is the ruthless overthrow of our Judaic-Christian heritage and the establishment of a world-wide Communist society. By its very nature, communism is expansionist and universalist. In fact, the Communists feel that they can find their true fulfillment only by conquering non-Communist areas and bringing the whole planet under their dominion.

This overriding Communist goal of universal domination becomes the key to Party activities. Feeling that history has destined communism for ultimate victory, the Communists believe that permanent peace with non-Communists is impossible, that life must be an inevitable struggle between the two. "It is inconceivable," Lenin proclaimed, "that the Soviet Republic should continue to exist for a long period side by side with imperialist states. Ultimately, one or the other must conquer." ("The Communist Menace: Red Goals and Christian Ideals," *Christianity Today,* October 10, 24, November 7, 1960 issues, reprint, p. 1.)

WORLD CONQUEST—COMMUNIST GOAL. It is an incontestable fact that our country, the symbol of the free world, is the ultimate, priceless goal of international communism. The leaders of international communism have vowed to achieve world domination. This cannot be until the Red flag is flown over the United States.

If, for a moment, the grandiose Red plan is scoffed at as being fantastic, consider that one-fourth of the land surface of the world and one-third of the peoples of the earth are now controlled by the worldwide Communist-bloc.

Certainly, the Communist gains throughout the world are evidence enough that America, if it lowers its guard, may be someday an easy target for the Red threat. The Communist plan is to conquer the United States, if not today, then tomorrow; if not tomorrow, then the next day, next month, next year—there is no timetable, no "Five-Year Plan." This

255

is evident in the machinations of the Communist Party, USA, as shown by the analysis of its 17th National Convention published in this Bulletin. (*FBI Law Enforcement Bulletin,* March 1960, p. 1.)

WORLD CONQUEST. Nowhere is the hope for peace more sincere than in the hearts of all true Americans. But in our quest for peace we must never lose sight of the well-documented fact that every Red leader from Marx and Engels through Khrushchev, Mao, and the American Communist spokesman, Gus Hall, is dedicated to an ideology which upholds world conquest as its ultimate goal.

The Communists have never deviated from this objective. Despite the high-pressure campaign they have mounted behind Khrushchev's phrase of "peaceful co-existence," the Communist know that this is simply a propaganda slogan— one devised to further their own ends by stirring the hopes and emotions of those who seek an end to the turmoil, fear, and sorrow that world communism itself created.

Actions continue to speak louder than words, and certainly the Communists have shown no indication of a sincere quest for peace. (*Congressional Record,* Nov. 27, 1963, p. A7293.)

YOUTH. . . . the youth of our Nation are being singled out for special attention. The Party's chief hope for rapid growth and approval rests on its efforts to entice restless young men and women into its ranks, and the Communists already have good cause to be optimistic. Their campaign to blanket college and university campuses with Communist speakers—a program which has been accepted with palliative indifference by many persons—is a resounding success in the eyes of the Party. (*FBI Law Enforcement Bulletin,* October 1, 1966.)

In 1959, the Communist Party, USA, launched a major campaign with youth as its target. On May 30 and 31, 1959, approximately 20 young Communists from New York City, Baltimore, Chicago, Detroit, Los Angeles, and Philadelphia attended a conference with national leaders of the Party at Party headquarters in New York City. The purpose of the meeting was to devise a program to attract young blood—

teen-agers, students, and working youth—to the ranks of the Party.

After those May 1959 conferences, campuses throughout the Nation became prime targets for Communist infiltration and recruitment efforts. The Party began operating what amounted to a regular lecture bureau, with Party spokesmen seizing every opportunity to project their views on campuses across the country. (HCUA, "Communist Target—Youth," May 12-14, 1960, pp. 2-3.)

If for a moment any American considers the Communists to be blind to opportunity, let him consider this vile tactic which came out of the 17th National Convention:

It is obvious to the Communists that, if its Party is to survive, it must attract the youth of this Nation. As newspapers and other media reveal almost daily, many of America's juveniles are in a state of upheaval—adult authority and morality have been spurned to the point where juvenile arrests in this country in 1958 increased eight percent over the preceding year.

During the convention, an Illinois Communist took note of the juvenile delinquency situation and proposed that if "we" provide them with a place to go and with activities, they will not be so delinquent; "we" can move them in a positive direction.

What can be more despicable or dangerous to our democracy than this sort of Red Pied Piper trickery? (SISS, *Concerning the 17th National Convention, Communist Party, U. S. A., December 10-13,* 1959, p. 6.)

The Communist Party remains deeply interested in the American college student. At a press conference, Gus Hall was asked if the Party had made any inroads among college students. He replied that the Party had made gains in this field, adding that there has been a change in the thinking of college students toward "nonconformity." Hall added that he based this comment on the fact that a number of requests have been received from colleges for speakers. (*Ibid.,* p. 9).

Expanding its scope, the Party has revitalized its efforts to sway the thinking of the young people of America. Party functionaries have been visiting and speaking on college campuses at every opportunity. Leading the drive to subvert and recruit young people is Mortimer Daniel Rubin, national

257

youth director for the Party, who also is editing the magazine, *New Horizons for Youth,* a recently started monthly which the Party hopes will win over those students who are "sitting on the fence." (*FBI Annual Report, Fiscal Year 1961,* p. 26.)

Today, these rabid emissaries of Red Fascism are engaged in an intensive campaign to subvert the minds and win the support of American youth.

Foremost among the programs and activities currently being directed against our Nation's young people are:

A new Communist-oriented youth organization, The DuBois Clubs of America, which was founded last June at a special meeting in California dominated and controlled by the Communists; and

A continuation of the campus speech program which has contributed so successfully to the Party's efforts to reach the student bodies of American colleges and universities.

Why are Communist spokesmen so anxious to appear on college campuses, yet so tight-lipped before grand juries, committees of Congress and in our courts of law? Why do glib-tongued Party members suddenly lose their voices when placed under oath?

The answer is: They are afraid of the truth—just as they fear decency and justice and God! Let me repeat what I have said before: We are at war with the Communists and the sooner every red-blooded American realizes this the safer we will be. ("Our Heritage of Greatness," December 12, 1964, p. 6.)

"Give me a child for 8 years and it will be a Bolshevist forever." These words are attributed to the prophet of world communism, Nikolai Lenin, in a speech made in 1923. Now as a voice from the grave, the Communist Party, USA, a dedicated group of latter-day disciples of Lenin, acts with a determined program to recruit youth into the Communist conspiracy. Regarding our youth as a formless but pliable mass which can be shaped or molded, the Communist Party, USA has made clear its purpose and interests. The language jargon utilized is directed toward a single aim—the inculcation in young minds of a perverted theological faith in the ideals and objectives of a Communist society.

The Communist Party, USA plans to launch a recruiting drive to last from April 1, 1965, through July 1965. Emphasis will be directed toward the recruitment of Negro youth.

The Party also plans to hold a training school for youth in New York City in the summer of 1965 to give intensive Marxist-Leninist orientation to at least one youth from each Party district. Some of these youths will then be sent to other areas to train additional youths. In addition, certain Communist Party, USA youths will be asked to go to the South during the summer of 1965 to work with civil rights organizations. (*FBI 1966 Appropriation*, p. 55.)

YOUTH—APPROACH TO. This campaign is a skilfully contrived charade which seems to speak of truth but which is in reality a masked attempt to subvert our young people. For the truth is not important to the Communist except as it may serve his needs; it is important to youth, however, and the Communist, knowing this, has made it the premise on which he is waging this campaign. He knows that youth is a time of seeking after truth, of weighing new concepts and forming ideas; that youthful energies are impatient to be tested against the world's challenges and are quick to respond to proposals that seem to meet these challenges. He, therefore, caters to this impatience with cunning programs which seem to strike at social ills and international problems.

These programs are presented at meetings, social events, or wherever a susceptible group of young people is gathered. The Communist discusses his Party's concern for civil rights and civil liberties and speaks of its work to promote world peace and international disarmament. He portrays his organization as the defender of the underdog and the weak.

These are laudable objectives to which all Americans subscribe and so are particularly attractive to inexperienced young men and women who do not know of the sinister hypocrisy of the Party's propaganda. When youthful interest is aroused by these programs to the point of supporting the Party in its alleged espousal of humanitarian endeavors, then the stage is set for gradually bringing the deceived young people into other areas of the Party's activities which are more directly concerned with its main objective of subversion. ("Communist Youth Campaign," *Congressional Record*, August 17, 1962, p. A6288.)

YOUTH CAN BE VICTIMIZED. Particularly unfortunate is the fact that many youth and student groups in our Nation today are totally unaware of the extent to which they can be victimized and exploited by Communists. The sad proof of this fact was nowhere more apparent than in municipal court in San Francisco on June 1, 1960, when Judge Albert A. Axelrod dismissed riot charges against 62 of the persons arrested as a result of the mob violence which erupted during demonstrations protesting the hearings held in that city by the House Committee on Un-American Activities (HCUA), May 12-14, 1960.

The judge pointed out that there were ample grounds for conviction in the cases involving the 62 defendants, most of whom were college students, but he added that the defendants were, for the most part, "clean-cut American college students" who could well be haunted for the rest of their lives by the stigma which a conviction would attach to them. In response to this action on the part of the judge, 58 of the defendants signed a statement distributed immediately after he had rendered his decision. It read, in part: "Nobody incited us, nobody misguided us. We were led by our own convictions and we still stand firmly by them." (HCUA, *Communist Target—Youth, Communist Infiltration and Agitation Tactics,* 1960, p. 3.)

YOUTH—CLASSES. Of course, the Party's efforts to attract the younger generation are not limited to the appearances of Party leaders at college and university campuses. For example, one recruiting method employed by various Party districts is to conduct educational classes or study groups in Marxism for students or other young people who have exhibited an interest in politics, economics, and sociology. Participants are not always informed beforehand that the classes are conducted by Communists. (*FBI 1965 Appropriation,* January 29, 1964, p. 39.)

YOUTH—DEMONSTRATIONS. The successful Communist exploitation and manipulation of youth and student groups throughout the world today are a major challenge which free world forces must meet and defeat. Recent world events clearly reveal that world communism has launched a massive campaign to capture and maneuver youth and student groups.

260

The vigor and vitality of such groups constitute an explosive force of immense proportions. Channeled into proper outlets, this force can accomplish immeasurable good for a peace-loving world. Manipulated into destructive channels, this force can create chaos.

Communists have become experts at using this force to create chaos. In Japan, for example, Communists carefully nurtured and developed a growing body of students over a 10-year period, using them periodically in protest demonstrations. The culmination of this training was reached this year, when the highly organized and tightly disciplined rioters shocked the world with their uproarious displays.

The seeds for future large-scale demonstrations of this type have been planted by Communists in other countries. The small demonstrations staged by Communist-oriented students in Uruguay earlier this year—demonstrations which marred an otherwise cordial welcome extended to the President of the United States on the last stop of his Latin American tour—were reminiscent of Communist-instigated activities of student groups in Japan 10 years ago. Communists are hopeful that the seeds in Uruguay and other countries will sprout as they did in Japan, leading eventually to demonstrations of the type that rocked Japan. (HCUA, *Communist Target—Youth, Communist Infiltration and Agitation Tactics*, 1960, p. 1.)

YOUTH—DO. You might ask, "How can I, as a student in school, help in the fight against communism?"

In many ways. First of all, you should be a good student. Our Nation needs young people well-trained in mathematics, history, science, languages. This means doing a good job in school.

Second, you should be good citizens at home and in the community. This is most important. Too many of our young people are today becoming involved in criminal misbehavior. Such acts weaken our Nation. Crime is an important enemy of our national security.

Third, you should know more about the history of America, the principles on which this Nation was founded. The study of great men of our past, such as George Washington, Abraham Lincoln, and Theodore Roosevelt, helps us

261

understand the present and the future. We see the ideals which they pursued.

Lastly, you should be willing to do your share for your country. Too many citizens, old and young, shirk their responsibilities, saying, "Let George do it." This is wrong. Unless each of us does his part, the whole Nation is that much weaker. ("Young People Can Help Defeat Communism," *Junior Review*, April 16, 1962, reprint.)

YOUTH—IMPORTANCE TO COMMUNISTS. It has long been a basic tenet of Communist strategy to control for its own evil purposes the explosive force which youth represents. In the relentless struggle for world domination being waged by them, Communists are dedicated to the Leninist principle that "youth will decide the issue of the entire struggle—both the student youth and, still more, the working-class youth."

In the Soviet Union, for example, the reins on youth are held with a vise-like grip. In order to qualify for higher educational opportunities and better jobs in the Soviet society, young people must be members of the Young Communist League, the Komsomol. From their earliest days, young people must learn to accept the course dictated for them by the rulers of the only god they are permitted to know and worship—the almighty State.

Communist China is an even greater example of the Communist determination to make youth serve its objectives. There today, millions of children are being raised "the collective way." From the cradle to the factory, the youth of Communist China is being molded to serve the cause of world communism in its quest for world domination.

Projecting this Communist principle of strategy outward from behind the Iron and Bamboo Curtains, Communists strive with equal intensity to subvert the youth of other countries. The lures they use to do so are tempting and varied. There are, for instance, the World Youth Festivals, which have been held every other year since 1947. The seventh such affair, held last year in Vienna, attracted thousands of young people from America, Africa, and Asia, as well as those from the Soviet-satellite countries. (HCUA, *Communist Target—Youth, Communist Infiltration and Agitation Tactics*, 1960, pp. 1-2.)

262

YOUTH INFILTRATION. They have been exposed by a number of writers and columnists. I have in mind George Sokolsky and Fulton Lewis, Jr. One of the targets of the Communist Party is to step up its infiltration of youth organizations and the demonstration at San Francisco which occurred last year was typical of their efforts. At the same time there is a rather healthy sign I have observed which is developing at the high school and college level, where young men and women are learning about communism. I think this is a very healthy sign. The more one can learn about communism and its fallacies and its viciousness, the stronger our country will be.

I see two tides running.

In one is the group in favor of the false peaceful co-existence theory which functions through Communist-front organizations and the other is the group of young people operating through anti-Communist organizations. The questions these young people are asking show that they are beginning to realize communism is not all it has been portrayed to be. If we get them thinking and asking that kind of questions, it is a very healthy and wholesome condition.

Mr. Lipscomb. Will we be able to distinguish these different types of groups when they apply for the Peace Corps and programs of this sort? Will we be able to tell the intent of the people who desire to participate?

Mr. Hoover. It depends on what screening procedures are used in setting up the Peace Corps.

Mr. Lipscomb. It is important, in my opinion, they make some plans for screening.

Mr. Hoover. I think it would be desirable. (*FBI 1962 Appropriation*, pp. 67-68.)

YOUTH—MOST ARE LOYAL. The great majority of college students are proud of their American heritage and loyal to the traditions of democracy. However, it is basic communist strategy to further communist objectives with noncommunist hands, and this is exactly what is happening on some college campuses. The idealism of many American students is being cynically exploited for communist purposes; youthful exuberance is being channeled into unlawful riotous conduct; mocking disdain for democratic processes and moral values is being fed to inquisitive young minds—all under the guise

263

of seeking equal justice or some other noble cause. (*FBI Law Enforcement Bulletin,* February 1, 1967.)

YOUTH NEED TO UNDERSTAND. I present to the Committee a copy of this pamphlet entitled "What Young People Should Know About Communism." This presents a brief and meaningful message regarding the threat of Communists, the extent of communism, and some suggestions as to positive steps which young people and every citizen can take to combat this subversive organization.

It has always been our contention that in order to combat communism, one must know what it is and the steps that can be taken within the limits of our constitutional Government to thwart the goals of communism to take over this country either by propaganda or by force. (*FBI 1965 Appropriation,* January 29, 1964, p. 40.)

YOUTH—OBJECTIVE. Today, the Communists continue with impunity to breathe out lies and distortions against the United States. Their designs on American youth revolt and anger those steeped in our national ideals of freedom.

The peddling of their dishonest doctrine to high-minded, largely inexperienced, and basically eager to believe young people is not unlike the peddling of filth and dope in demoralizing effect. It can undermine patriotism, create doubts about our social and economic system, and mock the many wholesome youth organizations in this country.

The great majority of American youths are genuinely convinced that they would not fall for the Communist bait. Many never would. But there are others who might never know they were "hooked" until the enormous tragedy of their loss of faith dawned after bitter years of fighting the American way of life, almost unwittingly, as dupes of the Communists.

It has happened to idealistic Americans before. ("Faith in Freedom," *Congressional Record,* December 5, 1963, p. A7435.)

YOUTH PROGRESS. "This is a revolution which will be fought everywhere and we will win because there are more of us than there are of them."

The rallying cry of the Hungarian uprising of 1956? Not at all. These words were shouted by a young agitator in

264

December 1966 during riotous disorder on the campus of a large American university. In a continuing series of events, the academic community has been bombarded with civil disobedience, assaults, threats, and riots of unprecedented magnitude.

I think it is appropriate to quote two warnings from statements which appeared here in October 1964 and February 1966:

This academic year will undoubtedly see intensive Communist Party efforts to erect its newest facade   (the W. E. B. DuBois Clubs of America) on the Nation's campuses to draw young blood for the vampire which is international communism. (October 1, 1964.)

The unvarnished truth is that the communist conspiracy is seizing this insurrectionary climate to captivate the thinking of rebellious-minded youth and coax them into the communist movement itself or at least agitate them into serving the communist cause. (February 1, 1966.)

Has this strategy paid off? The answer, unfortunately, must be a definite yes. Today the communist conspiracy is reaping large dividends from its persistent efforts to gain a toehold on college and university campuses and from its dogged determination to disrupt, through mass agitation, the orderly processes of our educational systems. (*FBI Law Enforcement Bulletin*, February 1, 1967.)

YOUTH—U. S. SOME SUCCESS. In the United States, the Communist Party is jubilant about success it has had recently in developing and exploiting youth and student groups. A spokesman at one of the Party's national executive committee meetings earlier this year stated that "there has been a breakthrough as far as young people are concerned, particularly in colleges where students want to know what socialism is."

Unfortunately, there is some truth in what the Party's spokesman has said. There has been a limited "breakthrough" as far as the efforts of the Communist Party to infiltrate youth and student groups in this country are concerned. It is attributable neither to chance nor to a stroke of good luck for the Party. Instead, it is the result of careful planning and a concentrated effort by the Party. (HCUA, *Communist Target—Youth, Communist Infiltration and Agitation Tactics,* 1960, p. 2.)

Chapter Three

J. EDGAR HOOVER'S BRIEF ON THE COMMUNIST PARTY

STATUS OF THE COMMUNIST PARTY UNDER THE ACT OF CONGRESS APPROVED OCTOBER 16, 1918

(A) Federal Statute Applicable to the Communist Party

The act of Congress approved October 16, 1918, amending the immigration laws of the United States, provides among other things that (1) aliens who disbelieve in or advocate or teach the overthrow by force or violence of the Government of the United States shall be deported; (2) aliens who are members of or affiliated with any organization that entertains a belief in, teaches, or advocates the overthrow by force or violence of the Government of the United States shall be deported.

(B) Proposition

The Communist Party is an organization advocating and teaching the overthrow by force or violence of the Government of the United States and members thereof believe in and advocate and teach the overthrow by force or violence of the Government of the United States.

(C) Introduction

During the year of 1918 a considerable amount of dissension arose in the Socialist Party between the conservative and extreme elements. In a subtle and discreet manner an ultrarevolutionary movement gained headway within the ranks of the Socialist Party of America, with the result

266

that on November 7, 1918, a Communist propaganda league was organized and established a publication, *The Revolutionary Age*. In this publication an agitation was started against the so-called "reactionary Socialists," but, with the exception of the Foreign Language Federation, it met with little response for some months. The pages of *The Revolutionary Age* called upon the Socialist Party to adopt the revolutionary Communist tactics. In February, 1919, there was organized in New York City the leftwing section of the Socialist Party. On February 16, 1919, the foreign language branches and a few of the English branches of the leftwing section issued a manifesto to the members of the Socialist Party. Attached hereto and marked as "Exhibit 1" is a copy of the manifesto of the leftwing section of the Socialist Party. Examination of the manifesto throws considerable light upon the purposes of this organization, which later grew into the Communist Party.

I shall now set forth certain extracts taken from the manifesto as illustrative of its purposes:

"Revolutionary Socialists hold, with the founders of scientific socialism, that there are two dominant classes in society, the bourgeoisie and the proletariat; that between these two classes a struggle must go on until the working class through the seizure of the instruments of production and distribution, the abolition of the capitalist state, and the establishment of the dictatorship of the proletariat, creates a socialist system. Revolutionary Socialists do not believe that they can be voted into power. They struggle for the conquest of power by the revolutionary proletariat."

It will thus be seen that it is expressly stated that the revolutionary Socialist planned to seize the instruments of production and distribution and the abolition of the capitalist state.

"Between the capitalist society and the Communist lies the period of revolutionary transformation of the one into the other. This corresponds to a political transition period, in which the State can not be anything else but the dictatorship of the proletariat . . .

"We assert with Marx that the 'class struggle is essentially a political struggle,' and we can only accept his own oft-repeated interpretation of that phrase. The class struggle, whether it manifest itself on the, industrial field or in the direct struggle for governmental control, is essentially a struggle for the capture and destruction of the capitalist state. This is a political act. In this broader view of the term 'political' Marx includes revolutionary industrial action. In the sense that it aims to undermine the bourgeois state, which 'is nothing less than a machine for the oppression of one class by another and that no less so in a democratic republic than under a monarchy.' "

Particular attention is to be noted of the doctrine of Marx, wherein it is specifically stated that not only will the class struggle manifest itself on the industrial field but that it will also direct its energies toward the struggle for Government control and for the capture and destruction of the capitalist state. Attention is particularly called to this expression of Marx's for the reason that Communists often allude to their propaganda and program as being political and, therefore, not a violation of the present Federal statutes. It will be noted, however, that Marx, the spokesman of Communists and the formulator of the original Communist manifesto, explains the class struggle as being an essentially political struggle in that its end is the destruction of the political state, but that the means of accomplishing such an end is not to be accomplished through political means, but by direct and mass action.

"Political action, revolutionary and emphasizing the implacable character of the class struggle, is a valuable means of propaganda. It must at all times struggle to arouse the revolutionary mass action of the proletariat—its use is both agitational and obstructive. It must on all issues wage war upon capitalism and the State. Revolutionary socialism uses the forum of Parliament for agitation, but it does not intend to and can not use the bourgeois state as a means of introducing socialism; this bourgeois state must be destroyed by the mass action of the revolutionary proletariat. The proletarian dictatorship in the form of a soviet state is the immediate objective of the class struggle.

"Marx declared that 'the working class can not simply lay hold of the ready-made state machinery and wield it for its own purposes.' This machinery must be destroyed. But 'moderate socialism' makes the state the center of its action."

268

From the above quotations we again see that the left wing section of the Socialist Party in February of 1919 stated that the bourgeois state must be destroyed by the mass action of the revolutionary proletariat. Later in this brief, a detailed explanation of mass action will be given, but it is illuminating to note that the word "destroy" runs throughout the first manifesto issued by the left wing section of the Socialist Party, and it is conceded by all parties concerned that the reference to the bourgeois state refers to the Government of the United States, as at the present time there is but one State existing in the United States namely, the Government, and as will be pointed out later, "the state" is synonymous with "capitalist state" and "bourgeois state."

It will be noted from the above quotations that the left wing, in its first manifesto, advocated industrial action for political purposes and that they place the ballot as a secondary action for propaganda purposes only. After the issuance of the manifesto, the left wing began to take in members and the propaganda intensified, particularly in the foreign languages, and on May 10, 1919, they published the manifesto of the first congress of the communist international held at Moscow on March 2 to 6, 1919. A detailed analysis of this manifesto will later be made in this brief. It is sufficient at this point to state, however, that the manifesto of the third international called upon the proletariat to immediately seize government power and substitute in its place the power of the proletariat, and that mass action with force and violence as incidents thereto was openly advocated. In the list of eligible organizations to participate in the International Communist Congress we find but three names of organizations in the United States as considered eligible for such participation, namely, the Industrial Workers of the World, the Workers' International Industrial Union, and the left wing of the Socialist Party. Upon examination of the call for the International Communist Congress we will note the peculiar similarity between the doctrines enunciated in the call of the International Communist Congress and the call of the left wing of the Socialist Party of New York.

Following the issuance of the manifesto of the left wing of the Socialist Party the national executive committee of the Socialist Party commenced to take cognizance of the revolutionary movement within its organization and started counter propaganda. On May 24, 1919, the so-called reactionary section of the Socialist Party convened in Chicago for the purpose of discussing the so-called fraudulent election for delegates to the international congress, and also to discuss the left wing. This conference lasted from May 24 to 29, inclusive, and expelled approximately 6,000 leftwing members from Michigan and 30,000 from the Foreign Language Federations. They also set August 30 for a special convention in Chicago.

This action caused the left wing to issue a call on May 31, 1919, for delegates to attend a national leftwing convention to be held in New York on June 21.

This call was responded to immediately, and when this conference convened, on June 21, there were delegates representing approximately 45,000 members. The conference lasted from June 21 to 24, inclusive, the principal discussion being as to whether a Communist Party should be organized at once or whether it would be more advisable to agitate in the Socialist Party until the special convention and then withdraw. It was finally decided to wage a struggle in the Socialist Party until September in order to rally all the revolutionary elements for a Communist Party, meanwhile organizing temporarily as the leftwing section of the Socialist Party. At this time they issued a manifesto and program.

In this manifesto it will be noted that practically the same wording and phraseology is used as was used by the Bolsheviks for the International Communist Congress, which will be analyzed later. The manifesto attacked social patriots scoffing at parliamentary action and advising mass action in conquering, suppressing, and overthrowing the bourgeois state, establishing the dictatorship of the proletariat for the transitory period. The following are some of the extracts from this manifesto, which show the nature of the organization:

"Revolutionary socialism, on the contrary, insists that the democratic parliamentary state can never be the basis for the introduction of socialism; that it is necessary to destroy the producers, which will deprive the bourgeoisie of political power and function as a revolutionary dictatorship of the proletariat.

"But there is a more vital tendency—the tendency of the workers to initiate mass strikes—strikes which are equally a revolt against the bureaucracy in the unions and against the employers. These strikes will constitute the determining feature of proletarian action in the days to come. Revolutionary socialism must use these mass industrial revolts to broaden the strike to make it general and militant; use the strike for political objectives, and finally develop the mass political strike against capitalism and the State.

"The mass strikes of the American proletariat provide the material basis out of which to develop the concepts and action of revolutionary socialism.

"Our task is to encourage the militant mass movements in the American Federation of Labor, to split the old unions, to break the power of unions which are corrupted by imperialism and betray the militant proletariat. The American Federation of Labor, in its dominant expression, is united with imperialism. A bulwark of reaction, it must be exposed and its power for evil broken.

"Our task, moreover, is to articulate and organize the mass of the unorganized industrial proletariat which constitutes the basis for militant socialism.

"The class struggle is a political struggle in the sense that its objective is political—the overthrow of the political organization upon which capitalistic exploitation depends and the introduction of a new social system. The direct objective is the conquest by the proletariat of the power of the State.

"Revolutionary socialism does not propose to 'capture' the bourgeois parliamentary state, but to conquer and destroy it. Revolutionary socialism, accordingly, repudiates t h e policy of introducing socialism by means of legislative measures on the basis of the bourgeois state. This is a bourgeois state, the organ for the coercion of the proletarian by the capitalist. How, then, can it introduce socialism? As long as the bourgeois parliamentary state prevails, the capitalist class can baffle the will of the proletariat, since all the political power, the Army and the police, industry and the press are in the hands of the capitalists, whose economic power gives them complete domination. The revolutionary proletariat must expropriate all these by the conquest of the power of the state by annihilating the political power of the

271

bourgeoisie before it can begin the task of introducing socialism.

"Revolutionary socialism, accordingly, proposes to conquer by means of political action—political action in the
revolutionary Marxian sense, which does not simply mean
parliamentarism, but the class action of the proletariat in
any form having as its objective the conquest of the power
of the state.

"But parliamentarism can not conquer the power of the
state for the proletariat. The conquest of the power of the
state is an extraparliamentary act. It is accomplished, not
by the legislative representatives of the proletariat, but by
the mass power of the proletariat in action. The supreme
power of the proletariat inheres in the political mass strike,
in using the industrial mass power of the proletariat for
political objectives.

"The final objective of mass action is the conquest of
the power of the state, the annihilation of the bourgeoisie
parliamentary state, and the introduction of the transition
proletarian state, functioning as a revolutionary dictatorship
of the proletariat.

"Dictatorship of the proletariat.—The attitude toward
the state divides the anarchist (and anarcho-syndicalist), the
moderate socialist, and the revolutionary socialist. Eager
to abolish the state (which is the ultimate purpose of revolutionary socialism), the anarchist (and anarcho-syndicalist)
fails to realize that the state is necessary in the transition
period from capitalism to socialism. The moderate socialist
proposes to use the bourgeois state, with its fraudulent democracy, its illusory theory of the 'unity of all the classes,' its
standing army, policy, and bureaucracy oppressing and baf-
fling the masses. The revolutionary socialist maintains that
the bourgeois parliamentary state must be completely destroyed, and proposes the organization of a new state, the
dictatorship of the proletariat.

"The state is an organ of coercion. The bourgeois
parliamentary state is the organ of the bourgeoisie for the
coercion of the proletariat. The revolutionary proletariat
must, accordingly, destroy this state. But the conquest of
political power by the proletariat does not immediately end
capitalism or the power of the capitalists or immediately

socialize industry. It is therefore necessary that the proletariat organize its own state for the coercion and suppression of the bourgeoisie.

"The old machinery of the State can not be used by the revolutionary proletariat. It must be destroyed.

"The state of proletarian dictatorship is political in character, since it represents a ruling class, the proletariat, which is now supreme; and it uses coercion against the old bourgeois class. But the task of this dictatorship is to render itself unnecessary; and it becomes unnecessary the moment the dictatorship of the proletariat performs its negative task of constructing the old order; it performs the positive task of constructing the new. Together with the government of the proletarian dictatorship there is developed in the old sense, since it concerns itself with the management of production and not with the government of the persons. Out of workers' control of industry, introduced by the proletarian dictatorship, there develops the complete structure of Communist socialism—industrial self-government of the communistically organized producers. When this structure is completed, which implies the complete expropriation of the bourgeoisie economically and politically, the dictatorship of the proletariat ends, in its place coming the full and free social and individual autonomy of the Communist order."

From the above we see that the left wing of the Socialist Party, which later became the Communist Party, specifically states that it does not intend to capture the bourgeoisie parliamentary state, but to conquer and destroy it, and that the final objective of mass action is the medium intended to be used in the conquest and destruction of the bourgeoisie state to annihilate the parliamentary state and introduce a revolutionary dictatorship of the proletariat. In another quotation, it is specifically stated that the proletariat must organize its own state for the "coercion and suppression of the bourgeoisie." Throughout the above manifesto, advocation of force and violence is sponsored by the leftwing party.

After the conference, at which the above manifesto was formulated, the efforts of the Socialist Party intensified and the national executive committee of that Party continued to expel members.

273

On July 19, 1919, the left wing of the Socialist Party issued a call for a convention to be held in Chicago on September 1, for the purpose of organizing a Communist Party. Attached hereto and marked "Exhibit 2" is a copy of *The Communist* for July 19, 1919, containing the call for the national convention. I will not advert to the contents of this call other than to point out that its phraseology and meaning was consistent with all the documents we have previously examined and that they again talk of conquering and destroying the state by mass action, thereby establishing clearly that they were following the lead of the Bolshevik and the first congress of the Communist International.

On August 30, 1919, the Socialist Party of America convened in Chicago for the purpose of discussing and, if possible, harmonizing the dissatisfied elements within its organization. The left wing of the Socialist Party tried to be seated and capture the convention, but were defeated in their attempt, with the result that they bolted the convention and convened the Communist Party convention on September 1, 1919, which lasted until September 7, 1919. Approximately 129 delegates attended this Communist convention, representing 55,000 members. Officers were elected and a manifesto and program adopted which was consistent with all of the manifestos and programs previously issued by the left wing of the Socialist Party. The official manifesto and program will later be analyzed in this brief. Immediately at the close of this convention the Communist Party proceeded with an extensive propaganda, issuing a large number of pamphlets, not only in English but also in foreign languages, and immediately established the publication of *The Communist*, the official organ of the Communist Party, a periodical issued weekly from the headquarters of the organization in Chicago. The energies of the Party were immediately directed toward the acquisition of new members, and to date the Communist Party has added to its original membership hundreds of new members, and is at present carrying on a most extensive and intensified propaganda.

(D) COMMUNIST INTERNATIONAL

Reference has previously been made to the third international or to the first international congress of Communists, and I will later show that the Communist Party of America is actually affiliated and adheres to the teachings, program, and tactics of the third international. In order that an intelligent understanding may be had of the principles of the third international, it will be necessary to analyze in detail various provisions of the manifesto which was issued in connection with this international.

The first congress of the Communist International was held at Moscow from March 2 to 6, 1919, and on March 10, 1919, a manifesto was issued, signed by Charles Rakovsky, N. Lenin, G. Zinoviev, Leon Trotsky, and Fritz Platten. Attached hereto and marked as "Exhibit 3" is a translation of the manifesto of the Communist International. The manifesto calls upon the proletariat to seize all Government power and substitute in its place the power of the proletariat. It is noted that the manifesto is addressed not only to the proletariat of Russia but to the "proletariat of all countries." It proceeds with a discussion in which the statement is made that the proletariat recognizes neither inherited privileges nor rights of property. It urges the formation of workers', soldiers' and peasants' counsels to oppose them to the State apparatus and to achieve "the same conditions as exist in Soviet Russia." Later in the manifesto we find the following statement: "The working class must answer blow for blow, if it will not renounce its own object and its own future, which is at the same time the future of all humanity." Immediately following this quotation is found the following statement: "This makes necessary the disarming of the bourgeoisie at the proper time, the arming of the laborer, and the formation of a Communist army as the protector of the rule of the proletariat and the inviolability of the social structure."

It will be particularly noted that the quotations set forth above directly advocate force and violence in acquiring the ultimate aim of the proletarian dictatorship. I call particular attention to these particular quotations at the present time, for I shall later point out that each member of the Communist Party of America pledges himself to the principles and tactics set forth in the Communist International.

Later in the manifesto of the Communist International we find open advocation of mass action, and the following quotation is particularly interesting: "It must end the domination of capital, make war impossible, wipe out State boundaries, transform the whole work into one cooperative commonwealth, and bring about real human brotherhood and freedom." This quotation is followed by the following statement: "This monstrous new conspiracy of the capitalist class must be met with the proletariat by seizure of the political power of the State, turning this power against its class enemies, and using it as a lever to set in motion the economic revolution." The next division of the manifesto is headed "The conquest of political power," and the following is the explanation of what is meant by the conquest of the political power:

"Seizure of political power by the proletariat means destruction of political power of the bourgeoisie. The organized power of the bourgeoisie is in the civil state, with its capitalistic army under control of bourgeois junker officers, its police and gendarmes, jailors and judges, its priests, Government officials, etc. Conquest of the political power means not merely a change in the personnel of ministries but annihilation of the enemy's apparatus of government; disarmament of the bourgeoisie of the counter revolutionary officers, of the White Guard, soldiers, the Red arming of the proletariat, the revolutionary Guard of workingmen, displacement of all bourgeois judges and organization of proletarian courts; elimination of control by reactionary Government officials and substitution of new organs of management of the proletariat. Victory of the proletariat. Victory of the proletariat consists in shattering the enemy's organization and organizing the proletarian power; in the destruction of the bourgeois and upbuilding of the proletarian state apparatus. Not until the proletarian has achieved this victory and broken the resistance of the bourgeoisie can the former enemies of the new order be made useful by bringing them under control of the Communist system and gradually bringing them into accord with its work."

From the above it will be noted that by the seizure of political power is meant the destruction of the political power of the bourgeoisie. It specifically advocates the elimination of government officers, police, judges, and priests. It urges the arming of the proletariat and the creation of a Red Guard. There is no effort to accomplish in this instance the ultimate aim by parliamentary action, but it is conclusive that in order to attain the aim desired that force and violence will be resorted to as a means of acquiring the desire. Later in the manifesto we find the following quotation:

"As the opposition of the bourgeoisie is broken, as it is expropriated and gradually absorbed into the working groups, the proletarian dictatorship disappears, until finally the State dies and there are no more class distinctions."

It will thus be seen from the foregoing quotation that the Communist International borders virtually upon the borders of anarchy, in that it contends through its efforts there will be no necessity of a state or government.

In the manifesto we find open advocation for the expropriation of the means of production and the distribution of such means into the common property of the proletarian state. It specifically advocates the expropriation of factories, mines, and estates, and, to use the words of the manifesto, advocates the "transfer of the large mansions to the local workers' councils and move the working people into the bourgeois dwellings." Thus we see an utter disregard of the rights of property.

Under the heading of "The way to victory," which closes the manifesto, the following statement appears:

"The revolutionary era compels the proletariat to make use of the means of battle which will concentrate its entire energies, namely, mass action with its logical resultant direct conflict with the governmental machinery, in open combat. All other methods, such as revolutionary use of bourgeois parliamentarism, will be of only secondary significance."

Thus we come to the close of the Communist international manifesto, and find that parliamentarism is to be considered victory in the drive of the Communists for worldwide control and that it openly advocates mass action which will result in direct conflict with the governmental machinery in open conflict. There can no longer remain any doubt in even the mind of a reader who gives but casual note to the manifesto of the Communist International, that it openly advocates the overthrow of the Government of the world by force or violence.

(E) Communist Party of America

Now that we have examined the manifesto of the Communist international, the next phase of the Communist movement which should be considered is the manifesto and program of the Communist Party of America. Attached hereto and marked as "Exhibit 4" is a copy of said manifesto and program, as issued by the Communist Party from its general headquarters at Chicago, Illinois. The essence of the Communist program is that the proletariat must be so directed and educated that by mass action they will at one sweep destroy the State and establish a dictatorship of the proletariat in the form of soviets, which will exist until the bourgeois is suppressed and destroyed, and the proletariat is organized into the working groups and the Communist commonwealth is established. They will only use parliamentary action (the ballot) as propaganda.

I will now endeavor to analyze in detail the manifesto of the Communist Party as adopted at its first national convention in Chicago, September 1, 1919.

On page 1 of the manifesto we find the following statement: "The struggle is between the capitalist nations of the world and the international proletariat, inspired by Soviet Russia." Thus we see behind the movement of the Communist Party in this country the inspiration of the Bolshevik forces now at work in Russia.

On page 3 of the manifesto reference is made to the attitude of the Socialist Party of America during the war. An examination of page 3 shows that the Communists lack patriotism for the Communist Party is founded upon internationalism and not nationalism.

On pages 5 and 6 of the manifesto we find the urging of the establishment of the dictatorship of the proletariat, which will be of particular significance in view of the advocation of such dictatorship by the Communist international above discussed in detail.

On page 6 we find set forth in the manifesto of the Communist Party what communism considers its conception of the State, and the following is a quotation taken from page 6:

"There is a common policy that characterizes moderate socialism; that is, its conception of the State. Out of the conception that the bourgeois parliamentary State is the basis for the introduction of socialism developed a directly counterrevolutionary policy.

"Communism rejects this conception of the State. It rejects the idea of class reconciliation and the parliamentary conquest of capitalism. The Communist Party alone is capable of mobilizing the proletariat for the revolutionary mass struggle to conquer the power of the State."

Thus we see that the Communist Party of America rejects parliamentary actions as its means to accomplish its end and directly sponsors mass action in its campaigns.

On page 8 of the manifesto we find the advocation of strikes and the seizure of the functions of industry and Government by the strikers as was done in the Seattle-Winnipeg general strikes.

On page 9 we find the following statement: "Laborism is as much a danger to the proletarian as moderate petty bourgeois socialism."

Again on page 9 we learn of the attitude of the Communist Party toward the fomenting of dissatisfied unrest:

"But there is a more vital tendency toward the workers to start mass strikes—strikes which are equally a revolt against the bureaucracy of the unions and the capitalists. The Communist Party will endeavor to broaden and deepen these strikes, making them general and militant, developing the general political strike."

This is of particular significance due to the fact that in the great coal and steel strikes which have been existing in the United States for the past several months, investigation has shown that the Communist Party has been actively engaged in its propaganda in fomenting industrial unrest, a doctrine specifically advocated in its manifesto and to which, as I will later show, each and every member of the Communist Party pledges himself to adhere.

On page 9 of the manifesto under the heading "Political action" we find the following statement:

"It is a political struggle in the sense that its objective is political — overthrow of the political organizations upon which capitalist exploitation depends, and the introduction of a proletarian State power. The objective is the conquest by the proletariat of the power of the State. Communism

279

does not propose to 'capture' the bourgeois parliamentary State, but to conquer and destroy it."

Thus we find that the Communist Party of America specifically pledges itself not only to capture the bourgeois parliamentary State but also to conquer and destroy it. Virtually the same language is found here as is found in the manifesto of the Communist International.

On page 10 of the manifesto we find the statement that the use of parliamentarism is only of secondary importance, and that the conquest of the power of the State is to be accomplished by the mass power of the proletariat, resulting in the mobilizing of this control against capitalism, which means the initial form of the revolutionary mass action that will conquer the power of the State.

On page 11 we find the particular significant statement of organization along the industrial lines rather than along craft lines, showing its similarity to the Industrial Workers of the World.

Pages 12 and 13 of the manifesto contains illuminating passages upon the doctrine of mass action, from which I will merely quote one sentence thereof, although all of the passages appearing on the pages mentioned are pertinent: "Therefore it is necessary that the proletariat organize its own State for the coercion and suppression of the bourgeoisie." The above concludes the manifesto of the Communist Party of America, and it is now necessary for us to examine in detail the program adopted at the Chicago convention.

On page 14 of the pamphlet attached and marked as "Exhibit 4" we find the program of the Communist Party, starting out with the following statement: "The Communist Party's aim is to direct this struggle to the conquest of political power, the overthrow of capitalism, and the destruction of the bourgeois State."

On page 15 the following statement appears: "The Communist Party maintains that the class struggle is essentially a political struggle; that is, a struggle to conquer the power of the State."

On page 16 we find the Communist Party's program pledged to the fomenting of mass strikes and the establishment in each industrial center and each industrial plant of a local committee for the purposes of stirring up the unrest.

On pages 16 and 17 we find the Communist Party against the unionism of the American Federation of Labor, to use the language of the program, as follows: "The Communist Party recognizes that the American Federation of Labor is reactionary and a bulwark of capitalism."

On page 17 of the program we find the Communist Party embracing the Industrial Workers of the World and militant unions of the American Federation of Labor.

Page 17 also contains the fact that the Communist Party will use their efforts to agitate among the unskilled workers so as to obtain their support.

Page 18 of the program we find the following statement: "The Communist Party will carry on among the Negro workers agitation to unite them with all class conscious workers." Thus we see the cause of much of the racial trouble in the United States at the present time.

The program closes with the following statement: "There must be close unity with the Communist International for common action against imperialism."

From the above we see that not only is the Communist Party of America pledged to overthrow the Government of the United States by force and violence, but that it is also pledged to foment industrial unrest through mass strikes and to stir up and agitate racial prejudices throughout the entire country.

In Exhibit 4, in which is contained the manifesto and program of the Communist Party, we find also the constitution of this Party, from which I will quote but one section:

"Sec. 8. No person shall be accepted as a member who enters into the service of the National, State, or local government bodies otherwise than through the civil service or by legal compulsion."

The last part of Exhibit 4 contains a report by Louis C. Fraina, international secretary of the Communist Party of America, to the executive committee of the Communist International. Thus we see that the Communist Party of America reports directly to the Communist International, with which it is affiliated according to its constitution and program.

(F) MASS ACTION

Numerous references have above been made to the term "mass action," which we find employed not only in the manifesto of the Communist International, but also in the manifesto of the Communist Party of America. In order that there may be no misunderstanding as to the direct meaning of the term "mass action," we will now consider the explanation of the term "mass action." As set forth in report by Louis C. Fraina, under subtitle "Unions and mass action," we find the following statements appearing in Fraina's work:

"It is the unity of all forms of proletarian action, a means of throwing the proletariat, organized and unorganized, in a general struggle against capitalism and the capitalist state.

"The value of this mass action is that it shows the proletariat its power, weakens capitalism, and compels the State largely to depend upon the use of brutal force in the struggle, either the physical force of the military or the terrorism; this emphasizes antagonisms between proletarian and the capitalist, widening the scope and deepening the intensity of the proletarian struggle against capitalism.

"Organizations, political and economic, have a tendency to become conservative; a tendency emphasized, moreover, by the fact that they largely represent the more favored groups of workers. The organizations must be swept out of their conservatism by the elemental impact of mass action, functioning through organized and unorganized workers, acting instinctively under the pressure of events and in disregard of bureaucratic discipline.

"A vital feature of mass action is precisely that it places in the hands of the proletariat the power to overcome the fetters of these organizations, to act in spite of their conservatism, and through proletarian mass action emphasize antagonisms between workers and capitalists and conquer power.

"MASS ACTION IS THE PROLETARIAT ITSELF IN ACTION

"The class power of the proletariat arises out of the intensity of its struggles and revolutionary energy. It consists, moreover, of undermining the bases of the power and morale of the capitalist state, a process that requires extra-parliamentary activity through mass action.

"It is the concentration of proletarian forces that makes mass action the method of the proletarian revolution.

"The proletarian revolution is a test of power, a process of forcible struggles, an epoch in which the proletariat requires a flexible method of action, a method of action that will not only concentrate all its available forces, but which will develop its initiative and consciousness, allowing it to seize and use any particular means of struggle in accord with a prevailing situation and necessary under the conditions.

"Socialism will come not through the peaceful, democratic, parliamentary conquest of the State but through the determined and revolutionary mass action of a proletarian minority.

"Parliamentarism in and of itself fetters proletarian action; organizations are often equally fetters upon action; the proletariat must act and always act; through action it conquers.

"Mass action is a dynamic, pliable, creative; the proletariat, through mass action, instinctively adapts itself to the means and the tactics necessary in a prevailing situation. The forms of activity of the proletariat are not limited and stultified by mass action; they are broadened, deepened, and coordinated. Mass action is equally a process of revolution and the revolution itself in operation.

"It will be noted by an examination of the above that the basis of the so-called mass action is primarily industrial and economic in function, but actually political in purpose. It basically functions on the industrial and economic field through mass action (meaning the general strike, or direct action) to force concessions from the so-called bourgeois state, considering parliamentary action but secondary at best. Hence, if mass action is to be the principal method used to bring about the Communist commonwealth, with parliamentary action (the ballot) as a poor secondary method, we can conclude but one thing, and that is: Mass action is the very essence of force and violence."

The above needs little or no comment, as the substance of same is well expressed in its last phrase, "Mass action is the very essence of force and violence." It is to be borne in mind that the above exposition of mass action is given by Louis C. Fraina, the official head of the Communist Party of America, and a man who directs its purposes and energies.

(G) Membership of the Communist Party of America

From the examination of the above documents, namely, the manifesto of the Communist International and the manifesto of the Communist Party of America, we find advocation of doctrines for the overthrow of the Government of the United States, not by parliamentary action but by direct action or mass action, which, as above shown, means force and violence. Thus the Communist Party of America stands indicted under the act of October 16, 1918. However, in order that there may be no doubt as to the responsibility of individual members of the Communist Party of America, we have but to examine the application for membership which each member must sign upon entering the organization. The following is a statement taken from the application: "The undersigned, after having read the constitution and program of the Communist Party, declares his adherence to the principles and tactics of that party and the Communist International; agrees to submit to the discipline of the party as stated in its constitution; and pledges himself to engage actively in its work."

Thus we see from the above that each and every member accepted for membership in the Communist Party pledges himself not only to the constitution and program of that party, but also to the principles and tactics of the Communist International, and further pledges himself to engage actively in the work of carrying out such principles and tactics.

Attached hereto and marked as "Exhibit 5" is an application for membership of the Communist Party of America.

Attached hereto and marked as "Exhibit 6" is a copy of the membership card issued to each member of the Communist Party of America, on which it will be seen that the statement appears, "Affiliated with the Communist International."

From the above examination of the membership we find that each member of the organization knowingly accepts the principles and tactics of the organization and pledges himself to the purpose of not only the Communist Party of America, but also of the Communist International, which is the ruling power of Soviet Russia.

(H) ACTIVITIES OF COMMUNIST PARTY OF AMERICA

In order that we may gain a view into the actual propaganda work of the Communist Party of America, we have but to examine a few samples of its literature.

Attached hereto and marked as "Exhibit 7" is a leaflet issued by the Communist Party of America, entitled "The capitalist challenge you, workingmen." This circular, it will be noted, bears upon the steel strike at Gary, Indiana, and urges the workers to resort to mass action. Of particular significance is the following statement appearing in the circular: "The National Government—the capitalist State—has stepped in." Thus we see that the Communist Party uses the "capitalist State" as a term synonymous with the National Government. The circular urges the workingmen to express opposition to law and order, and ends with the statement, "The workers must capture the power of the State."

Attached hereto and marked as "Exhibit 8" is a circular issued by the Communist Party of America, entitled "Your shop." In this circular we find the workers urged to take over the shops and urged to adopt mass action in accomplishing this purpose. Further, we find the workers urged to establish in this country the present conditions existing in Russia.

Attached hereto and marked as "Exhibit 9" is a copy of a circular entitled "The State—strike breaker." This circular was printed in Detroit, Michigan, on November 3, 1919, and through the efforts of the Federal authorities was never actually circulated. It will be noted that the circular was issued after the injunction had been issued by the court upon the coal strike, and yet we find the Communist Party of America openly violating that injunction. The examination of the circular shows an attitude of satire upon the Government of the United States. The miners are urged to take over the mines and the circular incites the workers against the Government. The following statement appears: "The workers must conquer that power (the State). The workers are urged to establish a dictatorship of the proletariat." The same phrasing is used in this circular as was used by the Communist International.

Attached hereto and marked as "Exhibit 10" is a copy of a circular issued to the workers of the world by the executive committee of the Communist International, with which the Communist Party of America is affiliated, according to its own statement, and wherein protest is again made against the Versailles peace treaty. It is also further urged in the proclamation to the workers of the world that there should be a worldwide revolution, like that existing in Russia, with a resultant destruction of the bourgeois state. The above is but a small sample of the literature circulated by the Communist Party of America, but is sufficient to definitely establish its type of propaganda.

(I)   PUBLIC OPINION ON COMMUNIST PARTY OF AMERICA

The Communist Party of America has been in existence for so short a time that few States have as yet been able to proceed against members of the organization; however, in New York State, under the criminal-anarchy law of that State, a large number of the members of the Communist Party of America have been indicted, and the following is a quotation from the opinion of Chief Magistrate William McAdoo upon the nature of the organization.

"The Communist Party is intended to destroy organized government and it appeals for class hatred, and the Communist Party is an organized conspiracy against the United States Government and the State of New York, and each member of the party is guilty and responsible for the acts, writings, and sayings of each and every member, just as handed down years ago in the famous Lord George Gordan case, following the no-property riots in London, in which each member of the mob that followed him through the streets was held guilty.

"I hold that the Communist Party has declared a state of war against the United States and the Government of the State of New York and that the establishment of the Communist Party in the State of New York is the highest crime known to our law, and I will not reduce the bail one dollar.

"If the Communist Party is an organization intended to destroy the Government of the United States and preparing the way by appeals to class hatred and by preventing members from taking part in Government and impliedly preventing their using constitutional methods to bring about a change, then every member is responsible for the acts and sayings of every other member. This is a well-established principle of law.

"The common impression that these men are held because they have membership cards in an organization is erroneous. There are some well-meaning citizens who have gotten the idea that these men are being mistreated; that all that they have done is join some organization just as anyone might join the Elks.

"These men are recruited into barracks, into which they make a declaration against the Government of the United States before they can become a member."

It will thus be noted from the above that the nature of the Communist Party of America has been recognized by the judiciary and that its obnoxious and insidious propaganda has borne fruit.

(J) CONCLUSION

From examination of the various documents analyzed above the following is definitely established:

(1) That the Communist Party was the outgrowth of the left wing of the Socialist Party of America.

(2) That the Communist Party is an integral part of the first congress of the Communist International, which was formed by the Bolsheviks.

(3) That through its history as the left wing, the Communist Party constantly followed the doctrines of mass action and the advocation of the dictatorship of the proletariat.

(4) That the first congress of the Communist International directly advocated the overthrow of all the governments of the world by force and violence through its advocation of mass action.

(5) That the Communist Party of America, in its manifesto and program officially adopted at its convention

287

in Chicago held September 1, 1919, advocated the overthrow of the Government of the United States by force and violence.

(6) That each and every member of the Communist Party of America pledges himself knowingly to the tactics and principles of the Communist Party of America and to the tactics enunciated in the manifesto of the Communist International.

(7) That the Communist Party of America, through the propaganda being actively carried on at the present time, is advocating the overthrow of the Government of the United States by force and violence.

It is respectfully submitted that the Communist Party of America and persons members thereof fall within the provisions of the act of October 16, 1918, in that it openly advocates the overthrow of the Government of the United States by force and violence.

Respectfully submitted.

J. E. Hoover,
Special Assistant to the Attorney General.

(House Committee on Rules, *Attorney General A. Mitchell Palmer on Charges made Against Department of Justice by Louis F. Post and Others,* Part 2, Washington: Government Printing Office, 1920, pp. 321-331.)

CHAPTER FOUR

ONE NATION'S RESPONSE TO COMMUNISM
(September, 1960)

Pattern for Expansion

Within the comparatively short period of four decades, international communism has seized control of approximately one quarter of the land area of the world and now boasts of its control over almost a billion people. Its goal is eventual world domination. Its methods are any tactics—legal or illegal, moral or immoral, open or clandestine. Its agents are the 36 million members of the communist parties now operating in 86 nations throughout the world.

Throughout the non-communist world, there is a growing realization that communist boasts of eventual world domination must not be taken lightly. This is particularly true in many areas of the world which, until recently, were generally assumed impervious to communist conquest. Although the enemy is a common one, the nature of the threat—of necessity—varies from country to country according to geographical location and the strength of the local communist party, as well as the social, political, and economic environment.

THE COMMUNIST PARTY, USA

In the United States, the international communist movement is represented by the Communist Party, USA. As the history of the communist movement in the United States proves, the Communist Party, USA, has been inspired and completely controlled by the fountainhead of world communism, the Soviet Union. Every major phase of the Party's historical development has been determined, not by any factor indigenous to the United States, but rather by the exigencies of communist imperialism.

Formative Years

The Communist Party in the United States was organized in 1919. From 1919 until 1929, this conspiratorial Party experienced its birth pangs and growing pains. Its entrance on the stage of American life was characterized by defiant militancy. It openly proclaimed its revolutionary goals and pursued them with action. The communists participated in strikes and, boring from within, fomented social unrest. Internal dissension broke out as various individuals struggled for control of the communist movement in the United States. From this internal conflict, the Party early assumed the rigid, dogmatic, intolerant form which has characterized it down to the present time.

The Communist Party of this Nation was inspired by the success of the Bolshevik Revolution of 1917, through which, in the Soviet Union, the first communist government seized power. For the communist movement in the United States, the newly formed Soviet Government was not an abstract ideal. It was, and still is, a living, guiding example of what communism hopes to achieve in this country.

The Communist International* was organized in Moscow in 1919 to insure the discipline of the international communist movement. Comintern representatives were dispatched to the United States to guide the American communist movement in its formative years. By 1921, when a sufficient degree of unity had been achieved, the Communist Party in the United States was admitted to the Comintern. As part of the requirements for membership, the Party agreed that it would support the Soviet Union rather than the United States in the event of a war between the two nations and that it would be bound by all decisions of the Comintern. Orders from the Comintern led the Party, which had been operating largely underground from shortly after its organization until 1924, to establish an "open" organization. Com-

---

* Usually referred to as the Comintern.

intern instructions and Soviet financial assistance were responsible for the establishment of the Party's newspaper. During the 1920's, Party leaders made regular pilgrimages to the Soviet Union for guidance and instruction. Throughout all this period, the Party repeatedly called on the United States to grant diplomatic recognition to the Soviet Government.

The Soviet Union intervened even more decisively in selecting the Party's leaders. Although the Party was outwardly united, a factional struggle continued until 1929, when Stalin himself decreed that Earl Browder and William Z. Foster, whose subservience could be depended upon, were to "direct" the communist movement in the United States.

Operational Training

In 1929, the Comintern proclaimed that a capitalist economic crisis was beginning and called on all communist parties to take advantage of this situation. The Communist Party, USA, concentrated on exploiting the economic and social unrest of the early 1930's. Party members organized and participated in strikes, bonus marches, unemployment demonstrations, and similar activities. These tactics were used by the Party to intensify the social and economic difficulties and to spread communism. Through these militant tactics, the Party developed into a closely knit, strictly disciplined, tightly organized, and highly flexible group. Openly proclaiming that it had predicted the economic collapse, the Communist Party claimed that its revolutionary program offered the only solution to what it describes as the problem of recurrent economic crisis under capitalism.

Gaining "Respectability"

In 1935, the Soviet Union decreed that all communist parties should adopt a united front against fascism. Concerned by then over the threat to its own security from the fascist regimes in Germany and Italy, the Soviet Union promulgated this directive through the Seventh World Congress of the Comintern. Adopting the "Trojan-horse" technique, the Party discontinued the open advocacy of its revolutionary program. Party propaganda appealed to non-communists to ignore the differences between democratic and communist principles in order to unite against the common fascist enemy. By exploiting this issue, the Party was able, not only to comply with Soviet instructions, but also, in the very process, to cloak itself with an aura of respectability and to masquerade as a legitimate political party.

By the late 1930's, the Party had been successful in maneuvering itself into the mainstreams of American life. Communist influence was exercised through a myriad of interlocking front groups, ostensibly designed to counter the threat of fascism, but covertly manipulated by the Party for its own purposes. Many prominent educators, writers, artists, entertainers, clergymen, and others influential in molding public opinion were duped, not only into supporting communist causes, but also into stifling anti-communist views. Party members were successful in infiltrating even some of the most sensitive agencies of the United States Government. Party propaganda went so far as to claim that communism was "20th Century Americanism."

Perhaps the most striking communist success during this period occurred in the American labor movement. By infiltrating certain unions in the newly formed Congress of Industrial Organization (CIO) during the 1930's, the Party laid the groundwork for its eventual control of 11 large labor unions. When these communist-dominated unions were expelled by the CIO during 1949 and 1950, their total membership exceeded 700,000.

Even during this united-front period when it was purportedly cooperating with the Government, the party did not neglect its obligations to the international communist movement. Approximately 1,500 Party members fought in the Spanish Civil War (1936-1939) to further the aims of the international communist movement.

Communist-Fascist Alliance

The signing of the Nazi-Soviet nonaggression pact in August, 1939, signaled another major change in the tactics of the world communist movement. After recovering from its initial shock, the Communist Party, USA, did an abrupt about-face from its policy of ostensibly cooperating with the Government. Now that the fascists and communists were allies, the threat of fascism disappeared from the Party's propaganda. A few months later when World War II broke out in Europe, the Party, in line with Soviet policy, labeled it as an "imperialist war" in which the United States had no interest. By instigating strikes in basic industries, the Party delayed the defense preparations of the United States and obstructed American efforts to aid democratic nations of Western Europe.

In November, 1940, the Communist Party held an emergency convention at which it withdrew from the Comintern. However, the Party made it explicitly clear that it still approved the aims of the Comintern and that it was withdrawing solely because of the provisions of the Voorhis Act. This law, enacted that year, provided that any organization in the United States which was engaged in political activity and which was subject to foreign control would be required to register with the Attorney General of the United States. As is evident, the Party's disaffiliation from the Comintern was merely a tactical maneuver designed to thwart enforcement of the Voorhis Act.

The "Superpatriots"

The German invasion of the Soviet Union in June, 1941, caused another major reversal in international communist tactics. With the fatherland of communism under attack, what had been an "imperialist war" was magically transformed into a "just war." Even before the Japanese attack on Pearl Harbor in December, 1941, the Communist Party, USA, was agitating for the United States to enter World War II. Once the United States had entered the conflict, the communists became "superpatriots." Instead of instigating strikes, they completely sacrificed the interests of the American workers by advocating that the labor movement adopt a no - strike pledge for the duration of the war. In effect, World War II provided the communists an opportunity to become both Soviet and American "patriots." In typical totalitarian fashion, they subordinated all other considerations, even such basic ones as human dignity, justice, and civil liberties, to the cause of victory. They did this, however, not with the aim of promoting the war effort of the United States, but rather with the goal of preserving the Soviet Union at all costs.

In 1943, the Soviet Union, in dire need of military assistance, dissolved the Comintern as a tactical gesture of wartime cooperation with its Western allies. The Comintern, the tangible organizational structure of the world communist movement, had long irritated all non-communist nations. The dissolution of the Comintern together with the Soviet desire for wartime unanimity apparently led Earl Browder, then the Party's general secretary, to foresee an extended postwar period of international cooperation. He proposed that the Party actually dissolve and become a political-action organization. Browder's recommendation was adopted in 1944 by the Party's national convention, and the Party changed its name to the Communist Political Association.

Pretense Abandoned

Moscow ordered the reconstitution of the Communist Party, USA, as a Marxist-Leninist revolutionary group in 1945, when it became apparent that the defeat of the fascist Axis was imminent. With the end of the war in Europe in sight, the Soviet Union was no longer in desperate need of the economic and military assistance which had prompted its temporary war-time collaboration with non-communist allies. Instead of the postwar era of cooperation envisioned by Browder, the Soviet Union was already preparing for a return to a period of traditional communist revolutionary activity based on the international class struggle.

In April, 1945, shortly after he returned from Moscow, the French communist leader, Jacques Duclos, wrote an article for a French communist publication. This article severely criticized Browder for his role in the dissolution of the Communist Party, USA. Duclos characterized the wartime dissolution of the Communist Party, USA, as an unwarranted revision of Marxism-Leninism and called on American communists to reconsider their action. The leaders of the Communist Political Association dutifully admitted their error in following Browder and, at a special convention in July, 1945, reconstituted the Communist Party, USA. For his deviation from Marxism-Leninism, Browder was expelled from the Party shortly thereafter.

Back on Course

In 1946, Stalin decreed the beginning of the cold war when he announced that the Soviet wartime alliance with the West had been based on political expediency and was not to be interpreted as an indication of long-range postwar cooperation. In 1947, at the founding conference of the Information Bureau of the Communist and Worker's Parties (Cominform),* Soviet delegate A. A. Zhdanov was even more specific when he divided the world into the "imperialist camp" led by the United States and the "anti-imperialist camp" headed by the Soviet Union. Guided by these explicit instructions, the Communist Party, USA, has attempted to obstruct every measure which the United States has taken to protect itself and other non-communist nations against the threat of further communist aggression. The Party has opposed the Marshall Plan, aid to Greece and Turkey, the Point Four Program, the United Nations intervention in Korea, and the military alliances the United States has made with other non-communist nations.

Post-Stalin Developments

Soviet domination of the Communist Party, USA, continued even after Stalin's death. The Soviet Union intervened in the factional dispute within the Communist Party, USA, in 1956. Arising out of Khrushchev's reappraisal of Stalin, this factional dispute had been intensified by evidences of anti-Semitism in the communist nations and the intervention of Soviet troops to suppress the uprising in Hungary. During this period, the most open discussion in the Party's entire history took place as rank and file members subjected the Party, its policies, and its leaders to extensive criticism, much of it public. During this discussion, three divergent views over future Party tactics developed.

The left-wing faction, led by Party Chairman William Z. Foster, called for the continuation of the Party as a strong Marxist-Leninist organization with close ties to the Soviet Union. The middle - of - the - road group, headed by General

---

* From 1947 until its dissolution in 1956, the Cominform served as an international press and propaganda organ of the international communist movement.

Secretary Eugene Dennis, advocated a modified Marxist-Leninist organization to cloak the Party in a new look. The right-wing faction, led by John Gates, *Daily Worker** editor, openly called for the transformation of the Party into a political-action organization which could appear to act independently of the Soviet Union. All three factions agreed that world communism was still the goal. They disagreed only on the means to this end.

Realizing the danger to its continued control of the Party if the right wing prevailed, the Soviet Union exerted influence in several ways. *Pravda,*** fully aware of all the deference accorded to its pronouncements, hailed William Z. Foster as a "noted theoretician and Marxist historian." At the Party's Sixteenth National Convention in February, 1957, the Party's future policy was one of the principal topics of discussion. As in 1945, the French communist leader, Jacques Duclos, warned against any revisionist tendencies in the Communist Party, USA. Foster told the convention that Duclos' warning was correct. In the light of Duclos' role in 1945, his intervention was clearly designed to support Foster's pro-Soviet faction. When the proposal to transform the Party into a political-action organization was defeated at the convention, *Pravda* hailed the defeat of the "reactionary forces" who had supported that view. Later in 1957, the authoritative Soviet theoretical periodical, *Kommunist,* published an article attacking the position of John Gates and another article by Foster defending his own position in the factional dispute. When Gates finally resigned from the Party in January of 1958, the victory of the left-wing, pro-Soviet faction became a foregone conclusion.

The year 1959 was a momentous one in the Party's history. In September, Soviet Premier Nikita S. Khrushchev visited the United States. The Party claimed that his visit gave a tremendous boost to the morale of its members by revitalizing their confidence in themselves and in the ultimate victory of communism in the United States. In December, 1959, shortly after Khrushchev's visit, the Party's 17th Na-

---

* Former eastcoast communist newspaper.
** Organ of the Central Committee of the Communist Party of the Soviet Union.

tional Convention was held. This convention achieved a reconciliation of the factional dispute and welded the Party into a more solidly unified, militant organization, led by its new general secretary, Moscow-trained Gus Hall.

Under Hall's vigorous leadership, there has been a resurgence in all phases of Party activity—recruiting new members, promoting the circulation of Party publications, expanding the Party's internal educational program, and laying the groundwork for the formation of a new nationwide Marxist youth organization.

Soviet Domination

The one inescapable conclusion which must be drawn from this brief review of the major phases of the history of the Communist Party, USA, is that the Party is the direct and willing instrument of the Soviet Union. Every significant change of direction and emphasis in its policies since its formation in 1919 has been dictated, not by any reference to its American environment, but either by a specific Soviet directive or by an almost automatic reflex action in defense of the Soviet Union, regardless of the consequences to its own fortunes.

TOTAL IMPERIALISM

Any definitive analysis of the world communist movement which considers the relationship between the fountainhead of communism — the Soviet Union — and the various communist parties acting as its agents in other countries must arrive at the inevitable judgment that here is the most all-embracing demonstration of imperialism ever known to mankind.

The classic imperialism of the nineteenth century was, in essence, an economic phenomenon. There were, of course, other consequences, but both the motives and the effects were largely economic. This is not true of communist imperialism. Here is a form of total subjugation never dreamed of by either a merchant prince or a trading combine. Communist imperialism imposes its will on all nations by methods and practices which involve every phase of man's existence. In short, with the rise of world communism, led by the Soviet

Union, mankind has come face to face with a new type of imperialism—the total imperialism of communism.

International Solidarity

This total imperialism has a horizontal and a vertical aspect held together by communist ideology. On the horizontal plane, Marxism-Leninism demands close fraternal relations among and between the communist parties in 86 nations throughout the world in order to further the eventual goal of communist world domination.

Fraternal relations among and between the individual communists parties are maintained in various ways. The announcement of the dissolution of the Cominform in 1956 specifically instructed individual communist parties and groups of parties throughout the world to "find new useful forms of establishing relations and contacts among themselves" and to "exchange views." Party congresses, conventions, and other high-level meetings serve as convenient occasions for visits by Party leaders to other nations. Thus, two representatives of the Communist Party, USA, attended the Twenty-first Congress of the Communist Party of the Soviet Union in Moscow in 1959, along with delegates from practically every other communist party in the world. Meetings of this type provide an excellent opportunity for discussions of international, regional, and national policies. As another example, in 1958, the Communist Party of Argentina held an indoctrination school which was attended by communists from six other Latin-American republics, as well as by students from Poland, Spain, and Italy. These official contacts are frequently supplemented by additional meetings of a less formal nature. Finally, a communist party in one country is frequently in a position to furnish financial and even military assistance to the communist party of another nation.

The major Soviet publications serve as clearinghouses for policy guidance on theoretical and tactical questions for the world communist movement. The periodical, *Problems of Peace and Socialism,** was specifically designed to promote the exchange of views between all communist parties. It is

---

* The English language edition is entitled *World Marxist Review.*

298

now published in 19 different languages and receives world-wide circulation. Officials of one communist party frequently contribute articles to the publications of another. The November, 1959, issue of *Political Affairs*, the theoretical publication of the Communist Party, USA, includes, for example, articles by a Soviet professor of economics and a prominent French communist theoretician.

This international cohesion among and between all communist parties under the guidance of the Soviet Union explains the close coordination in all communist propaganda. In our own hemisphere, for example, the propaganda of all communist parties, including the Communist Party, USA, claims that the United States is attempting to impose its economic and political domination over Canada and Latin America in order to swell the profits of the "American monopolists." This allegation completely ignores the independence of the Philippine Islands and the commonwealth status of Puerto Rico, both freely chosen by the people of these former territorial possessions of the United States. Nor is communist propaganda limited to the printed word. In September 1959, members of the Communist Party, USA, picketed the Mexican Consulate in New York City to protest the arrest of a communist leader by the Mexican Government.

Unquestioned Allegiance

On the vertical plane of relationships between the Soviet Union and all communist parties, the control of the Soviet Union is uncontested.* This point has been amply demonstrated by the history of the Communist Party, USA, and similar examples could be cited from the histories of other communist parties. Allowing for specific local differences, the history of the Communist Party, USA, mirrors the history of most other communist parties throughout the world on this point. All have defended the Soviet Union with blind obedience, regardless of the cost to themselves in the loss of membership, influence, and prestige.

---

* At the present time, Yugoslavia, although a communist nation, does not recognize the supremacy of the Soviet Union.

For its part, the Soviet Union takes for granted the unquestioned subservience and allegiance of the communist parties throughout the world. Rarely, if ever, does it consult with other communist parties prior to any major change of policies. As a result, the world communist movement was stunned by such events as the signing of the Nazi-Soviet non-aggression pact and the reappraisal of Stalin. Soviet advantage has always been paramount, and the individual parties are willingly sacrificed, if necessary, to promote some aspect of Soviet foreign or domestic policy.

In spite of this cavalier treatment by the Soviet Union, the communist parties have provided convincing evidence of their complete subservience to the Soviet Union and their dedication to the communist goal of world domination, even to the extent of engaging in activities which are essentially treasonable. When France fell before the Nazi onslaught in 1940, the French communists hailed the German victory as an opportunity for a communist seizure of power. The revelations of Soviet defectors Igor Gouzenko, in Canada, and Vladimir Petrov, in Australia, definitely linked the communist parties in both those nations to Soviet espionage activities.

Inspirational Symbol

The acceptance of Soviet leadership by the rest of the world communist movement can be explained by the fact that the Soviet Union, as the first communist nation, blazed the trail which all other communist parties confidently expect to follow. To cut the tie which binds them to the Soviet Union would be, for the other communist parties, to forego their share, vicarious though it may be, in the achievements of the Soviet Union, recently enhanced by Soviet scientific and technological advances. For all communists, the Soviet Union looms as the heroic symbol of the Marxist-Leninist vision. Failure by other communist parties to support the Soviet Union would constitute, in effect, a rejection of Marxism-Leninism itself. The defense of the Soviet Union, then, is a psychological necessity for communists, because to lose this vision and their identification with it would be to lose everything.

Marxism-Leninism is the cement which binds together the vertical and horizontal aspects of communist total imperialism. By demanding a close association among and between parties, this ideology, at the same time, strengthens the control of the Soviet Union over each individual party. Complete control over this international conspiracy assures the Soviet Union of world-wide support for all of its domestic and foreign policies, particularly within the noncommunist nations. Moreover, Marxism-Leninism provides the rationale for communist total imperialism by justifying the use of any tactics whatsoever to achieve its goal of world domination.

Betrayed Promise

Communists do, indeed, hold out the promise of an "ideal" society, one in which complete equality, social justice, and material abundance will prevail. They say, in effect, that what they have to offer is so good for all mankind that any means is justified in achieving it and that man must be prepared to endure any sacrifices necessary for its attainment. But, what they actually offer is a Utopian dream which has already been proved a nightmare by the reality of life under communism. The imperialistic communist empire now controls approximately one quarter of the land area of the world. Yet, the almost one billion people under its tyranny were given no opportunity to accept or reject this totalitarian system.

Latvia, Lithuania, and Estonia were forcibly incorporated into the Soviet Union against the will of the people of those countries. The communist governments in China, North Korea, and North Vietnam gained power by outright armed warfare. The communist governments in the European satellite nations were imposed against the will of the majority by brute force, represented by the presence in overwhelming strength of the Red Army; by diplomatic pressure of the Soviet Union; and by the suppression of noncommunist political groups through the terrorism of the communist-dominated secret police. The brutal suppressions of the uprisings in East Germany, Hungary, and Tibet are forceful examples of the only way in which communist control can be maintained.

Communist total imperialism is insatiable. Ideologically committed to world domination, it relentlessly presses forward on all fronts. All noncommunist nations are constantly subjected to continuous communist pressures of one type or another. Recently, the emphasis has been placed on a new-type political, economic, and psychological offensive woven around the themes of peaceful coexistence and peaceful competition. Designed to lull noncommunists into a false sense of security, this new campaign has supplemented, not superseded, the traditional communist methods of seizing power.

The communist parties in all noncommunist nations are engaged in a continuous effort to subvert, by any means, existing governments. Their subversive activities are complemented by communist espionage activities designed to obtain the technological, scientific, and military secrets of the free world. This espionage is carried out by agents who, under aliases and with false passports, gain illegal access to noncommunist nations. At the same time, other communist intelligence agents are operating under the cover of diplomatic immunity. Soviet defectors have estimated that 70 to 80 percent of Soviet-bloc diplomats in foreign countries have intelligence assignments. The close interrelation of communist subversion and espionage was highlighted in 1959 when Mexico and Argentina found it necessary to expel communist diplomats who, in collusion with local communists, were fomenting social and economic unrest.

COMBATING COMMUNISM

The basic question of protecting the internal security of any nation is not a new one. It has challenged men since the earliest attempts to establish order through government. The United States has been no exception. We have been faced with different internal security problems during various phases of our history. Laws necessary to protect the very existence of any government — against espionage, sabotage, treason, and sedition—are, of course, in effect. The fundamental laws were passed before the Communist Party, USA, was organized. Others, such as Trading with the Enemy Act, no doubt would have been enacted whether or not a communist party ever operated in the United States. Still others, the Voorhis Act, for example, were adopted to meet the specific threat to the Nation's internal security posed by the international communist conspiracy.

Federal Action

The approach to counteracting the threat of communism must be the product of every nation's unique historical development. Of necessity, therefore, the methods will vary in different nations. American views on internal security have been strongly influenced by the traditional legal principles that guilt is personal and laws apply to every individual and organization with equal force.

The principle that guilt is personal means simply that organizations, as such, cannot be held accountable for criminal acts. Should an organization be guilty of criminal activity, any penalty which is imposed must fall upon the responsible members of the organization. The Internal Security Act of 1950, in brief, would require any communist action organization or communist front group to register its members, disclose its finances, and label its propaganda as communist. However, any sanctions imposed as a result of any organization's failure to comply with the provisions of this act are specifically directed against the responsible officials of the organization and, ultimately, against the rank-and-file members.

The principle that laws apply with equal force to everyone is self-explanatory. Laws, for example, against burglary and robbery are meticulously drafted so that they are applicable without any distinction to all persons who may commit those crimes. Again, this principle is applied with equal vigor in the field of internal security. The Smith Act, in brief, prohibits the teaching and advocacy of overthrowing the Government by force or violence, and also membership in such an organization with knowledge of this purpose. Significantly, nowhere in its provisions does it single out any specific organization. Leaders of the Socialist Workers Party, a Trotskyite group, as well as leaders of the Communist Party, USA, have been convicted of violating this law.

Another practical application of the principle that laws apply with equal force to all can be found in the various security programs established by the Federal Government. In the complex, modern American civilization, the wide variety of factors which have a direct bearing on security problems has occasioned a number of programs designed to protect vital operations from penetration by any individuals whose activities could adversely affect the national security. Thus, members of the Armed Forces; employees of the Federal Government; employees of private defense facilities who have access to classified information; and individuals in maritime, waterfront, or atomic-energy employment are subject to inquiry, the extent of which is determined by the security requirements of the specific position involved.

State Action

Antisubversive activity has not been limited to the Federal Government. Several states have established special committees to investigate subversive activities and recommend necessary legislation. In this process, these state committees, like their congressional counterparts in the Federal Government, have served to focus public attention on the true nature of communist activity. Other states have enacted legislation which excludes from the ballot candidates of any organization which advocates altering the form of government by force and violence.

Legal Restraint

As is evident, the Communist Party, USA, is not outlawed. However, its activities — and the activities of any other organization bent on the illegal seizure of power—are circumscribed and restricted by legal measures enforced by both the national and local governments.

However, experience has demonstrated that the sheer volume of laws relating to internal security is not necessarily a valid measure of their effectiveness. This is particularly true where communism is involved. Communists are adept at evading any laws designed to restrict their activities. At times, too, there is an unavoidable delay between the time when a specific threat to security is recognized and when legal action to meet the danger can be taken. Finally, most laws relating to internal security are based on past experience rather than on an anticipation of future problems. Communists, on the other hand, are long-range conspirators, always planning far into the future. Consequently, legislation, in and of itself, will not guarantee the internal security of a nation. This is particularly true in the United States.

Under our system, the concept by which people delegate powers to their Government not only limits the power which the Government has, but also restricts the areas in which it may exercise these delegated powers. This limitation on govermental authority—a heritage of freedom Americans jealously guard—necessarily and desirably shifts the burden of responsibility for internal security squarely upon the individual citizen.

Local Action

Under the American system, local community action is fundamental. On this basic level, the private citizen, individually and through his civic, labor, religious, educational, and similar organizations, acts to influence the life of the entire Nation. His participation in public affairs is the innate strength of the American system. As a consequence, some of the most effective anticommunist action has sprung from the initiative of private citizens acting without any Government intervention. One of the worst setbacks inflicted on the Communist Party, USA, was the expulsion from the CIO in 1949 and 1950 of the 11 communist-dominated unions. This action was originated and carried out by the CIO entirely on its own initiative. Communists have also been removed from positions of influence in various phases of American life, for example, education, entertainment, and other media which influence public opinion, through the individual and group efforts of noncommunists.

Diverse Approaches

The American approach to the problem of internal security is, as has been shown, an outgrowth of the entire historical development of this Nation. Moreover, this approach has been influenced by the very practical considerations of the nature and extent of the threat to the United States posed by communist total imperialism. It is not surprising, therefore,

305

that our methods have not been, and probably could not be, applied universally with equal effectiveness. While it is vitally important for each nation to protect itself against both the internal and the external threats of communism, the specific measures adopted must be formulated in the light of each nation's historical background, cultural tradition, economic development, social environment, and geographical location.

The Basic Issue

The ultimate guarantee against communist encroachment is a deep and abiding awareness on the part of all noncommunists that freedom is inherently superior to communism. The communists falsely pose the issue as one between communism and capitalism. In reality, the struggle is between communism and freedom.

The communists would have us believe that freedom can be attained only under their system. Yet, the history of every nation under a communist regime demonstrates conclusively that the communist version of freedom is only a new form of total slavery. Moreover, the people of the noncommunist world who enjoy freedom under various forms of government prove that the "either-or" alternative of communism is spurious. Freedom is possible under many types of government, ranging from republics to constitutional monarchies. Because these diverse forms of government are freely chosen, they reflect the history, culture, traditions, ideals, and aspirations of their own people rather than the tyrannical will of an alien, self-appointed elite—the leaders of the world communist movement.

The full realization of the advantages of freedom over communism can galvanize the entire noncommunist world into a purposeful program against the inroads of communism. This program, under responsible leadership, must be expressed through the indigenous institutions of each nation —the government, the churches, the schools, the labor unions, and other groups—working in close cooperation. While the details will obviously vary in different countries, each will experience a revitalization and a reinforcement of its own national traditions. This in turn, will generate the determi-

306

nation in each nation to pursue its own destiny, not by following the stereotyped communist blueprint, but according to its own freely chosen values and ideals.

(Adapted from an article by Mr. Hoover which was translated into Spanish and distributed in Latin America by the United States Information Agency.)

CHAPTER FIVE

THE NEW LEFT

In discussing our field investigative work, I will first turn to our widespread and important internal security work which during the past year has been highlighted by stepped-up activities of the New Left movement, continuing antiwar activity, various kinds of demonstrations, and the proliferation of mass membership organizations, such as certain militant black nationalist groups, whose programs have the effect of undermining respect for law and order.

New Left Movement

During 1968, the New Left movement in the United States continued to reveal itself as a firmly established subversive force dedicated to the complete destruction of our traditional democratic values and the principles of free government. This movement represents the militant, nihilistic and anarchistic forces which have become entrenched, for the most part, on college campuses and which threaten the orderly process of education as the forerunner of a more determined effort to destroy our economic, social, and political structures.

The discontent expressed by the movement in this country is also found in other countries. As a result, the New Left movement is a new specter haunting the Western World. It is a movement that is united to some degree by common issues, such as the Vietnam war, civil rights matters, so-called capitalist corruption, and a so-called archaic university system.

308

FINANCES

New Left funds are generally obtained from contributions, dues, sales of literature, benefits, advertisements, and its publications and fund drives. The main sources of revenue are contributions, and it is estimated that nearly 60 percent of Students for a Democratic Society (SDS) funds, for example, come from this source.

Although the majority of gifts are in the $10 to $50 range, wealthy benefactors who have acquired their fortunes in the United States have contributed substantial amounts in support of the New Left movement and in support of the activities of the SDS in particular. Included among these, for example, are a Cleveland industrialist who has long been a Soviet apologist; the wife of an attorney in Chicago who is a millionaire; an heiress in the New England area who is married to an individual prominent in the academic community who has been active in New Left activities; and a wealthy New York lecturer and writer who for years has been linked to more than a score of Communist-front organizations and has contributed liberally to many of them. These individuals alone have contributed more than $100,000 in support of New Left activities.

The New Left has also received money from several foundations. A very prominent foundation in New York, for example, has contributed more than a quarter of a million dollars from 1961 to 1968 to various individuals and groups, most of which have been identified as either present or past members or sympathizers of the Communist Party—U.S.A. or New Left movement.

Demonstrations are frequently financed by fundraising and collections. For example more than $25,000 was collected from participants and spectators by the organizing committee during the march on the Pentagon in 1967. The organizing committee raised $10,000 from the sale of buttons during an anti-Vietnam war demonstration early in 1967 in New York City.

Funds for antidraft activity by the New Left also have been supplied by organizations such as that known as Resist, located in Cambridge, Mass. This group was formed in 1967 by approximately 300 professors, writers, ministers, and others who signed a statement pledging to raise funds to aid youths who resist the draft and denounce the Vietnam war.

Communist Party—U.S.A. leaders have recently urged party members to give time and money to "New Left demonstrations and causes."

Much of the nationwide travel engaged in by prominent New Left leaders is paid for by honorariums paid to them, generally out of student funds, for their guest speaker appearances on college campuses.

STUDENTS FOR A DEMOCRATIC SOCIETY (SDS)

At the core of the New Left movement in the United States is the Students for a Democratic Society, an organization which became well known in 1968 for its disruptive tactics at a number of universities in this country, the main one being Columbia University in New York City. And if the leaders of the Students for a Democratic Society have their way, they will attempt to create chaos on many more campuses. Their desire is to let the "Columbia Spirit" prevail.

The Students for a Democratic Society advocates, in the terminology of a considerable number of its leaders and members, revolutionary communism. Along this line, at the organization's 1968 national convention, two of the newly elected national officers publicly identified themselves as Communists "with a small c," as many New Left adherents do to signify that while they are Communists they are a brand apart from those in the old-line Communist movement.

While the distinction may seem important to them, it is irrelevant to the rest of Americans because the basic objective of both New Left and old-line Communists and their adherents in our society is to completely destroy our form of Government.

The militant mood of the 1968 national convention of the Students for a Democratic Society was obvious from the subjects discussed and the suggestions made at its various workshops. For example, at a workshop dealing with sabotage and explosives, the participants discussed such things as disrupting selective service and police facilities during riots; mailing letters dipped in combustible materials; flushing "bird bombs" in toilets to destroy plumbing; using sharp, tripod - shaped instruments to halt vehicles; jamming radio equipment; firing Molotov cocktails from a shotgun; using electronic firing devices; and inserting "thermite bombs" in manholes to destroy communications.

The same militant mood was evident in suggestions made for a proposed pamphlet by participants in a workshop on self-defense and internal security. Suggested articles included starting rifle and karate clubs; infiltrating right-wing organizations; starting rogues' galleries of police officers; and spotting plainclothesmen by observing them as they testify in court.

The 1968 SDS convention also adopted a resolution on the military. This resolution created a project for "GI organizers" and established a coordinating office for the project in New York. The project will support individuals who wish to continue the "struggle against imperialism" by entering the military service in order to "politicize" and organize those in military service to resist authority. The project is to establish "GI drop-in centers" near military facilities in order to offer a political program to aid servicemen in their organizing efforts within the military.

In addition, the resolution encourages local SDS chapters to organize a campaign to involve servicemen in social and political activities; establish a military counseling service; provide support for deserters; and give support through demonstrations and publicity to radicals within the military service.

The meeting of the National Council of the Students for a Democratic Society held in Ann Arbor, Mich., over the recent Christmas holidays was highlighted by a power play by SDS members who are also members of the pro-Peking Progressive Labor Party (PLP). The struggle concerned two main issues. One was the participation in proposed demonstrations at the time of the Presidential Inauguration. The resolution for SDS support and participation in the Inaugural demonstrations was defeated and generally regarded as a PLP victory. The PLP considered the SDS to be unprepared for a confrontation with authorities and also their action would endanger black revolutionary work in the Nation's Capital.

The other issue stemmed from the advocacy by the PLP element for the creation of a broad-based revolutionary group consisting of students and workers. While this resolution was unsuccessful, its defeat by an extremely narrow margin was indicative of the PLP's increasing attempt to influence the SDS and the student New Left.

An SDS National Council meeting was held in Austin, Tex., from March 27, 1969, to March 30, 1969. Michael Klonsky, SDS national secretary, among other things stated, "Our primary task is to build a Marxist - Leninist revolutionary movement." The PLP continued in its bid to control SDS, however, was unable to pass many of its resolutions. This organization still continues to wield considerable influence in SDS; however, it is now receiving competition from the Communist Party - U.S.A. and the Young Socialist Alliance (youth affiliate of the Trotskyite Socialist Workers Party). The influence of these two groups in competition with PLP is growing in SDS circles and by the time the next SDS annual national convention convenes in June 1969, it can be expected that there will be considerable dissension within SDS ranks as to what course to follow.

It can be fully expected that old-line Communists groups will make every effort to insure SDS follows Marxist-Leninist doctrine for guidance in their activities and building a revolutionary movement.

Although the PLP represents a minority of the SDS members, it is able to wield a disproportionate influence on the national office level due to the militancy of its members and the cohesiveness of its Maoist line. The PLP's ability to seize upon situations ripe for violence was certainly revealed by the Columbia University riots when it attempted to guide the riot leadership.

The PLP is one of several Communist splinter extremist groups formed during recent years to enunciate the tenets of Communist China and Mao Tse-tung. The majority have been ineffectual paper organizations. The PLP, however, is one group which has emerged with a broad-based membership making significant organizational strides in major U.S. cities and on a number of college campuses. It is headed by such devoted revolutionaries as Milton Rosen, one - time labor secretary of the Communist Party, New York State, who was expelled from the Communist Party for extremist views, and William Epton, who, following his participation in the Harlem race riots of 1964, was found guilty of conspiracy to riot, conspiracy to advocate criminal anarchy, and advocating criminal anarchy. Apropos of the strong rapport existing between the PLP and the Communist Party of Communist China, the latter group informed top-level PLP members in 1967 that it considers the PLP the only revolutionary Marxist-Leninist party in the United States.

There can be no doubt that the New Left movement is a threat to established law and order and to the stability of our society. Through it a comparative handful of revolutionaries have displayed total disregard for the rights and privileges of the overwhelming majority of millions of dedicated and responsible college students. The Students for a Democratic Society will continue to be at the forefront of the organizations making up the New Left movement in taking every opportunity to foment discord among the youth of this country.

Mr. SMITH. Mr. Chairman, I will have to leave in a few minutes and I wonder if I may ask a couple questions?

Mr. ROONEY. Yes, Mr. Smith.

Mr. SMITH. A couple years ago, I thought we were told the Students for a Democratic Society were about to be put on the Attorney General's list.

Mr. HOOVER. They have never been put on the Attorney General's list.

Mr. SMITH. Are they likely candidates to be placed on that list?

Mr. HOOVER. I do not know. The Internal Security Division of the Department would determine that based on all the material we have sent to them.

Mr. SMITH. That is all.

Mr. HOOVER. I now turn to the antiwar and antidraft activities.

ANTIWAR AND ANTIDRAFT ACTIVITY

Antiwar and antidraft protests and activities continued throughout 1968. Scarcely a day passed that did not see demonstrations by various "peace" groups.

The major antiwar demonstrations held in cities throughout the United States in April 1968 grew out of proposals made at a conference of the Student Mobilization Committee to End the War in Vietnam which was held in Chicago, Ill., in January 1968. This conference was attended by leading young members of the Communist Party - U.S.A.; the Socialist Workers Party and its youth group, the Young Socialist Alliance; the Student Nonviolent Coordinating Committee, a militant black nationalist group; and the Students for a Democratic Society.

Nearly 50,000 individuals participated in a New York City demonstration. Many of the demonstrators carried Viet Cong flags and photographs of Ho Chi Minh and "Che" Guevara. A demonstration at Los Angeles, Calif., attracted some 2,500 individuals who heard speakers, including a member of the Communist Party - U.S.A., urge withdrawal of all U.S. troops from Vietnam. At San Francisco, Calif., approximately 10,000 individuals heard Fred Halstead, the Socialist Workers Party presidential candidate, denounce U. S. foreign policy.

In May 1968, the National Mobilization Comittee To End the War in Vietnam, which is headed by David Dellinger who is self-described as a Communist although not the Soviet variety, and which includes representatives of various subversive organizations, such as the Communist Party, U.S.A. a n d t h e Socialist Workers Party among its members, planned its Summer of Support. This is a program to establish coffeehouses near military installations throughout the United States for the purpose of attracting military personnel and to serve as alternatives to the "militaristic, drab, occasionally violent Army town environment." Some such coffeehouses have been set up.

Rennie Davis, one of the leaders of the Join Community Union, the community action group of the Students for a Democratic Society, was selected to head Summer of Support. A letter issued by the group explains that Summer of Support is a national program to support GI's and their right to come home. Sponsors of it include the Reverend James Bevel, an official of the Southern Christian Leadership Conference who has been active in antiwar demonstrations; Marlon Brando, a prominent actor; the Reverend William Sloane

Coffin, Jr., who has been convicted for a violation of the Selective Service Act; and David Dellinger.

The Student Mobilization Committee To End the War in Vietnam, which is controlled by members of the Young Socialist Alliance, the youth group of the Socialist Workers Party, sponsored anti-Vietnam war demonstrations in various cities throughout the United States from April 4 to 6, 1969. Many antiwar protest groups participated in the demonstrations which had two main themes—namely, to bring servicemen home from Vietnam and to achieve free speech for servicemen advocating antiwar sentiments. The principal demonstrations were conducted at New York City; Chicago, Ill.; and San Francisco, Calif. At New York City, 30,000 individuals participated in a march and rally. Among the demonstrators were members of the Communist Party, the Socialist Workers Party and its youth group, and Students for a Democratic Society (SDS). At Chicago, approximately 10,000 individuals participated in a march and rally. One of the principal speakers at the rally was an official of the Black Panther Party. At San Francisco an estimated 10,000 demonstrators marched through San Francisco to the Presidio, a military base. Several arrests were made by the San Francisco Police Department and several military policemen were injured when the marchers attempted to force their way into the Presidio.

ACTS OF VIOLENCE

During the past year we have seen some protest groups turn more and more to violent plans and tactics.

In December 1967, Greg Calvert, a national representative of the Students for a Democratic Society, stated at an SDS chapter meeting in Oklahoma that the SDS and other New Left groups were organizing and planning efforts to disrupt the national "warmaking effort" all over the country.

In January 1968, a pamphlet entitled, "What Must We Do Now? . . . An Argument for Sabotage As The Next Logical Step Toward Obstruction and Disruption of the U.S. War Machine," was prepared in Canada and copies were mailed from Toronto, Canada, to anti-Vietnam war groups in this country. The pamphlet referred to the need for increased radicalization of the antiwar movement and urged the utilization of incendiary devices to immobilize local draft boards, Reserve Officers' Training Corps (ROTC) buildings, other Government agencies and war industries. Other acts of violence were also proposed and detailed instructions and diagrams were contained in the pamphlet for the construction of simple incendiary devices. The pamphlet strongly emphasized the clandestine nature of such violent activity and urged that only two or three persons be knowledgeable of any action in order to preclude compromise.

In September 1968, within a 5-day period three ROTC establishments were sabotaged and a fourth threatened at diverse points across the Nation. On September 13, 1968, Callahan Hall, the Naval ROTC building at the University of California at Berkeley, was damaged by explosives which caused in excess of $25,000 in damage. Two previous attempts were made to firebomb this building in 1968. On September 15, 1968, several firebombs were thrown into the ROTC armory at the University of Delaware damaging or destroying 300 military uniforms and public address system equipment. On September 18, 1968, a fire of undetermined origin caused extensive damage in Clark Hall, the Naval ROTC building at the University of Washington in Seattle. Prior to this date members of the SDS at this university had announced the Naval ROTC unit as one of their "targets." Furthermore, at the scene of the fire, Robbie Sterns, self-described SDS activist, was observed chanting, "This is No. 1 and the fun has just begun; burn it down, burn it down."

In Storrs, Conn., a source reported that SDS was planning to blow up the ROTC building on September 17, 1968, at the University of Connecticut; however, the bombing attempt did not take place.

On September 29, 1968, the local CIA office at Ann Arbor, Mich., was bombed. Ann Arbor is the home of the University of Michigan where there have been numerous New Left activities in the past several years. The New Left at the university, and specifically SDS, has claimed credit for the bombing of this CIA office.

The New Left by innuendo made additional claims of violence in September 1968, when on September 29, at a Navy and Marine ROTC unit at Eugene, Oreg., a crane was dam-

316

aged with explosives and several military vehicles were destroyed by being set afire. On September 10, 1968, five heavy army trucks were destroyed in explosions and fires at the National Guard armory at Van Nuys, Calif.

A 16-year-old narcotics addict advised the Detroit Police Department of identities of subjects involved in four recent bombings in the Detroit area. To date, over 10 New Left individuals have been charged with being implicated in these bombings which were: the September 10, 1968, bombing of a Selective Service Office, Roseville, Mich., and of a U.S. Army vehicle, Detroit, Mich.; the September 29, 1968, bombing of CIA headquarters at the University of Michigan; and the October 14, 1968, bombing of the Science and Technology building at the University of Michigan.

Five persons active in various phases of the New Left have thus far been charged with a number of bombings in the San Francisco, Calif., area, including the destruction of three Pacific Gas & Electric Co. towers in June 1968.

On February 20, 1969, Michael Siskind, a student at Washington University, St. Louis, Mo., and SDS member, on a plea of guilty in Federal court at St. Louis was sentenced to 5 years' imprisonment in connection with charges stemming from the attempted firebombing of the ROTC headquarters on the campus, December 3, 1968.

Between January 20 and January 28, 1969, high-power transmission towers were dynamited in and around Denver, Colo. On February 14, 1969 Cameron David Bishop, an SDS activist, was indicted by a Federal grand jury in connection with these incidents and is currently being sought as a fugitive.

It is certainly coincidental that in June 1968, at the SDS national convention, as I pointed out earlier, one of the workshops dealt with sabotage and explosives. Many of those who attended the SDS national convention returned to school in September 1968, and as noted previously, acts of violence occurred early in the school year. And the SDS continues to make available information regarding the use of explosives. For example, at a national council meeting of the SDS held in Boulder, Colo., from October 11, 1968 to October 13, 1968, copies of a pamphlet captioned "Sabotage" and setting forth instructions on how to make bombs and incendiary devices were left on the stage of the auditorium where the meeting was held.

The selective service facilities of this country have also been the targets of antiwar violence by individuals, including clergymen, resulting in destruction of or damage to selective service facilities or records.

Other acts of violence have occurred during some of the numerous demonstrations erupting on various college campuses since the beginning of 1968. These protest actions have ranged from those directed against the school administration, to those matters relating to the defense effort, such as the war in Vietnam, the draft, and the appearance of military and war industry recruiters on campus. Several of these demonstrations resulted in severe damage to school facilities. For example, the total costs of the riots at Columbia University in April and May 1968, by the Students for a Democratic Society and other New Leftists, were approximately $500,000. This amount included damages to grounds, furnishings, and buildings and other related expenses.

Those incidents which concern damage to Federal facilities or property receive our immediate investigative attention and the results of the investigation are turned over to the Attorney General for prosecutive consideration. Where no Federal jurisdiction is involved, the matter rests with the local authorities.

DISTURBANCES AND RIOTS

There has been no lessening of racial tension in the United States. A particularly aggravating factor in the past few years has been the increased activity of emboldened Negro agitators and revolutionaries affiliated with black extremist groups who exhort and promote hate and violence. Their appeal to destructive action and guerrilla warfare has intensified, spreading a mood of lawlessness among sympathetic followers and among the young criminal element, thereby increasing the potential for violence.

For example, the assassination of Martin Luther King, Jr., on April 4, 1968, was seized upon by extremist and criminal elements in Negro areas throughout the country as an excuse to riot, loot, vandalize, burn, snipe, and kill. Violence

318

in varying degrees, ranging from minor disturbances to major riots erupted in more than 100 cities across the land following King's death. In the remaining months of 1968, serious disturbances occurred in more than 40 other cities across the Nation.

The April outbreaks and the subsequent disorders resulted in more than 60 deaths, injuries to thousands of persons, and millions of dollars in property damage. In a number of instances, the summoning of the National Guard and Federal troops to help restore law and order was found necessary. Acts of violence and disorder on college campuses and in the lower schools by black student groups, often aided by outside agitators, have reached alarming proportions and have added to the racial strife.

I would like to point out that in connection with recurring disturbances and riots, we have no jurisdiction over the protection of persons and property nor do we have responsibility for the policing or controlling of riotous conditions. Our responsibilities center around the development and dissemination of intelligence data concerning these situations, being ever alert to the detection of violations of Federal laws over which the FBI has investigative jurisdiction, including violations of the antiriot provisions of Public Law 90-284 which was approved on April 11, 1968.

As to intelligence data, through expanding coverage a great deal of valuable information relating to a variety of cases of violence and planned violence has been developed. This information is widely disseminated throughout the executive branch of the Government. In addition, where pertinent, State and local authorities have been kept advised of information developed in this field and the prompt dissemination of such information often enables them to take preventive measures to forestall acts of violence and to combat violence as it develops.

We were able, for example, through our coverage to provide the Baltimore, Md., Police Department identifying data regarding several members of the extremist Black Panther Party from New York City who were reportedly responsible for the firebombing of a supermarket in Baltimore, Md.. in late August 1968.

Demonstrations at the National Democratic Convention

Months before the National Democratic Convention was held at Chicago, Ill., in August 1968, all appropriate Federal and local authorities were fully aware that the convention was the target for disruption and violence by various dissent groups and individuals from throughout the United States.

It was clear from the information received that these groups and individuals desired to deliberately bring about a hostile confrontation with the established authority. Pre-convention plans for various demonstrations by New Left, antiwar, subversive, and other militant groups were made. In addition to these plans, allegations involving assassination plots against Vice President Humphrey, Senator Eugene McCarthy, and some prominent Negroes were also received. In view of this background, authorities were compelled to devise necessary and effective security precautions.

Numerous groups and their members were involved, in varying degrees, in the activities aimed at disrupting the convention. These included such organizations as the Communist Party - U.S.A., Student Nonviolent Coordinating Committee, Youth International Party (also known as Yippies), Students for a Democratic Society, Black Panther Party, and the National Mobilization Committee To End the War in Vietnam.

This latter organization, a coalition organization representing a variety of antiwar, New Left and subversive groups, emerged as the dominant coordinating force in planning disruption at the convention. It is the organization, headed by David Dellinger, which I spoke of earlier and which has sponsored a number of major demonstrations — some of them violent — including the mass assault on the Pentagon during the March on Washington in October 1967.

Although the organizers boasted of having from 100,000 to 200,000 supporters converge on Chicago, only some 10,000 at the most actually appeared. These, however, were well organized for disruption.

Demonstrations held during the convention period included taunting of the police: they were referred to as "pigs," they were spat upon, obscenities were shouted at them and they were the targets of all kinds of unbelievable abuse; on several occasions undisciplined mobs intent on marching to the convention site without legal authority had to be repulsed by the police and National Guard. Reportedly many of the hippies used drugs regularly.

The demonstrations resulted in mass arrests. Also, there were numerous police and demonstrators injured. Approximately 650 arrests were made by local authorities and nearly 200 police officers were injured during the confrontations with the demonstrators. It has been estimated that more than 900 persons obtained emergency treatment for injuries received during the disorder.

Although the disorders were violently disruptive, it should be noted that not one life was lost. Also not to be lost sight of is the fact that the convention itself was not interrupted and the city was not paralyzed.

As an outgrowth of the confrontations with the authorities, numerous allegations were made of violations of Federal civil rights and antiriot law statutes. As to civil rights violations, the FBI investigated over 150 civil rights cases involving more than 200 victims.. Nearly 1,300 antiriot law cases were investigated. More than 3,400 reports totaling over 26,000 pages setting out the results of more than 12,000 interviews were submitted. A Federal grand jury at Chicago on March 20, 1969, returned indictments charging eight persons with violating the new antiriot laws, seven police officers with violating civil rights statutes, one police officer for committing perjury before the grand jury and a former employee of the National Broadcasting Co. for concealing a microphone in a meeting room at the time of the Democratic National Convention.

Indicative of the tremendous drain placed on our manpower, the handling of civil rights and antiriot laws cases stemming from the convention demonstrations involved not only virtually our entire Chicago office special agent staff of some 275 in addition to 45 special agents brought in on special assignment, but the investigation was so widespread that general instructions as to the handling of it went to all of our offices.

Demonstration at Presidential Inauguration

Subsequent to the violent demonstrations at the Democratic National Convention, the National Mobilization Committee to End the War in Vietnam headed by David Dellinger addressed a paper to groups active in protesting the war in Vietnam. This paper called for demonstrations during the election campaign and called for a national action on January 20, 1969, during the Presidential Inauguration. Subsequent planning by the committee led to a program calling for workshops and conferences on January 18, 1969; rallies, a march, and a counterinaugural ball on January 19, 1969; and an "organized presence" along the inaugural parade route on January 20, 1969.

Rennie Davis, an official of the National Mobilization Committee, was appointed coordinator of the inaugural demonstrations. Local chapters of Students for a Democratic Society and other militant organizations, such as the Coalition for an Anti-imperialist Movement, the Yippies, and Women Strike for Peace, endorsed the demonstrations.

The demonstration activity at Washington, D.C., over the inaugural weekend began on January 18, 1969, with 600 to 1,000 individuals participating in workshops and conferences which were described as completely disorganized and chaotic. Among other activities on January 19 were a march by approximately 4,000 individuals and demonstrations including one at the Smithsonian Institution where a reception was being held for Vice President Agnew and his wife. Some of the demonstrators threw clods of dirt and other items and, as a result, it was necessary for police to break up the demonstration. During the meetings on January 19, 1969, several of the demonstrators called for a confrontation with the police on January 20, 1969. The counterinaugural ball, which was held by the demonstrators on the evening of January 19, 1969, was poorly attended and disorganized.

On January 20, 1969, 600 to 800 of the demonstrators positioned themselves along the inaugural parade route, particularly from 12th to 15th Street on Pennsylvania Avenue. They attempted to disrupt the parade by throwing objects, including a few smoke bombs, but were unsuccessful in their attempts. However, their actions made it necessary for police to disperse them.

During the 3 days of demonstrations, 119 individuals were arrested, the majority on charges of disorderly conduct. During the 3 days, six of those arrested were charged wth mutilation, burning, or desecration of the U.S. flag. Of those arrested, 10 were juveniles.

It is interesting to note that a source advised that David Dellinger, the leader of the demonstrations, and his group, the National Mobilization Committee, lost control of the activities of the demonstrators during the inaugural parade.— (*FBI, 1970 Appropriation,* April 17, 1969, pp 51-61).

IMPACT OF NEW LEFT AND BLACK EXTREMIST STUDENT MOVEMENTS

While the phenomenon of revolutionary "protest movements" manifested by campus rebellions and riotous demonstrations throughout the world, some of which I have briefly described, reached a new peak during the past year, it has been building up for a decade. The wave of extremism, which has been marked by growing violence and lawlessness, has without a doubt had a harmful impact on this country in a number of ways. It has impaired the successful and speedy prosecution of the Vietnam war effort; jeopardized the struggle for civil rights and increased animosity between blacks and whites; severely disrupted the normal processes of our academic system; and has served to advance Communist causes both national and international.

At the same time, the New Left and black extremist student protest activity has contributed greatly to the development of a lawless and insurrectionary atmosphere which has encouraged widespread contempt for established authority and promoted criminal, violent behavior. Overall, it is apparent that these groups are clearly subversive forces which represent an ever increasing danger to our national welfare and security.

In this regard, we have developed information on a number of occasions whereby nonstudents appeared on campuses during periods of student agitation to participate in campus disorders. Information has also been developed indicating

323

that extremist agitators have traveled from one campus to another exhorting students to protest the administration of their schools, and some students have participated in disorders on campuses other than their own.

Information concerning the activities of such individuals is furnished to the Department of Justice for determination as to whether violations of the antiriot laws or other Federal violations exist.—(*FBI, 1970 Appropriation,* April 17, 1969, p. 72).

DATE D

1988